American Jewish Historical Society

Publications of the American Jewish Historical Society

Nomber 24

American Jewish Historical Society

Publications of the American Jewish Historical Society
Nomber 24

ISBN/EAN: 9783337033507

Printed in Europe, USA, Canada, Australia, Japan

Cover: Foto ©ninafisch / pixelio.de

More available books at **www.hansebooks.com**

PUBLICATIONS

OF THE

AMERICAN

JEWISH HISTORICAL SOCIETY

NUMBER 24

PUBLISHED BY THE SOCIETY

1916

The Lord Baltimore Press
BALTIMORE, MD., U. S. A.

JEWISH DISABILITIES IN THE BALKAN STATES

AMERICAN CONTRIBUTIONS TOWARD THEIR REMOVAL, WITH PARTICULAR REFERENCE TO THE CONGRESS OF BERLIN

By MAX J. KOHLER AND SIMON WOLF

A paper presented at the twenty-fourth annual meeting of the American Jewish Historical Society

1916

AMERICAN JEWISH HISTORICAL SOCIETY.

LIST OF OFFICERS.

President:
Dr. CYRUS ADLER, Philadelphia, Pa.

Vice-Presidents:
Hon. SIMON W. ROSENDALE, Albany, N. Y.;
Prof. RICHARD J. H. GOTTHEIL, New York;
Rev. Dr. DAVID PHILIPSON, Cincinnati, O.;
Hon. JULIAN W. MACK, Chicago, Ill.

Corresponding Secretary:
ALBERT M. FRIEDENBERG, 38 Park Row, New York.

Recording Secretary:
SAMUEL OPPENHEIM, New York.

Treasurer:
Hon. N. TAYLOR PHILLIPS, New York.

Curator:
LEON HÜHNER, New York.

Additional Members of the Executive Council:

(Term expiring with the 25th Annual Meeting.)
CHARLES J. COHEN, Philadelphia, Pa.;
Dr. HERBERT FRIEDENWALD, Denver, Colo.;
Prof. MAX L. MARGOLIS, Philadelphia, Pa.;
Prof. ALEXANDER MARX, New York.

(Term expiring with the 26th Annual Meeting.)
LEE M. FRIEDMAN, Boston, Mass.;
Prof. J. H. HOLLANDER, Baltimore, Md.;
MAX J. KOHLER, New York;
Dr. A. S. W. ROSENBACH, Philadelphia, Pa.

(Term expiring with the 27th Annual Meeting.)
Rabbi HENRY COHEN, Galveston, Texas;
L. NAPOLEON LEVY, New York;
Hon. MAYER SULZBERGER, Philadelphia, Pa.;
Hon. SIMON WOLF, Washington, D. C.

Hon. OSCAR S. STRAUS, New York, *ex-officio,*
   as Past President of the Society.

OBJECTS.

The object of this Society is to collect and publish material bearing upon the history of America, and to promote the study of Jewish history in general, preferably so far as the same is related to American Jewish history or connected with the causes of emigration from various parts of the world to this continent. It is known that Jews in Spain and Portugal lent no inconsiderable aid to the voyages that led to the discovery of America, that a few accompanied the earliest discoverers and that Jews were among the first settlers on this continent, and in its adjacent islands. Considerable numbers saw service in the Colonial and Revolutionary wars, some of them with great distinction. Others contributed liberally to the Continental treasury, at critical periods, to aid in the establishment of Independence. Since the foundation of our government, Jews have played an active part in the political affairs of the country, and have been called upon to hold important public positions. The records of the achievements of these men will, when gathered together, prove of value and interest to the historian, and perchance cast light upon some obscure parts of the history of our country.

PREFACE.

The present work arose out of a paper prepared by Max J. Kohler and Hon. Simon Wolf, bearing the title "American Contributions Toward the Removal of Jewish Disabilities in the Balkan States." It was presented by Mr. Kohler at the twenty-fourth annual meeting of the American Jewish Historical Society held at Philadelphia, Pa., on February 20, 1916. Since that date he has considerably recast it and somewhat widened the scope of its inquiry so as to conform it to the new title under which it is now submitted to the public.

The subject-matter of this volume has practical importance as well as historical interest. It shows that the disabilities in some of the Balkan States which prevailed prior to the Berlin Congress of 1878 were removed; that the United States more than forty years ago, when its power and importance were much less than at present, was nevertheless willing to make strenuous exertions on the grounds of humanity in the interest of oppressed Jews in Eastern Europe. Unfortunately the efforts made on behalf of the largest population of Jews settled in any Balkan country, namely, Roumania, were without result, and the conditions in Roumania are still much as they were before Roumania obtained independence. The present volume may perhaps assist in bringing the unfortunate condition of the Jews of Roumania to the attention of the statesmen and thinkers of the world, and will furnish to those who are engaged in the struggle for full rights for the Jews the needed information wherewith to conduct their fight for justice.

The publication committee charged with the issuance of this volume consists of Albert M. Friedenberg, chairman; Prof. Alexander Marx and Dr. A. S. W. Rosenbach. Because of the present-day value of the subject, the chairman has bent his efforts to secure a prompt publication of the book. An extra printing of it has been made for the use and at the charge of the American Jewish Committee. The next volume of our *Publications,* No. 25, to comprise the usual papers, notes and necrologies, is now in course of preparation and may be expected to appear with all convenient speed.

CYRUS ADLER,
President.

PHILADELPHIA, PA., *June 12, 1916.*

CONTENTS.

	PAGE
Preface	ix

Jewish Disabilities in the Balkan States. American Contributions Toward Their Removal, with Particular Reference to the Congress of Berlin. *Max J. Kohler* and *Simon Wolf* ... 1

I. Benjamin F. Peixotto's Mission to Roumania 2
II. Three International Jewish Conferences, 1872-1878 25
III. The Congress of Berlin, 1878 40
IV. Secretary Hay's Roumanian Note of 1902 and the Peace Conference of Bucharest of 1913 80
Appendix I. Petition of the Roumanian Jews to the Chamber of Deputies; 1872 98
Appendix II. Memorial submitted to the Conference of the European Powers at Constantinople by the Conference of Israelites held at Paris (1876) 102
Appendix III. Memorial of *Alliance Israélite Universelle* of Paris to the Congress of Berlin 105
Appendix IV. Hon. Oscar S. Straus' Memoranda Preceding Dispatch of the Hay Roumanian Note 108
Appendix V. The Jews of Roumania and the Treaty of Berlin. Extracts from an address by the Hon. Walter M. Chandler, in the House of Representatives 114
Appendix VI. Memorandum on the Treaty Rights of the Jews of Roumania Presented to Sir Edward Grey by the London Committee of Deputies of the British Jews and the Council of the Anglo-Jewish Association 137
Index 155

JEWISH DISABILITIES IN THE BALKAN STATES.
AMERICAN CONTRIBUTIONS TOWARD THEIR REMOVAL, WITH PARTICULAR REFERENCE TO THE CONGRESS OF BERLIN.[1]

BY MAX J. KOHLER AND SIMON WOLF.[2]

American aid towards Jewish emancipation in the Balkan States has been much more important and continuous than is generally recognized, and it constitutes an important chapter in the history of international endeavor to establish religious liberty all over the world. Moreover, a study of these contributions is singularly timely, and fraught with special significance for our own day, for, as Bolingbroke so well said, " History is philosophy teaching by examples." For convenience, we may group these contributions around four incidents: (a) Benjamin F. Peixotto's mission to Roumania as U. S. Consul at Bucharest; (b) three International Jewish Conferences held abroad between 1872 and 1878, largely at Peixotto's instance, and at all of which American Jews were represented; (c) provision on behalf of the persecuted Jews of Eastern Europe at the Berlin Congress of 1878, which was in turn largely pro-

[1] A paper presented at the twenty-fourth annual meeting of the American Jewish Historical Society, Philadelphia, February 20, 1916.

[2] To avoid misunderstanding, Mr. Kohler assumes sole responsibility for this study, Mr. Wolf's share having been to place valuable unpublished correspondence at Mr. Kohler's disposal, and to give him other useful information, and both he and Mr. Kohler, independently, selected this subject. Valuable unpublished material was also secured from Dr. Cyrus Adler, Lewis M. Isaacs, Louis Marshall, Jacob H. Schiff, Hon. Oscar S. Straus, and through the courtesy of Assistant Secretary Alvey A. Adee, of our Department of State.

moted by these Jewish conferences and to which our own government directly contributed; and (d) Secretary Hay's Roumanian Note of August 11, 1902, and subsequent events, including the Peace Conference of Bucharest of 1913. All four of these incidents relate chiefly to Roumania, though other Balkan States, particularly Serbia and Bulgaria, are also involved.

I.
Benjamin F. Peixotto's Mission to Roumania.

Peixotto's mission to Roumania is unique in diplomatic history, for he was appointed U. S. Consul at the Roumanian capital for the express purpose, and accepted the post avowedly, in order to secure an amelioration of the condition of the Jews of Roumania. The year 1870 was signalized by shocking Roumanian Jewish persecutions, which stirred the whole civilized world. These demonstrated how little had been accomplished, after all, by the illusory promises that had been made by Prince Charles of Roumania during the preceding decade to the two great Jewish philanthropists, Adolphe Crémieux and Sir Moses Montefiore. As one of the founders of that noble international Jewish charitable organization, the *Alliance Israélite Universelle,* Crémieux had personally visited Roumania some years before this, in 1866 and again in 1869, and investigated conditions on the spot. In 1867 the venerable Sir Moses Montefiore had personally appealed to the Roumanian Government, on behalf of his coreligionists, at the risk of imminent mob violence, as was then freely reported. The English and French Governments had made strong representations to Roumania, England largely at the instance of Sir Francis Goldsmid, France on Crémieux's special appeal. Napoleon III, in 1867, had even telegraphed to Prince Charles:

I must not leave your Highness in ignorance of the public feeling created here by the persecutions of which the Jews of Moldavia are said to be the victims. I cannot believe that the enlightened

Government of your Highness authorizes measures so opposed to humanity and civilization.[3]

Under these conditions, efforts were made to enlist the active intermediation of the United States Government on behalf of the persecuted Roumanian Jews, which, by Secretary William H. Seward's direction already in 1867 had made representation through Minister Morris at Constantinople, at the request of the Board of Delegates of American Israelites, concerning Roumanian and Serbian Jewish persecutions.[4] The able and intelligently directed efforts of the United States Government on behalf of Jewish emancipation in Switzerland, especially through the campaign of education waged there by Minister Fay, had contributed greatly, not long previously, to securing equality of rights for the Jews of the Swiss Cantons.[5]

[3] *Aus dem Leben König Karls von Rumänien*, Stuttgart, 1894-1900, abridged English translation, edited by S. Whitman, New York, 1899; I. Loeb, *La Situation des Israélites en Turquie, en Serbie et en Roumanie*, Paris, 1877; Great Britain, State Papers, 1877, vol. 89: "Correspondence respecting the Jews in Servia and Roumania, 1867-76," 359 pp.; Hansard's Debates, third series, vol. 191, p. 1267. See Lord Derby's utterances quoted *infra*, pp. 104, 112; also appendices V and VI, pp. 114, 137.

[4] "Foreign Relations of the United States, 1867," vol. ii, pp. 2, 3, 9. *Cf.* "Great Britain, State Papers, 1877," *supra.* See also Hansard's Debates, *supra*, vol. 210, pp. 1592, 1593; D. W. Marks and Albert Löwy, "Memoir of Sir Francis Henry Goldsmid," London, 1879; Bernard Levy, *Die Judenfrage in den Donaufürstenthümern*, Berlin, [187?].

[5] See S. M. Stroock's able paper, "Switzerland and American Jews," in *Publications of the American Jewish Historical Society*, No. 11, p. 7 *et seq.*, which should be supplemented by a reference to Holland's rejection of a commmercial treaty with Switzerland, because of anti-Jewish discriminations, largely in consequence of the efforts of her distinguished Jewish minister, Michael H. Godefroi. ("The Jewish Encyclopedia," vol. vi, p. 16; necrology by Dr. M. Kayserling, in *Allgemeine Zeitung des Judentums*, 1882, p. 524.) Mr. Stroock incidentally emphasized the refusals of France and England to permit such discriminations against their

Moreover, even previously, in 1840, our government had recognized the fact that its absolutely non-sectarian character made its representations on behalf of foreign victims of religious persecution particularly in order, and, in instructing our Minister at Constantinople to use his good offices on behalf of Turkish Jews at the time of the Damascus blood accusations, Secretary Forsyth, under date of August 17, 1840, used these noble words:[6]

The President [Martin Van Buren] is of the opinion that from no one can such generous endeavors *proceed with so much propriety and effect* as from the representative of a *friendly power, whose institutions, political and civil, place upon the same footing, the worshippers of God of every faith and form, acknowledging no*

Jewish subjects by Switzerland. See also Arthur K. Kuhn's "International Law and the Discriminations Practiced by Russia under the Treaty of 1832," Washington, 1911, quoting a report made to the French Senate on Swiss discriminations against French Jews, in which a commission of which Ferdinand de Lesseps was Chairman, reported in 1864:

"No discrimination may be recognized in the enjoyment of civil and political rights between a French Jew and a French Catholic or Protestant. This equality of rights must also follow a citizen beyond the frontier; and the principles of our Constitution do not authorize the Government to protect its subjects in a different manner according to which faith he professes."

This and other precedents (including one of September, 1815, when Metternich acquiesced in Turkey's claim that Ottoman Jews should not be treated differently than other Ottoman subjects by Austria, because Austria treated her own Jewish subjects differently than those of other creeds) were reviewed in the French Chamber of Deputies on December 27, 1909, in a discussion of Russian discriminations against French Jewish citizens, at the conclusion of which the Minister was instructed to continue negotiations to stop these practices. (*Debats parlementaires*, Paris, 1909, pp. 3763-80; *American Jewish Year Book*, for 1911-1912, pp. 66-76.)

[6] *Publications, supra*, No. 9, pp. 163-164; see *ibid.*, No. 8, pp. 141-145, and Dr. Cyrus Adler's valuable work on "Jews in the Diplomatic Correspondence of the United States," *ibid.*, No. 15, pp. 4-6.

distinction between the Mohammedan, the Jew and the Christian.
Should you, in carrying out these instructions, find it necessary or proper to address yourself to any of the Turkish authorities, you will refer to *this distinctive characteristic of our government as investing with a peculiar propriety and right, the interposition of your good offices in behalf of an oppressed and persecuted race*, among whose kindred are found some of the most worthy and patriotic of our citizens.[1]

---

[1] It is interesting to observe that during the very first decade of our existence as a nation, we emphasized this non-sectarian character of our government in our foreign relations. As Oscar S. Straus aptly points out in an address on " Religious Liberty in the United States " in his volume, " The American Spirit," New York, 1913 (p. 264): " On November 4, 1796, during the presidency of Washington, a treaty was concluded with Tripoli, which was ratified by the Senate under the presidency of John Adams, on June 4, 1797, wherein it is provided: 'As the government of the United States is not in any sense founded on the Christian religion; as it has itself no character of enmity against the laws, religion or tranquility of Mussulmen . . . . it is declared by the parties that no pretext arising from religious opinions shall ever produce an interruption of harmony existing between the two countries.' 'This disclaimer by Washington,' says Rev. Dr. Samuel T. Spear, an able writer on constitutional law, 'in negotiating, and by the Senate in confirming, the treaty with Tripoli, was not designed to disparage the Christian religion, or indicate any hostility thereto, but to set forth the fact, so apparent in the Constitution itself, that the government of the United States was not founded upon that religion and hence did not embody or assert any of its doctrines.'" Mr. Straus, *ibid.*, also quotes the utterances of Thomas F. Bayard when Secretary of State, that " religious liberty is the chief corner-stone of the American system of government, and provisions for its security are imbedded in the written charter and interwoven in the moral fabric of our laws. Anything that tends to invade a right so essential and sacred must be carefully guarded against, and I am satisfied that my countrymen, ever mindful of the sufferings and sacrifices necessary to obtain it, will never consent to its impairment for any reason or under any pretext whatever." See, also, Mr. Straus' address on " Humanitarian Diplomacy of the United States," in the same work, which contains a reference to the provisions of the Congress of Berlin (p. 35), and

These precedents made it particularly proper for the government of the United States to lend its aid in 1870, when fresh outbursts of anti-Semitic persecution in Roumania were called to its attention. Accordingly, we learn from *The Jewish*

---

other references to our intercession on behalf of the victims of religious persecution.

It was merely an application of this principle that led to our abrogation of our treaty with Russia in December, 1911, after many years of negotiations failed to induce Russia to cease denying to American citizens of the Jewish faith, the rights conferred thereunder upon all our citizens, regardless of race or creed. (See Hearings before the Committee on Foreign Affairs of the House of Representatives, December 11, 1911, on " Termination of the Treaty of 1832 between the United States and Russia," [including addresses at Carnegie Hall Meeting of December 6, 1911] 336 pp.; 62d Congress, 2d Session, House Report No. 179 on " The Abrogation of the Russian Treaty "; and U. S. Senate Hearings before Committee on Foreign Relations on " Treaty of 1832 with Russia," December 13, 1911, 50 pp.; " The Passport Question," in *American Jewish Year Book*, for 1911-1912, pp. 19-128; *ibid.*, for 1912-1913, pp. 196-210, 295-298; *Congressional Record*, December, 1911.)

An admirable outline history and exposition of the American principle may be found in Rev. Dr. Philip Schaff's " Church and State in the United States " (New York, 1888). In a paper by David Dudley Field, one of our most distinguished American jurists and publicists, on " American Progress in Jurisprudence," read at the World's Fair in Chicago in 1893, published in *American Law Review*, vol. xxvii, p. 641, and quoted in Max J. Kohler's " Phases in the History of Religious Liberty in America with Special Reference to the Jews," in *Publications, supra*, No. 11, p. 59, it was said: " The greatest achievement ever made in the cause of human progress is the total and final separation of the state from the church. If we had nothing else to boast of, we could claim with justice that first among the nations, we of this country made it an article of organic law that the relations between man and his Maker were a private concern into which other men had no right to intrude. To measure the stride thus made for the emancipation of the race, we have only to look back over the centuries that have gone before us, and recall the dreadful persecutions in the name of religion which have filled the world with horror." In the article last cited, an effort was made by me to trace the effect of

Times of April 1, 1870,[5] that Simon Wolf, who had just received stirring appeals, there reprinted, from Adolphe Crémieux, as President of the *Alliance,* on behalf of persecuted European Jews, was

---

American religious liberty, and particularly of the emancipation of the Jews in America, upon the establishment of religious liberty in France, and particularly Jewish emancipation there. While the United States was the first country to establish both religious liberty and complete Jewish emancipation in the modern world, France was a close second in both respects, though a large measure of religious and political liberty for the Jews had been developed long previously in Holland and England. An admirable and convincing study of the indebtedness of the French Declaration of Rights of 1789 to its American precedents, and particularly to the earliest constitutions adopted by the American states immediately following the declaration of our Revolutionary War, especially as regards religious liberty provisions, is to be found in Georg Jellinek's *Die Erklärung der Menschen- und Bürgerrechte,* 2d edition, Leipzig, 1903, and English translation by M. Farrand entitled "The Declaration of the Rights of Man and of Citizens," New York, 1901. In England, Macaulay's famous *Edinburgh Review* essay on "Civil Disabilities of the Jews" (January, 1831), referred to the good results of America's precedent in this field, and Peixotto had this essay translated and extensively circulated in Roumania in the early seventies. Emilio Castelar, the distinguished Spanish statesman, in his life of Columbus (*Century Magazine,* 1892, p. 589), in commenting upon the fact that Columbus' voyage of discovery began at the very time that the Jews were expelled from Spain, refers to Columbus' fleet as "bound in search of another world, whose creation should be new-born, a haven be afforded to the quickening principle of human liberty and a temple reared to the God of enfranchised and redeemed conscience. . . . . Following their narrow views, the powers of the Middle Ages denied even light and warmth to the Jews at the same time that they revealed a new creation for a new order of society, that was predestined by Providence to put an end to all intolerance and to dedicate an infinite continent to modern democracy." See also Francesco Ruffini's "Religious Liberty," New York, 1912, and Sir Frederick Pollock's "Theory of Persecution," in "Essays in Jurisprudence and Ethics," London, 1882.   M. J. K.

[5] Vol. ii, p. 70.

about to bring the attention of the President of the United States to the deplorable condition of our brethren in Roumania, and hoped to enlist our Government in their behalf, at least to have our consuls instructed to use their influence in mitigation.

In the following May, Mr. Wolf reported at the annual meeting of the Board of Delegates of American Israelites [9] that he had called on President Grant in reference to Roumanian Jewish persecutions, and that Adolph Buchner, a Jewish resident of Bucharest, who had served as secretary to the former United States Consul, would be appointed United States Consul there, and be instructed to look into the matter of Roumanian Jewish persecutions. On June 3, 1870,[10] Mr. Wolf called on the Secretary of State, who deplored the news of fresh Roumanian Jewish persecutions, which had just been published, and Mr. Wolf brought these reports to the attention of every member of Congress, and particularly to Charles Sumner's, who was then Chairman of the Senate Committee on Foreign Relations, urging prompt legislative action, in accord with our precedents. Numerous mass meetings had been held about this period throughout the United States, and Congressional action urged. Sumner offered a resolution of inquiry, directed to the President, which was adopted, and expressed the hope that the reports would prove to be exaggerated, and added these striking words:

It is important, however, it seems to me, *in the interest of humanity and in that guardianship of humanity which belongs to the great Republic,* that we should possess ourselves at once of all the information attainable on the subject.[11]

In the House, Mr. Winchester offered the following resolution:[12]

Resolved, That the House of Representatives learns with profound regret and disapproval of the gross violations of the great

---

[9] *Ibid.*, p. 201.
[10] *Ibid.*, p. 229.
[11] *Congressional Globe,* 41st Congress, 2d Session, Pt. 5, pp. 4044-45.
[12] *Ibid.*, p. 4062.

principle of religious liberty by some of the people of the province of Roumania in Turkey, in their late persecutions and outrages against the Israelites, and hereby expresses the earnest hope that they will speedily cease.

Fortunately, the early reports, which referred to thousands of Jews as having just been massacred in Roumania, proved to be exaggerated, and President Grant transmitted a letter from the Secretary of State, in answer to the Senate inquiry, stating he had no official information.[13]

On June 17, 1870, *The Jewish Times* announced the withdrawal by President Grant of the nomination of Mr. Buchner as Consul, and the substitution of the name of Benjamin F. Peixotto.[14] Early in the year 1870, Mr. Peixotto had received an earnest appeal from Crémieux to aid the famine-stricken Jews of Russia, the letter having been addressed to him under the mistaken impression that he was still Grand Master of the Independent Order of B'nai B'rith,[15] and it is probable that Crémieux's unconscious influence was felt, in impelling him to assume the ordeal of the Bucharest consulate.

A private, unpublished letter dated San Francisco, June 28, 1870, from Peixotto to Simon Wolf eloquently outlines Peixotto's purposes in accepting the mission, and refers to Peixotto's earlier letter to Wolf, which led to his appointment. Some excerpts from this letter, following the appointment, are pregnant with meaning. Peixotto wrote:

Heaven hath not placed it in my power to show the extent of the sacrifice I would make for suffering humanity, for persecuted Israel. Were I possessed of fortune and luxurious home, then to go to Bucharest would be still greater proof of my devotion. But

---

[13] Richardson's " Messages and Papers of the Presidents," Washington, 1898, vol. vii, p. 63.

[14] See sketches of Benj. F. Peixotto in Markens' " Hebrews in America," New York, 1888, and " The Jewish Encyclopedia "; Dr. Adolf Stern's *Denkrede über Benj. F. Peixotto*. Bucharest, 1891, translated from the Roumanian, and memorial addresses in *The Menorah*, vol. ix, 1890, p. 336 *et seq.*

[15] *The Jewish Times*, vol. i, Ferbuary 11, 1870.

even as it is, it is no trifle, for here in California, I have found many warm and true, though new, friends, and my prospects for the future are most promising, and though the immediate present bears no fruit, I feel that with time the seed will bear and the reaping be not in vain. Nay, probably every true friend I have in America to-day would persuade me to remain in this land of liberty and hope, and not go an exile to regions of despotism and a land of darkness, especially among my own people who are doubtless sunk in depths of superstition and wedded to forms—a hand people—in truth letters have come to me expostulating—begging me not to dream of going, &c. But none of these and few among the countless thousands who may have read the dispatch in the daily papers, can appreciate my motive. Mine in wishing to go, yours in obtaining the appointment. Surely you would not have done this thing, if your soul had not been in unison with mine. Thank God, all heroism is not dead. Thank God! there still lives in the world the sublime principle of unselfishness, springing from love and patriotism. . . . .

The many poor Jews must be assisted with money and counsel—thus they will learn to love me and through me that religious liberty of which as an Israelite, I am a type. Schools, à la Alliance Israélite, must be planted throughout Roumania, and modern education, liberalizing thought and hopes beyond the mere present, introduced. We can commence and by degrees make these schools powerful instrumentalities for revolutionizing the social and religious life of our people and effectually securing their civil and political rights. There, now you have the object of my mission. Were I to write folios they would contain but repetitions of this thought. The salvation of the people of Israel in all countries where despotism rules, lies in the emancipation from the superstitions, forms and ceremonies of the past, their moral, social and religious reform and elevation, and the only positively effectual means to accomplish this salvation is by the introduction of schools, the sowing the seed of modern thought, which in its germs carries the light of liberty, the new life of mental freedom, social elevation and equality or the hope thereof. . . . . . There is to me nothing humiliating in being thus sustained since our Government affords no adequate means to sustain its civil-international representative. Ours is not a government that concerns itself with the political misfortunes of the peoples of other lands. It cannot. It can only put its representative in a sort of semi-civil commercial international position. Therefore it becomes those who would aid the suffering people of Roumania, to make the office of the Government representative, effective for good. I think you will fully understand and correctly interpret my view. It is not me, you must understand, whom they sustain— it is the cause. If God gives me strength to serve that cause, it is a threefold blessing. So—you now must realize my position. To go to Roumania without the means of doing good would be like uttering words of commiseration, but being helpless to effect relief. I await events, ready to bear what may be the will of Him who I believe designs and fashions what is best. Let me only say your part in this work was not ended when the appointment was obtained. Put not a barren sceptre in my hand. It is your duty to make good the appointment you have secured, to get it confirmed. Mr. Seligman has telegraphed Senators Cole and Casserly from his own prompting; would have been done so 10 days ago but supposed you would have no difficulty securing the confirmation.

Before Peixotto left on his mission (which had no emoluments connected with it), Mr. Jesse Seligman took the lead in collecting funds to be placed at the disposal of the new Consul, in order to enable him to carry out his very elaborate plans for Roumanian Jewish relief; correspondence on this subject appeared in *The Jewish Times*.[16] This appeal led to the organization in December, 1870, in New York City, of the American Roumanian Society, with Joseph Seligman as President, Barnett L. Salomon, Vice-President, Adolph Hallgarten, Secretary, and Lazarus Rosenfeld, Treasurer, and this society, and the Board of Delegates of American Iraelites, together with the Independent Order B'nai B'rith (the last to an even greater extent) raised the funds requisite for the maintenance of the agencies organized by the " Consul Missionary," during his five years' services."[17] The I. O. B. B. lodges, during a series of years, raised funds for this undertaking, largely on Mr. Wolf's personal appeal throughout the country. It is to be regretted that letters received by Dr. Max Lilienthal at this period from Senators Carl Schurz and Sumner regarding this mission [18] have apparently not been preserved.

---

[16] Vol. ii, 1870, pp. 390-391, 405.
[17] *Ibid.*, pp. 662, 651 *et seq.*
[18] *Ibid.*, p. 312.

It is at this point that we may conveniently turn to Mr. Peixotto's own narrative in *The Menorah*,[19] written many years later, beginning in 1886, entitled " Story of the Roumanian Mission," which unfortunately, however, ended abruptly without explanation, in narrating the early stages of the mission.[20] His personal correspondence of the period with Mr. Wolf and the Board of Delegates of American Israelites,[21] both largely extant, supplements and extends the narrative, however, as do also the files of the diplomatic correspondence of our Government and of Great Britain's, above cited, and the Jewish newspapers of the day, especially *The Jewish Times*, and this is particularly true of the able and interesting Memorial Address, delivered soon after Peixotto's death, by Dr. Adolf Stern, of Bucharest, who served as his secretary during his consulate.

Peixotto, near the beginning of his narrative, quotes President Grant's sympathetic words to him before he left on his mission, as follows:[22]

Respect for human rights is the first duty of those set as rulers over nations, and the humbler, poorer, more abject and more miserable a people be, be they black or white, Jew or Christian, the greater should be the concern of those in authority, to extend protection, to rescue and redeem them and raise them up to equality with the most enlightened. The story of the sufferings

---

[19] Vol. i, p. 22 *et seq.*

[20] Vol. iv, 1888, p. 430.

[21] Through the courtesy of Mr. Lewis M. Isaacs I have been enabled to examine the files of the Board of Delegates of American Israelites, of which his father, the late Hon. Myer S. Isaacs, was Secretary for many years. These include numerous interesting letters from Peixotto to the Board and to Judge Isaacs personally, and related letters from Crémieux, Isidore Loeb, Sir Moses Montefiore, Sir Francis Goldsmid, Dr. A. Benisch, Ritter Josef von Wertheimer, Isaac Seligman, Joseph Seligman, Julius Bleichroeder, Charles Netter, Narcisse Leven, Adolph Buchner, Simon Wolf and Adolphus S. Solomons, besides excerpts from the *Rumänische Post*. Unfortunately it appears that Peixotto's correspondence with the Seligman family has not been preserved.

[22] *Ibid.*, vol. i, p. 26.

of the Hebrews of Roumania profoundly touches every sensibility of our nature. It is one long series of outrage and wrong; and even if there be exaggeration in the accounts which have reached us, enough is evident to prove the imperative duty of all civilized nations extending their moral aid in behalf of a people so unhappy. I trust Prince Charles and his ministers and the public men of that country, may be brought to see that the future of their nation lies in a direction totally opposite to those Draconic laws and persecutions, whether great or petty, which have hitherto so invidiously marked its character. It is not by Chinese walls or Spanish expatriations that nations, great or small, can hope to make progress in our day. I have no doubt your presence and influence, together with the efforts of your colleagues of the Guaranteeing Powers, with whom in this matter you will always be prompt to act, will result in mitigating the evils complained of, and end in terminating them. The United States, knowing no distinction between her own citizens on account of religion or nativity, naturally believes in a civilization the world over, which will secure the same universal views.

President Grant also gave him a letter, written with his own hand in the presence of Mr. Peixotto and Mr. Wolf, which Peixotto later exhibited to the ruler of Roumania, reading as follows:[23]

EXECUTIVE MANSION,
Washington, D. C.,
December 8, 1870.

The bearer of this letter, Mr. Benjamin Peixotto, who has accepted the important, though unremunerative position of U. S. Consul to Roumania, is commended to the good offices of all representatives of this Government abroad.

Mr. Peixotto has undertaken the duties of his present office more as a missionary work for the benefit of the people he represents, than for any benefit to accrue to himself—a work in which all citizens will wish him the greatest success. The United States, knowing no distinction of her own citizens on account of religion or nativity, naturally believes in a civilization the world over, which will secure the same universal views.

U. S. GRANT.

In the course of a lecture entitled " What Shall We Do With Our Immigrants?" delivered and published in 1887, Mr.

[23] *Ibid.*, vol. ii, p. 250.

Peixotto records the following interesting conversation had by him with Prince Charles:

> Once, when I was speaking with the Prince, now King of Roumania, he asked me why it was that the Jews of Roumania could not be like those of England and America. "These people," he said, "seem to be so very low, and yet," he added, "it is curious, they are the best pupils in our public schools, and they are the brightest in all the professions to which they are admitted, and still look at them; see how grovelling and base they be," and when I directed the attention of his Highness to the fact that only in those countries where equality and liberty exist, the inhabitants show very little distinction, and also directed his attention to the fact that our country was a free country, and that men coming from Russia or Roumania, or from any other country of the earth, soon cast off old customs and became assimilated with the nation, and progressed with the moving tide of progress and science, he changed the subject, and said: "And you intend to go, Mr. Consul, into the interior?" I said "Yes." "Oh, I will give you an escort, you shall have a body-guard to go with you through the Provinces, and you shall see the true condition of these people." To which I replied: "I will not take a body-guard. I will go alone; I wish to see with my own eyes, their condition, and see whether it be true or not as to their treatment." So I went and found their condition to be deplorable past all words, and yet I tell you here to-night that the Israelites in Roumania, Russia and Poland are as good and worthy people as the Israelites of the United States of America, making every reservation in regard to their culture and associations and the conditions under which they live.

Less than a year after Peixotto's arrival at Bucharest, on June 5, 1872, an incident occurred, which caused serious injury to the Jews of Roumania; this was a theft and profanation at the church at Ismail, Roumania, committed by an apostate Jew, named Jacob Silberman. When arrested, and again on his trial, Silberman confessed that he alone was guilty, but under the influence of frightful torture, he implicated his employer and two other Jews, and, again, on a subsequent occasion, also the local rabbi, named Alter Brandeis, and the president of the congregation, David Goldschlager,[24] claiming that they had

---

[24] *Ibid.*, vol. iii, p. 399 *et seq.*

instigated the crimes. These unfortunates were all arrested, and horribly maltreated, and mobs fell upon the other hapless Jewish inhabitants of Ismail, pillaging, wounding and robbing them for three days, several towns following suit in the rioting. Peixotto at once intervened, and at his request Goldschlager was liberated, and Brandeis was released at the instance of the Austrian Consul-General as an Austrian subject. At the request of the foreign consuls, the chief rioters were in turn arrested. The Government, however, ordered even these Jews, after some interval, to stand trial, and they were brought before a jury at Buzeo. Although Silberman again admitted his guilt, and exonerated all his codefendants, and there was no evidence worthy of the name against the other defendants, the Attorney-General expressly conceding their innocence and asking for their acquittal,[25] the farcical trial resulted in a verdict of guilty against all the defendants and prison sentences were pronounced. The case has become a *cause célèbre*, and the account of the trial has been published in separate pamphlet form in several languages, including English. On the other hand, all the rioters were acquitted. The foreign consuls, with the exception of the Russian, jointly signed a vigorous protest to the Minister of Foreign Affairs, through Peixotto's influence, against such grave injustice, all the more dangerous because of the approaching Passover holidays, which

---

[25] A contemporaneous Jewish MS. review of this Silberman crime is before me, indicating that the entire incident arose through Russian intrigue, fomented for the double purpose of injuring the Jews and the administration of Prince Charles. Silberman, a Russian subject, had just left the army and was employed to commit this offence for these sinister purposes. Some such idea was also suggested in a contemporaneous discussion of the case by Sir Francis Goldsmid and Serjeant (afterwards Sir) John Simon in the English House of Commons. Hansard's Debates, *supra*, vol. 210, pp. 1589-1592, 1597-1599, 1601-1603. See Peixotto's account, *The Menorah*, vol. iii, pp. 398-409; vol. iv, pp. 58-60, 288-293, 340-350, 424-430; "The Jews in Roumania. Account of the Proceedings of the Trial of the Jews at Busen," London, 1874; and British State Papers cited in note 3, *supra*

have so often become periods for anti-Semitic riot. The various foreign governments, including our own (the latter through a message from Secretary Hamilton Fish, dated April 10, 1872, quoted *infra*), approved the action of their consuls in making representations in the matter, and the impending riots were averted.

The debate in the German Reichstag was particularly vigorous, a resolution of protest, offered by Deputy Ludwig Bamberger, and strongly supported by Eduard Lasker, being adopted in May, 1872.[26] In England, Sir Francis Goldsmid brought up the subject in a stirring speech in the House of Commons in April, 1872,[27] and a very important and fiery Mansion House meeting was held May 30, 1872, at which the Lord Mayor of London presided, and the Earl of Shaftesbury delivered a rousing speech, as did also the Bishop of Gloucester and others.[28] Earl Granville, Secretary of State for Foreign Affairs, proposed a conference of the Powers regarding these Roumanian Jewish persecutions, the Balkan States having been, even prior to the Congress of Berlin of 1878, under the protection of the Great Powers, though nominally still Turkish dependencies.[29] Italy seconded England's suggestion, which France also favored, but Russia opposed, suggesting a joint note instead, and no conference was held. On motion of Congressman Samuel S. Cox of New York, our House of Representatives unanimously passed a resolution on May 20, 1872:

> That the President of the United States be respectfully requested to join with the Italian government in the protest against the intolerant and cruel treatment of the Jews of Roumania.[30]

---

[26] *Aus dem Leben König Karls*, vol. ii, p. 265; *Allgemeine Zeitung des Judentums*, 1872, pp. 447-8. The Dutch Government also took action, Loeb, *supra*, pp. 361-2.

[27] *The Jewish Times*, vol. iv, p. 226; Hansard's Debates, *supra*, pp. 1595-1604.

[28] *The Jewish Times*, vol. iv, p. 325, reprinting addresses from *The Jewish Chronicle;* see *infra*, p. 112.

[29] *Ibid.*, vol. iii, p. 308, and British State Papers, *supra*.

[30] *Congressional Globe*, 42d Congress, 2d Session, p. 3655.

Both the Senate and the House of Representatives adopted resolutions, requesting the President to furnish information in March and May, 1872, which was done in published Congressional Documents, supplementing our published Foreign Relations for 1872.[31] In answer to the House resolution offered by Congressman Cox, Secretary Hamilton Fish reported that our Consul had already previously

> in common with the representatives of other powers, addressed a note of remonstrance to the [Roumanian] minister, and more recently united with the representatives of those powers (Italy being included), in a collective note to the Roumanian government, bearing date April 18, 1872, on the subject of these recent occurrences, and pointing out with marked but just severity, to the impunity which had been enjoyed by the perpetrators of the violence, which it characterized appropriately as unworthy of a civilized country.[32]

A number of detailed reports from Consul Peixotto, despatched in 1871 and 1872, were thus printed as early as 1872 by our Government. Already on October 5, 1871, Mr. Peixotto was able to report—what was true during the whole of his mission, with the exception of the riots of 1872, above referred to—that

> the sentiments of humanity he [the Prince of Roumania] was pleased to express, have been practically carried out in a more zealous regard for, and protection of, the rights of the oppressed Israelites. While it has been impossible to restrain prejudices fostered by designing men, mostly for political ends and in many instances for the purposes of robbery, every attempt at open violence has been promptly quelled, and effective measures taken to prevent outrage.[33]

On April 10, 1872, Secretary Fish addressed the following dispatch to Consul Peixotto:[34]

---

[31] Richardson, *supra*, pp. 167, 168; House Executive Documents, 1872, 42d Congress, 2d Session, No. 318, and Senate Document No. 75 of same session.

[32] House Executive Documents, *supra*.

[33] Senate Document, *supra*.

[34] *Ibid*.

DEPARTMENT OF STATE,
Washington, April 10, 1872.

SIR:

Among the large number of Israelites in this country, there are probably few whose sympathies have not been intensely excited by the recent intelligence of the grievous persecutions of their coreligionists in Roumania. This feeling has naturally been augmented by the contrast presented by the position of members of that persuasion here, who are equals with all others before the law, which sternly forbids any oppression on account of religion. Indeed, it may be said that the people of this country universally abhor persecution anywhere for that cause, and deprecate the trials of which, according to your dispatches, the Israelites of Roumania have been the victims.

This Government heartily sympathizes with the popular instinct upon the subject, and while it has no disposition or intention to give offense by impertinently interfering in the internal affairs of Roumania, it is deemed to be due to humanity to remonstrate against any license or impunity which may have attended the outrages in that country. You are consequently authorized to address a note to the minister of foreign affairs of the principalities, in which you will embody the views herein expressed, and you will also do anything which you discreetly can, with a reasonable prospect of success, toward preventing a recurrence or continuance of the persecution adverted to.

HAMILTON FISH.

On April 18, 1872, the foreign Consuls (except the Russian) at Bucharest, at Peixotto's instance, joined in the following note:[35]

The undersigned deem it their duty to address to the government of the Prince, collectively, and in the most formal manner, the verbal observations, which most of them have been ordered by their governments to present to it in relation to the Israelite question. They cannot, in the first place, help expressing their astonishment that the result of the investigation, ordered in Roumanian Bessarabia more than two months since, has not yet been communicated to them, notwithstanding the assurance contained in the note of the minister of foreign affairs, bearing the date of the 7-19th of February last.

---

[35] *Ibid.*

They have, moreover, learned with profound regret, that, after having condemned several Israelites to severe penalties, the prosecution of whom was abandoned by the public ministry itself, the court assizes at Buzeo has acquitted all the individuals who were charged with having ccmmitted the gravest excesses and crimes against the Jewish population of the town of Vilcova. The undersigned see in this double verdict, an indication of the dangers to which the Israelites are exposed in Roumania, the imminence of which, at the approach of the Easter holidays, justified the steps recently taken by them simultaneously near the government of the Prince.

The governments of the undersigned will judge whether the impunity which has been enjoyed by the assailants of the Jews is not of a nature to encourage a repetition of the scenes of violence quite unworthy of a civilized country, which, as such, ought to insure freedom and security to all religious denominations.

> THIDAN (Germany).
> SCHLECHTA (Austria-Hungary).
> PEIXOTTO (United States).
> G. LE SOUARD (France).
> J. GREEN (Great Britain).
> NEANES (Greece).
> ILLORIA (Italy).

Secretary Fish expressly approved of Peixotto's course in this matter, in the following vigorous note:[36]

> DEPARTMENT OF STATE,
> Washington, May 13, 1872.

SIR:

The Department has received your dispatch No. 30, of the 19th ultimo, accompanied by a copy of the remonstrance addressed by the representatives of foreign governments at Bucharest, to that of the principalities, against recent maltreatment of Israelites there.

The Department approves your taking part in that remonstrance. Whatever caution and reserve may usually characterize the policy of the Government in such matters, may be regarded as inexpedient when every guarantee and consideration of justice appear to have been set at defiance in the course pursued with reference to the unfortunate people referred to. You will not be backward in joining any similar protest, or other measure which

---

[36] *Ibid.*

the foreign representatives there may deem advisable, with a view to avert or mitigate further harshness toward the Israelite residents in, or subjects of, the principalities.

> I am, sir, &c., &c.,
> HAMILTON FISH.

B. F. Peixotto, Esq.,
United States Consul, Bucharest.

Our Government did not, however, rest with mere approval of such local action, but Secretary Fish wrote letters to our Ministers at Vienna, London, Paris, Berlin, Rome, St. Petersburg and Constantinople on July 22, 1872, of the following tenor:[37]

> DEPARTMENT OF STATE,
> Washington, July 22, 1872.
>
> SIR:
> It has been suggested to this Department, and the suggestion is concurred in, that if the sympathy which we entertain for the inhumanly persecuted Hebrews, in the principalities of Moldavia and Wallachia, were made known to the government to which you are accredited, it might quicken and encourage the efforts of that government to discharge its duty as a protecting power, pursuant to the obligations of the treaty between certain European states. Although we are not a party to that instrument, and, as a rule, scrupulously abstain from interfering, directly or indirectly, in the public affairs of that quarter, the grievance adverted to is so enormous, as to impart to it, as it were, a cosmopolitan character, in the redress of which all countries, governments, and creeds are alike interested.
>
> You will consequently communicate on this subject with the minister for foreign affairs of the Austro-Hungarian Empire, in such way as you may suppose might be most likely to compass the object in view. I am, &c.,
> HAMILTON FISH.

Minister John Jay reported August 31, 1872, that Austria had already joined other powers in a note to the Roumanian Government on the subject, and England had recently proposed further action, but Austria doubted the wisdom and efficacy of further proceedings.[38] Minister Elihu B. Washburne

---

[37] " Foreign Relations of the United States, 1872," p. 55, et seq.
[38] Ibid., pp. 62-3. Cf. British State Papers, supra.

at Paris entered into important correspondence with the French Government, which was also favorably inclined to effective intermediation, and this correspondence was widely printed at the time.[39] M. de Rémusat closed his letter to E. B. Washburne of August 30, 1872, with the encouraging words:

> You can say, sir, to Mr. Fish, that when the occasion presents itself, we shall insist that equal protection be accorded in Roumania to all creeds. I am happy to say that our intentions in this respect accord with the sentiments you have expressed to me.

George Bancroft reported similar sentiments on the part of the German Government.[40] Earl Granville told Minister Robert C. Schenck that unfortunately he could not pretend that the British Government's representations had met with much result, and that he

> believed a general expression of the public opinion of the world would have more effect than any particular means which governments could take.[41]

Russia again took an unfavorable stand, when our views were presented. The Turkish Government repudiated any sympathy with these persecutions.[42] Mr. Peixotto's note of June 24, 1872,[43] shows that it was on his recommendation that Mr. Fish sent the dispatches of July 24, 1872, above referred to.

In the course of a private letter to Mr. Wolf, dated August 4, 1871, Mr. Peixotto wrote:

> Even to any ordinary consul with purely commercial duties, the trial and task is enough, but to one with such a mission as mine—involving the fate of 250,000—it is a burden and a struggle few have any conception of. . . . . At the imminent risk of my life, I have visited those towns and villages where, during the last year and the three years preceding, the most violent outrages and robberies have been committed. . . . . You have doubtless received

---

[39] " Foreign Relations," *supra*, p. 184. See *Publications, supra*, No. 17, p. 200.
[40] " Foreign Relations of the United States for 1872," p. 194.
[41] *Ibid.*, p. 197.
[42] *Ibid.*, pp. 493-7, 678.
[43] *Ibid.*, p. 692.

the *Rumänische Post*, and have read my editorials and those (not written by my own hand) which I have directed. . . . . You have discovered the scope and character of this journal. Now, realizing that a purely Jewish paper would have no reading outside of Israel, and be powerless to effect political good, a strong paper from a national standpoint, gravely, but boldly written, would command attention and in due time become (as the *Post* has already become) an effective weapon. My reason for publishing it in the German, instead of the Roumanian, was that it might act as a censor, be a whip in my hand, to slash the vile enemies of our race naked through the world. . . . . I have set all Europe ablaze with the cause of our Roumanian brethren. All the great journals of England, Germany, Austria, France and Italy teem with articles on the persecutions and oppression of our people, and not only have parliaments been moved, but cabinets, and if I mistake not, some great results must follow.

Another contemporaneous letter refers to his corresponding on this subject with Sir Francis Goldsmid and Mr. A. Loewy of London, of the Anglo-Jewish Association, N. Leven of the *Alliance Israélite Universelle,* with Crémieux, Sir Moses Montefiore, Prof. Moritz Lazarus of Berlin, Baron Moritz von Königswarter, Ritter Josef von Werthheimer and Goldsmid of Vienna. Elaborate plans were also made, and foundations laid for improved Jewish education throughout Roumania, particularly through the Order Zion, affiliated with the I. O. B. B., and Peixotto was ever alert, fearless, and untiring in preventing attacks on Jewish rights and liberty.

Dr. Adolf Stern, who was Peixotto's secretary in Roumania and intimately in touch with all his work, ably summarized his services in the Memorial Address of 1891, above referred to. Only a few passages from this address can be utilized herein, supplemented by Peixotto's own reports and correspondence, the reports and files of the Board of Delegates of American Israelites and the contemporary Jewish newspapers.

Naturally, the very fact of an Israelite's holding office as representative of a great nation in Roumania, created a stir there, and Dr. Stern, as well as Mr. Peixotto, reports how the day of his first official reception by the Prince was turned into a Jewish holiday, as also his appearance in the interior on his travels. Moreover, he did not hesitate, consistently, to advise the Jews of Roumania to defend themselves with fire-arms, when necessary, as a protection against violence and assaults, the right of self-defence being recognized even by Roumanian law. Argument and friendly intercourse with influential personages in Roumania were resorted to by Peixotto, to establish a better feeling towards the Jews, and he entertained extensively. Largely through his influence, prefects whose inactivity had promoted anti-Semitic riots were removed, and new hostile legislation against the Jews was prevented. He vigorously combated the theory that native-born Jews could be treated as aliens in Roumania, and, moreover, as aliens without any foreign state obligated to protect them, but this benighted theory was nevertheless adopted by the Roumanian courts, and underlies Roumanian Jewish disabilities to this day. He recognized the need for superior education and educational facilities among the Jews, and agitated for their organization, and also founded, in 1871, the influential Roumanian Jewish benevolent society referred to, similar to and afiliated with the I. O. B. B., called Order Zion, which carried this programme into practice. His activity in connection with international Jewish conferences and their programmes for Roumanian Jewry will be presently considered, as also the related project of proposed wholesale emigration of Roumanian Jews to the United States in the early seventies.

When Peixotto resigned the consulate in 1875, there were numerous estimates published, reviewing the value of his services. While it was conceded on the one hand that he had aroused bitter enmities in certain quarters, and had met with opposition even from a minority of the Roumanian Jews themselves, while, on the other hand, many of his Roumanian co-religionists had formed unjustifiably high expectations as to what he would achieve, it was generally admitted that he had done much for the cause he had so enthusiastically espoused.

Atrocities against the Jews would have assumed much greater dimensions, and much more drastic anti-Jewish legislation would have been enacted, had it not been for his efforts. But his chief merit was recognized to have been his success in rousing all Europe, as well as the United States, against Roumanian anti-Semitic intolerance, and the importance of international action. Even *The Jewish Chronicle,* of London, stated* that " the international Jewish conference of Brussels [the first of a series] was certainly his work."

In a letter written by Sir Francis Goldsmid to Judge Isaacs on May 2, 1872, he referred to the fact that the American Roumanian Committee was responsible for the formation of the London Roumanian Committee to promote Peixotto's programme, the *Alliance Israélite Universelle* coöperating, and suggestions were made by Sir Francis for encouraging Peixotto's work. He said he felt sure

that you like ourselves are fully impressed with the value of the services rendered to our Roumanian brethren by Mr. Peixotto. . . . . We are certain that the Israelites of America, to whom is due the honor of having set this mission on foot, will not let it fall for want of material aid.

In the " Memoir of Sir Francis Henry Goldsmid," by Marks and Löwy, similar views are expressed as to the value of Peixotto's services (p. 161). Goldsmid was for many years the leading champion of the cause of the Balkan Jews, and this work contains much additional material of value. Mr. Wolf was, moreover, informed by Delegate Chief Rabbi Hermann Adler, in 1881, that Lord Beaconsfield had told the latter that what Peixotto had done was of material aid in securing the adoption of the Jewish rights provisions of the Berlin Treaty of 1878, and a close study of the history of the period confirms this view.

---

* Reprinted in *The Jewish Times*, vol. viii, 1877, p. 356.

II.
THREE INTERNATIONAL JEWISH CONFERENCES, 1872-1878.
A. THE INTERNATIONAL JEWISH CONFERENCE AT BRUSSELS, 1872.

As already indicated, Peixotto was in close correspondence with the Jewish leaders of public opinion in Europe, and on his way to Roumania had met a number of these communal guides, and placed himself in touch with them. In consequence, an international Jewish conference, probably the first in modern times, met at Brussels, October 29 and 30, 1872, at the suggestion of Prof. Moritz Lazarus, and on the call of a Berlin committee of which Julius Bleichroeder was temporary chairman, under date of September 19, 1872, for the purpose of considering the condition of the Jews in the Balkan States. Crémieux presided, and Prof. Moritz Lazarus of Berlin and Sir Francis Goldsmid of London, together with Dr. Leopold Kompert of Vienna were vice-presidents. The United States was represented by Mr. Peixotto and Isaac Seligman of London. Twenty-five of the delegates sat down at a banquet given in honor of the occasion, and one of the guests remarked, as indicative of their standing, that twenty-one of these Jews had been decorated. It was decided to encourage the submission of a petition from the Jews of Roumania for complete civil and political rights to the Roumanian legislature, and under the advice of the Conference, such a petition was drafted, and is hereto annexed in translated form as Appendix I (p. 98). An executive board, composed of members from various countries, was organized, with headquarters at Vienna, and an elaborate and thorough programme for educational and moral reforms among the Jews of Roumania was adopted. A project for the encouragement of immigration *en masse* of Roumanian Jews to the United States was unanimously disapproved of.[45]

[45] *The Jewish Times*, vol. iv, pp. 772, 816; "Final Report of Board of Delegates of American Israelites," New York, 1879, p. 30; Leven's History of the *Alliance Israélite Universelle*, Paris, 1911; Stern's *Denkrede über Benj. F. Peixotto*, Bucharest, 1891, pp. 27-33.

The proceedings of the Conference were conducted behind closed doors, after a full discussion of the *pros* and *cons* of such course. The Board of Delegates of American Israelites' annual report quoted the American delegates, Peixotto and Isaac Seligman, under date of November 13, 1872, to the effect that this was

> the first assemblage ever convoked, which included all shades of religious sentiment within the house of Israel and had no discord as to doctrine or dogma, but unanimously agreed on the broad ground of Judaism and humanity, never to rest until every enthralled Israelite stands forth a free man. . . . . It was a spectacle never to be forgotten to witness this conference of the best men drawn from all lands to deliberate for the emancipation of the down-trodden masses in Roumania.

The immigration resolution of the Conference calls for more extended consideration. Even before Peixotto went to Roumania, wholesale emigration of Roumanian Jews to the United States had been suggested in several quarters, and Rabbi Maurice Fluegel, a native of Bucharest, who had then resided for some years in the United States, published elaborate plans along these lines, some of which he had submitted to Crémieux and others. Peixotto, at the suggestion of the British Consul at Bucharest, had made an informal inquiry of the Roumanian Government whether it would permit the emigration of Jews, whereupon the premier, Costaforo, at once seized upon this expedient as a cure for the Roumanian Jewish problem, and announced publicly that his Government would welcome a total transmigration of Roumanian Jews to America, and that from August 18, 1872, until the next assembly of the legislature, free passports would be issued." Sir Francis Goldsmid, on September 12, 1872, addressed a public letter to Peixotto, pointing out the utterly impracticable nature of such a wholesale remedy, and the unfavorable impression it had made." A Roumanian Emigration Society had, meantime, been formed in the United States, but only such as were in-

---

[46] *The Jewish Times*, vol. iv, p. 628; Adolf Stern, *supra*.
[47] *The Jewish Times*, vol. iv, p. 729.

capable of supporting themselves, in general, came over under these auspices, so that Mr. Leopold Bamberger of New York, president of the society, wrote a letter, under date of August 6, 1873,⁴⁸ in which he gave his personal

opinion, based upon a practical experience of about nine months, that the flow of emigration to this country so far [from Roumania] has been a perfect failure, and in reality a misfortune to all those who were induced to leave Roumania,

and he reported that

of about 150 emigrants who have arrived here, more than 90% came as paupers and became a burden to our Society from the very day they landed on our shores,

and he had informed Mr. Peixotto of this, and urged that young and energetic men only should be encouraged to come over, and not those incapable of providing for themselves. This seems to be the first, and last, time that any wholesale, unselected Jewish emigration from abroad to the United States was encouraged, and, as seen, long before Mr. Bamberger's letter above quoted was written, the Brussels International Jewish Conference pronounced against it. Dr. Stern, misled by a few early comments in American newspapers, in favor of the encouragement of Roumanian Jewish immigration, vigorously criticised the action of the Brussels Conference in this respect, but, as seen, even Peixotto voted ultimately in favor of the resolution of disapproval, and this was long before our National Government adopted a law in 1907 forbidding societies and foreign states from encouraging emigration to our shores."⁴⁹

⁴⁸ *Ibid.*, vol. v, p. 373.

⁴⁹ Peixotto's attitude to this emigration project was ably expressed in a personal letter to Judge Isaacs, dated December 3, 1872. He stated that an unofficial inquiry as to what restrictions, if any, existed upon Jewish emigration was distorted into an alleged project for emigration *en masse*. On the other hand, he said that he was disposed to favor some emigration to the United States, and stated that an object lesson would have been afforded to Roumania, as many of her Jewish subjects were practically indispensable to

It appears that the petition to the Roumanian Chamber of Deputies was not submitted, after all, the Roumanian premier advising against its submission so late in the session, when its adoption was declared to be impossible, and many of the influential Roumanian Jews themselves feared that its discussion might lead to still further discriminatory laws. Nor did the Vienna executive board accomplish much, but differences of opinion developed between it and Peixotto, and the board declined to approve Peixotto's plans, which included founding an *Arbeits-bureau*, at an expense of $25,000 per annum, includ-

---

her. But he conceded that the emigration project, *en masse*, was strongly opposed, not merely by Sir Francis Goldsmid, but also by other distinguished European Jews, including Prof. Lazarus, Baron Rothschild, Königswarter and Bleichroeder. The Board of Delegates of American Israelites expressed their attitude towards the question in their published report of May, 1873, as follows: "This Committee embraced an early opportunity to deprecate indiscriminate emigration, but expressed the willingness of American Israelites to welcome to our shores Roumanians who may desire to establish themselves in a new country, and also are prepared to help themselves, and to appreciate the rights of citizenship." Judge Isaacs prepared a pamphlet on Roumanian discriminations entitled "The Jews in Roumania," New York, 1872, which the Board published in English and German. Mr. A. S. Freidus, of the New York Public Library, has kindly called my attention to a Hebrew work by Leon Horowitz, entitled "Roumania and America," favoring such emigration, published in Berlin in January, 1874, and dedicated to Peixotto. A fuller description of this work is contained (p. 122) in the excellent "List of Works Relating to the History and Conditions of the Jews in Various Countries," 278 pp., published by The New York Public Library in 1914 and prepared by Mr. Freidus. Horowitz's work is replete with Jewish information about Peixotto's troubles and struggles in Roumania. He wrote, besides, a biography of Peixotto in Hebrew, published in *Ha-Carmel*, vol. i, 1871, and separately reprinted. I am indebted to Mr. Freidus, Miss E. Cowen, Prof. Gotthard Deutsch, Albert M. Friedenberg, Leon Hühner and Arthur K. Kuhn for other references in this paper. I am also greatly indebted to my wife for valuable assistance in the preparation of this work.

M. J. K.

ing the conduct of a newspaper and extensive educational work, all under his direction.[50] Meanwhile it was reported that Roumanian Jewish immigration to the United States had practically ceased.[51]

B. THE INTERNATIONAL JEWISH CONFERENCE AT PARIS, 1876.

The assemblage of a Conference of the Powers at Constantinople, to take action regarding Eastern European affairs, and renewed Roumanian and Serbian Jewish persecution, led to the convening of a second International Jewish Conference, which met at Paris, December 11, 1876, being called together by the *Alliance Israélite Universelle* at the instance of the Anglo-Jewish Association.[52] Again some of the leading Jews of the day assembled, representing their coreligionists from all the chief countries, including America. Crémieux again presided, and the vice-presidents were Baron Henry de Worms. Chief Rabbi Lazard Isidor, Dr. Samuel Kristeller, Chief Rabbi Elie-Aristide Astruc and William Seligman. America was represented by William Seligman and Arthur Lévy of Paris, and J. M. Laurence of London. Again vehement discussions took place regarding the questions of meeting in executive session and excluding representatives of the press, both measures being again adopted, though subsequently a detailed report of the proceedings and of speeches at a banquet given in connection with the conference was published in booklet form. Baron Henry de Worms, one of the then ablest living authorities on the Eastern Question, suggested that the Conference of the Powers should be appealed to on behalf of the Jews, by submitting two different propositions: (a) protection and equal civil and political rights for all non-Mohammedans in the

---

[50] *The Jewish Times*, vol. v, 1874, p. 52.

[51] *Ibid.*, vol. vii, 1876, p. 214.

[52] See *ibid.*, vol. vii, pp. 708, 728, 144; Leven's History, *supra;* *Réunion au Faveur des Israélites de l'Orient*. Paris, December, 1876, 101 pp. A copy of the rare booklet, last cited, is in the New York Public Library, and contains a detailed report of this Conference.

Ottoman Empire, and (b) emancipation of the Jews in the Balkan provinces. Both propositions were adopted, though Baron de Worms' further suggestion was voted down, that the countries to be represented at the Constantinople Conference be severally appealed to, and not the Conference collectively. An able commission was appointed to prepare the proposed memorial to the Constantinople Conference, and consisted of Crémieux, Chief Rabbi Astruc of Brussels, Baron Henry de Worms, N. Leven, A. Loewy, B. Singer, Joseph Dérenbourg, Dr. Landsberg and F. Veneziani. A very strong memorial was prepared, a translation of which is hereto annexed as Appendix II (p. 102). Unfortunately, the Constantinople Conference itself accomplished practically nothing, a resort to arms between Russia and Turkey being the substitute adopted, though meantime M. Charles Netter went to Constantinople, on this mission, and copies of the memorial, as well as of Isidore Loeb's able book *La Situation des Israélites en Turquie, en Serbie et en Roumanie,* were handed to representatives of all the Great Powers. Particular support to these efforts was given by the publication, in a later edition of M. Loeb's book and elsewhere, of American official action, including the Washburne-Rémusat correspondence already referred to, and a letter written by U. S. Minister Horace Maynard to Mr. William Seligman, one of the American delegates,[33] reading as follows:

Dear Sir: *Constantinople, Jan. 9, 1877.*

I have received, by the last courier, your letter of the 2nd inst., containing a copy of the Memorial addressed to the Conference which is sitting at present in this capital. It is with pleasure that I will favor the object of this Memorial. In a conversation that I had yesterday evening with the Marquis of Salisbury, he has assured me of his sympathies for this question. All measures taken for the benefit of the non-Mussulman population of Turkey will equally aid, I am convinced, also the Jews there.

I am, etc.,

Horace Maynard.

---

[33] Loeb, *supra,* p. 369.

Mr. Maynard informed our Department of State that he had unofficially taken this matter up with delegates to the conference."

Mr. Maynard's letter to Mr. William Seligman was written by him in answer to one from the latter enclosing a copy of the Memorial, which letter was printed in our "Foreign Relations," [65] and a copy of the Memorial had also meanwhile been sent to our Department of State in Washington by Judge Isaacs on January 16, 1877, and its receipt was suitably acknowledged, after he had perused it, by Mr. Fish on February 16, 1877. In the letter in which Mr. Maynard acknowledged receipt of the correspondence between the Board of Delegates of American Israelites and the State Department, which the latter had transmitted to him, he distinguished between Roumania and Turkey proper, and added:

Justice to the Turks requires me to say they have treated the Jews much better than have some of the western Powers of Europe .... An impression prevails that under Turkish rule, the treatment of the Jews is better than that of the Christians. . . . . [The Turkish Minister of Foreign Affairs] protested that where the Turkish rule obtained, the Israelites have always enjoyed every privilege and immunity accorded by the laws to Ottoman subjects. His language in that sense was very emphatic. For their treatment in the provinces the Sublime Porte could not justly be held responsible. Yet, even there, in the late treaty with Servia, they had exacted from her a promise of justice to these much injured people.

Similarly, the Turkish Minister at Washington pointed out to the Board of Delegates of American Israelites, in May, 1877, that his Government was not responsible for the persecution of the Jews in Roumania, and that

the policy of the Porte towards the Israelites in the provinces under the direct sovereignty of the Sultan, is impartial and enlightened, and is characterized by the concession to them of civil and religious liberty.

---

[64] "Foreign Relations of United States, 1877," letter of June 26, 1877, pp. 593-4.
[65] *Ibid.*, pp. 596-7.

The unpublished correspondence between the Board of Delegates of American Israelites and Secretary of State Evarts, above referred to, was as follows:

I.

New York, May 1, 5637, 1877

Hon. WM. M. EVARTS,
    Secretary of State.

DEAR SIR: The beginning of war between Russia and Turkey, ostensibly for the protection by the former Power of the Christians resident in the dominions of the Porte, vividly suggests the danger and persecution to which the Israelites dwelling in the Turkish provinces are imminently exposed and reminds us of the fact that there is no friendly hand interposed to save these unhappy people from the foreign invader or from the mob in whose midst they dwell.

During many years, the State Department has generously and justly taken cognizance of the anomalous condition of the Hebrews in Roumania. In the interest of humanity, Mr. Peixotto, the late Consul of the United States at Bucharest, interposed, with the coöperation of his consular colleagues, to prevent the onslaught on the Hebrews begun in the villages and extending to the capital of Roumania. On several occasions, Mr. Peixotto's indefatigable energy proved the salvation of the unhappy Hebrews.

Already the intelligence reaches us that at Giurgewo, the Roumanians have killed eight and wounded eleven fugitive Israelites. There is no protection for these people in the cities or villages and when they seek refuge in flight, they are massacred.

Cannot our Government, so ably represented at Constantinople and Vienna and with a powerful naval force in the Mediterranean, accomplish something for the protection of the Hebrews dwelling in the Principalities?

Events march rapidly; and although there is an acting United States Consular Agent at Bucharest, a gentleman of zeal and discretion, he may be driven from his post and denied the opportunity or the right to intervene for humanity's sake.

It is a question of the life and liberty of two hundred thousand persons denied in the land of their birth or adoption the rights of man—denied these as *Hebrews*, because of peculiar treaty interpretations, oppressive and unprecedented local laws and a bigoted populace to intensify the terror of proscription and persecution.

Under such extraordinary circumstances we earnestly beg that the Department will instruct the United States Ministers and representatives near the Turkish provinces to coöperate with their colleagues in such measures as may be devised for the relief of the persecuted Hebrews of Roumania.

We are, with great respect,
for the Executive Committee:
MYER S. ISAACS, President.
SIMON WOLF, V. Pres.,
(of Washington, D. C.)

II.

DEPARTMENT OF STATE,
Washington, May 26, 1877.

MYER S. ISAACS, Esquire.

SIR: I have to acknowledge the receipt of your letter of the 1st instant, in relation to the hardships, outrages and persecutions of the Israelites dwelling in the Turkish provinces. In view of the oppression of these unhappy people, and of the dangers to which they are exposed, you appeal to the Department to instruct the United States Ministers and representatives near the Turkish provinces to coöperate with their colleagues in such measures as may be desired for the relief and protection of the Hebrews dwelling in the principalities, and you instance especially those in Roumania. Much of the misery that is now being endured is inseparable from the state of war in which the country is now engaged. The provinces are all more or less under military control and it is feared that ordinary diplomatic protests and representations cannot be made at present as effective as is wished by all who desire to see right, justice and humanity prevail.

In furtherance of your wishes the Department will refer a copy of your letter to our Minister at Constantinople with instructions to take such action in the matter as will in his judgment be best calculated to secure an amelioration of the condition of the oppressed people.

I am, Sir,
Your obedient servant,
WM. M. EVARTS.

At the same time Secretary Evarts forwarded the foregoing correspondence to Minister Maynard, and wrote him, as follows:

III.

DEPARTMENT OF STATE,
Washington, May 28, 1877.

HORACE MAYNARD, Esquire.

SIR: I transmit herewith for your information a copy of correspondence between the Department and the President of the Board of Delegates of American Israelites.

You will give such instructions to our Consular representatives in the Provinces as will be in your judgment, in view of the peculiar exigencies of the situation at present, best adapted to secure to the Israelites the desired protection.

I am, Sir,
Your obedient servant,
WM. M. EVARTS.

Responses were received from representatives of other Great Powers to the Paris Memorial, above described, as recorded in Loeb's work,[56] and in Narcisse Leven's able *Cinquante ans d'histoire. L'Alliance Israélite Universelle, 1860-1910.*

The answer of the English Government to the Anglo-Jewish Association was very explicit. Lord Derby said:

You may be certain, that, under the present ministry and, without any doubt, under every ministry that could be formed in this country, the policy of England in the future, will be, as it has been in the past, favorable to the abolition of all distinctions between the adherents of one religion and another. . . . .

Lord Derby promised to exert all England's influence in a manner which would seem to him the wisest and most practical for preventing in the future the persecutions of the past. He added:

The Roumanian and Servian question ought not to be confounded with that of the Turkish provinces. In what will be done for the internal administration of Turkey, I am certainly not prepared to concur with any measure of administrative reform which does not apply to all non-Mussulman subjects. As for Roumania and Servia, the position of semi-independence which they have acquired makes direct action for them more difficult.

---

[56] Pp. 365-8.

The Minister said, in short, that, having seen the Memorial for the first time the very morning of this conversation, he could not comment upon it in detail, but that he would send it to the Ambassador at Constantinople for such action as might be proper.

Melegari, the Minister of Foreign Affairs of Italy, declared to a Roman deputation of the *Alliance Israélite:*

No concession should be made to Servia and to Roumania, except on condition that they accord equality to the Israelites.

The German Secretary of Foreign Affairs, von Bülow, announced to the German delegates, in the name of Prince Bismarck, the Chancellor of the Empire, that the Memorial had been sent to the German plenipotentiary in Constantinople and declared that the

Imperial Government will support with pleasure the wishes concerning the equality of the Israelitish subjects of Turkey with those of other confessions, and will act in the same way, should the condition of the Israelitish population in Roumania and Servia enter into the conclusions of the deliberations of the Conference.[51]

Prince Orloff, Ambassador of Russia in Paris, most cordially received a deputation of the *Alliance,* which had sent him a copy of the Memorial, and expressed the conviction

that no measure would be taken in Turkey in favor of the Christians, which would not be extended equally to the Israelites.

The *Alliance* made a special request of the Minister of Foreign Affairs of France; it was to introduce to the French Ambassador in Constantinople, M. Netter, a member of the Central Committee of the *Alliance Israélite Universelle,* authorized to act in its name in Constantinople. Duke Decazes

---

[51] Already in 1868 Bismarck had officially expressed similar sympathy for this cause. Loeb, *supra,* p. 329. On February 28, 1878, von Bülow replied, in terms foreshadowing favorable action by the Powers, to a petition addressed to Bismarck by the leading Jewish congregations of Germany. See *Allgemeine Zeitung des Judentums,* 1878, pp. 157, 198, 426, 469-70.

answered "that he was eager to recommend M. Netter to the kindly welcome of the Ambassador," and added:

The sentiments of the French Government on the question with which the *Alliance* is engaged, are well enough known, so that there is no need of my adding that the support of our plenipotentiaries is assured in advance to the Israelites of the Orient, in the deliberations in which their interests and their rights could be the object.

The Russo-Turkish War brought much misery to the Jews of Eastern Europe in particular, the reports in the Jewish papers of that period reminding us greatly of war reports of our own time. The Board of Delegates of American Israelites called these conditions to the attention of our State Department, and the correspondence, given above, took place. This correspondence Secretary Evarts, as pointed out, communicated to Minister Horace Maynard. It produced newspaper reports of an exaggerated character, which were referred to in the following unpublished letters exchanged between Consular Agent Adolf Stern and our Department of State.

I.

Bucharest, May 30, 1877.

Hon. WILLIAM M. EVARTS.

SIR: On the 28th inst. I received from the Foreign Office a note wherein Mr. Kogalniceano, referring to the action of the deputation from the Board of Delegates of American Israelites in behalf of the Roumanian Jews, and giving me positive assurances that the alleged atrocities of Giurgewo have not occurred, requests me to "enlighten my Government and to state that those atrocities are a pure invention."

In reply I sent to the Foreign Office the note of which I beg to transmit an accurate copy.

Roumania is anxious to prove the legitimacy of her claims to the political independence which she has recently proclaimed; it is therefore natural that the Government should feel alarmed by anything which is calculated to create bad feeling abroad and revive the memory of the intolerance which has so frequently led to the gross outrages heretofore practiced on the Jews of Roumania.

I am, Sir, your obedient servant,

ADOLF STERN.

II.

Bucharest, May 27, 1877

Hon. WILLIAM M. EVARTS.

SIR: I learn from a newspaper that on May 2d a deputation from the Board of Delegates of American Israelites have waited upon his Excel. the President and yourself in behalf of the Israelites of Roumania, presenting a written statement respecting recent baruarities committed upon the Jews of Giurgewo and urging the Department to request our Representatives at Vienna, Constantinople and St. Petersburg to act in conjunction with the Representatives of those Powers in endeavoring to repress further atrocities.

While it is desirable that the Department, in compliance with the request of that deputation, should instruct the American Representatives abroad to interpose whenever required in behalf of the Roumanian Israelites, who labor under many disabilities and are exposed to frequent vexations, I must state that, from my own inquiries, no other atrocities have been practised on the Roumanian Jews, since November last, when several hundred Jewish inhabitants were driven away from the rural communes of the district of Washir in Moldavia. I have used my best influence and efforts to have the Government repress at once these inhumane expulsions; but only after they had been suffered to go on for about 4 months, was it possible to obtain the resignation (not dismissal) of the Prefect Lupashku, who had issued the orders for expulsion. In many instances the orders were withdrawn and several of the expelled Israelites, who were wandering shelterless about the country with their wives and children, exposed to cold and hunger, were allowed to return to their homes, where they found their property destroyed. They cannot expect compensation for their losses, nor redress for the wrongs practised upon them. These expulsions are all based upon Articles 8 and 12 of the Liquor Law, passed in 1873, which excludes from the liquor traffic in the rural communes "all persons not inscribed as electors in one of the Communes of Roumania," thereby virtually prohibiting all Israelites from continuing or engaging in this trade. The Government, on the representation of the Consuls here, repeatedly pledged itself not to enforce this law and to have the same repealed, but the law is still in force, and it only depends on the humor of a Prefect or other subaltern official to enforce those clauses, close the stores of the Israelites, confiscate their goods and expel them from their homes.

No persecution has, however, taken place at Giurgewo. The impression of such persecution originated probably in the reported murder of a Jewish family who, while flying from Giurgewo on account of its being exposed to bombardment by the Turks, were assaulted, grossly maltreated and killed on the highroad. Giurgewo is now nearly empty of inhabitants since the declaration of the war.

I am, Sir, your obedient servant,

ADOLF STERN.

III.

Bucharest, May 30, 1877.

MR. MINISTER:

I have received your esteemed note of the 22d instant, in which you inform me, according to the report published by a Vienna journal, of the representations made at Washington, by an Israelitic deputation, to the President of the Republic and the Secretary of State, in regard to certain atrocities alleged to have been committed against the Israelites in the town of Giurgewo, and request me to enlighten my Government and to state that the persecutions are pure invention.

I read myself, in a Vienna journal, with surprise, the news which you were pleased to communicate to me, and as I knew that the denunciations were unfounded, I did not think it necessary to await the confirmation of the statement published by the Vienna journal, and, previously to the receipt of your esteemed note, I had already enlightened my Government, in order that it might not be left under an erroneous impression.

I am happy to have thus fulfilled, in advance, the desire which you express in your note, but I must add that the murder of a Jewish family, which was recently committed on the highway between Giurgewo and Bucharest, seems to me to have been the source of the complaints referred to. I should therefore be obliged to you, Mr. Minister, if you would be pleased to furnish me with any details of which you may be in possession, in relation to this incident, which, being magnified and distorted, has perhaps alarmed and surprised the Israelites of Washington.

Be persuaded, Mr. Minister, that you can, on all occasions, rely upon my readiness and my earnest desire to dispel, to the best of my ability, any impression at variance with the truth, and calculated to be prejudicial to the interests of Roumania.

Be pleased to accept, Mr. Minister, the assurance of my high consideration.

STERN.

Mr. M. KOGALNICEANO,
   Minister of Foreign Affairs, etc.

The need of suffering Jews in the war zone was so great, that American Jews were appealed to, to contribute to the relief of Jews in the Ottoman Empire. In consequence of a conference held in 1878, a special committee was organized, of which Judge Myer S. Isaacs was chairman and Mr. Jacob H. Schiff treasurer, to collect funds, and over $7000 was raised and forwarded to Crémieux for distribution, through the *Alliance,* acting in coöperation with Baron de Hirsch and his aid, M. Venceziani. The idea of having Jewish organizations represented at Berlin, in connection with the Congress of Berlin, is claimed to have originated with the Board of Delegates of American Israelites, which suggested laying before such prospective Congress a full statement of the Jewish question, in a letter to the Anglo-Jewish Association in February, 1878, and an interchange of views to this end took place at London, between that organization and Mr. Peixotto, who was then on his way to begin the performance of his duties as United States Consul at Lyons.

C. THE INTERNATIONAL JEWISH CONFERENCE AT PARIS, 1878.

Before considering, in detail, the action taken at and in connection with the Congress of Berlin concerning the Jews of Eastern Europe, it will be convenient to disregard chronological order, so as to say a few words regarding the third International Jewish Conference, held at Paris, August 15. 1878. Crémieux again presided, and America was represented by Myer Stern, B. F. Peixotto and Rev. Henry S. Jacobs. Emigration to the United States was particularly considered, especially in papers prepared by Myer S. Isaacs, Henry Rice and Myer Stern. European organizations were warned against promoting indiscriminately the emigration of Jewish paupers incapable of supporting themselves, and plans for distributing Jewish immigrants were outlined.[54]

[54] "Final Report of Board of Delegates of American Israelites," New York, 1879; *The Jewish Chronicle,* August 16 and 23, 1878; *The Jewish Times,* October 11, 1878.

III.
THE CONGRESS OF BERLIN, 1878.

The Russo-Turkish War of 1877-78, following the unsuccessful Conference of Constantinople of 1876, began with Russia's declaration of war against Turkey on April 24, 1877, ostensibly on account of the persecution of Turkey's Christian subjects. After Russia had violated Roumanian neutrality, against Roumania's nominal protests, by sending her troops into the principality *en route* to Turkey, Roumania joined in the war against Turkey. The war ended with the Treaty of San Stefano of March 3, 1878, after Turkey had exhibited unexpectedly great, but futile, powers of resistance, but the other Great Powers were not represented in this treaty, and had not yet acquiesced in Turkey's recognition of Roumanian independence, and Austria and England had strong interests opposed to the terms of the Treaty of San Stefano. Accordingly Austria, on February 5, 1878, addressed a circular note to the Powers that had signed the Treaty of Paris of 1856 and the London protocol of 1871, suggesting a new international conference for establishing "the agreement of Europe on the modifications which it may become necessary to introduce into the above-mentioned treaties," and England, on April 1, 1878, declined to recognize the Treaty of San Stefano, unless the terms thereof were made the subject of a formal agreement among the parties to the Treaty of Paris, and took steps tending towards a declaration of war against Russia. Germany joined in these conference suggestions, and, despite Russia's opposition, such a Congress became essential, and was accordingly formally called by the German Government on June 3, 1878, to meet at Berlin, June 13, 1878. The Congress lasted just one month, with Prince Bismarck presiding. It was Germany's unexpected failure to sustain Russian demands, as expressed in Bismarck's announced purpose of remaining neutral in the rôle of "honest broker," that led to very considerable deviations, contrary to Russian and Roumanian interests, from the terms of the Treaty of San Stefano. Beaconsfield's unusual course of personally attending the Congress, though then Prime Minister, lent much significance to the deliberations.

As pointed out in Dr. Cyrus Adler's "Jews in the Diplomatic Correspondence of the United States,"[59] John A. Kasson, U. S. Minister to Austria, in an important dispatch to Secretary Evarts under date of June 5, 1878,[60] suggested that the United States Government should indicate its approval of having the Congress of Berlin decree equal rights to the Jews of Roumania, and this letter is probably the only official note, antedating the assemblage of the Congress, specifically suggesting such course. Mr. Kasson wrote:

It would be to the honor of the United States Government, if it could initiate a plan by which at once the condition of American Hebrews resident or travelling in Roumania, and the conditions of natives of the same race, could be ameliorated and their equality before the law at least partially assured.

The European Congress is about to assemble, and will be asked to recognize the independence of Roumania. Would there be any just objection to the United States Government offering on its part, if the European powers would on their part, make the same condition, to recognize the independence of that country, and to enter into treaty stipulations with its government, only upon the fundamental preliminary agreements:

1. That all citizens or subjects of any such foreign nationality shall, irrespective of race or religious belief, be entitled to equal rights and protection under the treaty and under their laws.

2. That all subjects or citizens under the jurisdiction of the Roumanian Government shall, irrespective of their race or religious belief, have equal rights of trade and commerce with the citizens or subjects of the foreign governments making such treaty; equal rights in the purchase, consumption, barter, or sale of the products of such foreign country, and in sales of Roumanian products to such aliens; equal rights to make contracts with the citizens or subjects of such foreign government, and to be equally protected by the laws in the exercise of the rights so secured?

---

[59] *Publications, supra*, No. 15, pp. v, 48-49.
[60] "Foreign Relations, 1878," p. 42.

To this extent, at least, it seems foreign governments would be justified by international law and the law of self-interest; while they would at the same time give effect to the humane instinct of all truly civilized and Christian nations. The persecuting and oppressive spirit is so strong in Roumania against the Jews that it requires united action by liberal and constitutional governments, as well as an appeal to the strongest desires of the Roumanian people, which are just now to be permitted to enter the family of nations, to bring relief and emancipation to this proscribed race.

Your own judgment will improve, doubtless, the form of action above suggested; but it will be sufficient, I hope, to attract your attention to a question, the favorable solution of which would greatly gratify the American people, and evoke especial gratitude from that race which has found in the United States absolute legal equality and security, and the occasion of the congress is most favorable for giving it effect, if approved.

The Congress of Berlin assembled eight days after this dispatch was written, so that there was not much time for formal action in the interim. We know, however, that the State Department at once acknowledged Mr. Kasson's letter, saying "that the subject is one eminently deserving of consideration, which it will receive."

Bayard Taylor took up the duties of his post as United States Minister to Germany shortly before the Congress of Berlin met, and he and his colleagues at other European capitals acted in line with Mr. Kasson's suggestion. Under date of July 15, 1878, Taylor reported to the State Department[61] as to the Treaty of Berlin, which he described as "perhaps the most important historical act since that of Vienna in 1815":

The chief interest which the Government and people of the United States have in the treaty is its enforcement of religious liberty in Roumania, Bulgaria and Eastern Roumelia. This is the only point which I felt at liberty to present unofficially to several members of the Congress, and I am glad to report that it was opposed by none of the statesmen present.[62]

---

[61] "Foreign Relations, 1878," pp. 227-8.

[62] See Mr. Taylor's impressions of the Congress, *ibid.*, pp. 221-2, and "Life and Letters of Bayard Taylor," Boston, 1885, vol. ii, pp. 745-7, 754.

Reports regarding the Congress and the significance of the treaty provisions were also transmitted by Mr. Kasson from Vienna,[63] Mr. Marsh from Rome,[64] and from our Minister at Constantinople.[65]

As far as Jewish disabilities and their removal were concerned, the Paris Jewish Conference of 1876, hereinbefore referred to, held in connection with the Constantinople Conference, had made arrangements for an international presentation of these grievances. However, vigorous opposition had meantime developed against the ratification of treaties with Roumania, negotiated by various leading powers, which would have had the effect of discriminating against Jewish subjects of such other powers, by applying against them, Roumania's own discriminations against her own Jewish subjects. England, France, Italy and Germany suspended ratification, pending modification, of these provisions, and in Germany particularly, a vigorous debate led by Eduard Lasker,[66] on May

---

[63] "Foreign Relations, 1878," pp. 50-1; *infra*, pp. 71-2.

[64] *Ibid.*, pp. 475-7.

[65] *Ibid.*, pp. 865, 886, 894.

[66] German anti-Semitic enemies of Eduard Lasker have made the absurd claim that his vigorous espousal of the cause of equal rights for his coreligionists in Roumania militated in some way against his German patriotism. The mere statement of this proposition carries its own refutation, for it was obviously an act of German patriotism, to insist that the German passport should be honored in Roumania, regardless of the creed of its holder. Nor is the championship of humanity and religious liberty even for distant climes in derogation of one's citizenship in one's own country. In fact, however, Lasker was no less zealous in struggling for the liberty and freedom of worship of non-Jews, and these incidents in his career were most beautifully treated by his friend, Andrew D. White, in an address at his funeral in New York in 1884, when he said that Lasker was " one whom we are proud to call in the highest sense our brother. This brotherhood he recognized. No barriers of creed could shut out from him the view of it. Never was he more vigorous than when he stood up for the rights of Roman Catholics in Parliament; never more eloquent than when he stood

14, 1878, in the Reichstag, a full report of which has been handed down to us, culminated in a reference of the treaty to a legislative commission, instead of ratification." In Austria and Hungary, Moritz Wahrmann and Dr. Ignaz Kuranda, both members of the legislature, started movements for the proposed abolition of Jewish disabilities through the forthcoming International Congress, which elicited assurances from Count Gyula Andrassy that, if opportunity offered, Austria would advocate equality of rights for all religions in the countries whose affairs the Congress would deal with,[68] and the German Minister of Foreign Affairs[69] gave similar assurances, as also the Italian Prime Minister. The *Alliance Israélite Universelle,* from its Paris office, forwarded a vigorous memorial, signed by Crémieux and his associates, to the Congress, a copy of which is annexed as Appendix III (p. 105).

---

by the grave of his Protestant friend Twesten. He came of that race which has upheld for thousands of years, against all temptations, all sophistry, all obloquy, all cruelty, the idea of the Divine unity; and he loved his race; but he rose superior to all the environments of race and creed. Like those men of different races and creeds, Baruch Spinoza and Hugo Grotius in the seventeenth century, like Moses Mendelssohn and Lessing in the eighteenth century, so did Eduard Lasker in the nineteenth century belong to the good and noble and true souls who have striven to make this earth better and more beautiful—who, whether Jew or Gentile, form the true elect of mankind, the very Israel of God." (*The American Hebrew*, January, 1884.)

[67] See *Allgemeine Zeitung des Judentums*, 1878, pp. 340, 356, 422, 566.

[68] *Ibid.,* pp. 387, 469-70; *The Jewish Chronicle*, June 28, 1878.

[69] " The Jewish Encyclopedia," *s. v.* Bismarck, quotes von Bülow, German Minister for Foreign Affairs, as stating to a Jewish delegation just before the Congress: " Gentlemen, '*toleration*' is an incorrect word; not toleration but *the unrestricted exercise of all their rights* shall we demand at the Congress for your coreligionists." Contemporary Jewish newspapers thus reported his remark: *Israelitische Wochenschrift*, Magdeburg, July 3, 1878, p. 221; *Allgemeine Zeitung des Judentums*, 1878, p. 426.

Lionel de Rothschild addressed an earnest letter to Lord Beaconsfield, dated May 31, 1878, urging action in favor of the removal of Jewish disabilities at the forthcoming Congress, the text of which has been preserved.[10] So, also, a brief Joint Memorial was addressed to England's representatives at the Congress, dated June 13, 1878, by J. M. Montefiore as President of the London Committee of Deputies of the British Jews and Henry de Worms, as President of the Anglo-Jewish Association.[11] About the same date, on June 16, Baron Henry de Worms made a public statement as to probable action at the Congress, as follows:[12]

---

[10] *The Jewish Chronicle*, June 14, 1878.

[11] *Ibid.*, June 21, 1878, p. 10.

[12] *Ibid.* Baron Henry de Worms, subsequently Lord Pirbright, was enabled to render services, the importance of which should not be underestimated in this connection. While he was, on the one hand, the President of the Anglo-Jewish Association, which was taking a leading rôle in this movement, and had, as we have seen, taken an important part at the Paris Conference of 1876, he was also one of the chief authorities relied on by the Conservative Party, in upholding its course on the Eastern Question in general, and enjoyed the confidence of Lord Beaconsfield and other political leaders. He was also an intimate of Count von Beust, the Austrian Ambassador at London, and subsequently, at his request, edited the English edition of the latter's "Memoirs," in which von Beust refers to his obligations to de Worms; in fact, even previous to this period, de Worms had enlisted von Beust's aid in presenting the Roumanian Jewish Question to the British Foreign Office, as an English blue book shows. References to his course, published herein, show that he was a wise and prudent statesman, and closely in touch with all efforts in this matter, both English and Continental, and even had important advance information before the Congress met. See as to his career, "The Jewish Encyclopedia"; necrology in *The Jewish Chronicle*, January 16 and 23, 1903, the English *Jewish Year Book* for 1903, and "Dictionary of National Biography," 2d supplement, vol. i, *s. v.* de Worms. Note also the references, *infra*, p. 59, to his book, "England's Policy in the East," London, 1877.

Earl Beaconsfield had taken the liveliest interest in the future condition of those Jews. He was happy to say that there was every indication that the work of the Board of Deputies and the Anglo-Jewish Association would be crowned with success. The Memorial addressed to Earl Beaconsfield and the Marquis of Salisbury had been forwarded by the Foreign Office to Berlin by Queen's Messenger. In the Memorial they had given the widest scope to their appeal. They had pleaded that religious toleration and political equality should be given to the members of all creeds alike, without any distinction of religion whatever. He ought also remark that Prince Bismarck had indirectly informed the Jewish gentlemen who had drawn his attention to the subject that he did not consider any settlement of the Eastern Question satisfactory, which did not place the Jews of Roumania upon a footing of perfect equality with their fellow citizens. It would be remembered that the German Parliament had refused to ratify a Commercial Treaty between Germany and Roumania, on the ground that the Treaty proposed to place German Jews on a different footing than other German citizens. The opposition to this Treaty had been led by Herr Lasker, himself a Jew. It would thus be seen that the spirit of toleration was abroad and growing. It must, however, never be lost sight of that the best way to successfully overcome prejudice was by showing that Jews were worthy, not of mere toleration, but of being placed upon a position of perfect equality with their fellow men.

On the same occasion, Baron de Worms stated that he had been personally ready to go to Berlin, to endeavor to interest members of the Congress in this cause, but he had learnt on high authority that this might prejudice, rather than aid, the cause, and similar advice was given to the Austrian Jewish delegates, the recommendation being that they should make their representations to their own Government. (*Israelitische Wochenschrift*, 1878, pp. 201, 220.) Perhaps " coming events had cast their shadows before," and they had been advised of the forthcoming humiliation to which the Roumanian Government was itself to be subjected by the Congress, which refused to receive its representatives even as petitioners, until after it had determined, in fact, to give effect to Russian ingratitude, and to deprive Roumania of conquered territory ceded to Russia by Turkey by the Treaty of San Stefano.

The *Alliance Israélite Universelle,* however, adopted a different course, and appointed MM. Netter, Kann and Veneziani to wait on individual members of the Congress at Berlin, Crémieux himself being prevented from attending by illness. Dr. Moritz Guedemann represented the Vienna branch of the *Alliance Israélite Universelle.* Probably the chief Jewish factor of all, however, was Baron Gerson von Bleichroeder, who exerted his potent influence in this cause on Prince Bismarck personally, as well as on other delegates, and his name appeared first on a letter of thanks to the Congress, transmitted by representative Jews after the clauses relating to religious liberty had been adopted.[13] The most detailed account of the

[13] See necrology in *The Jewish Chronicle,* February 24, 1893; "The Jewish Encyclopedia," *s. v.* Bleichroeder. In a private letter to an English correspondent, Bleichroeder wrote on July 5, 1878, of the Jewish emancipation provisions of the treaty: "The task performed by the Congress, notwithstanding the justice of the cause, has not been an easy one. It required the cooperation of all the Powers, and I must here repeat that Prince Bismarck was foremost in the work of humanity, and he has the greatest merit in its accomplishment." It is also interesting to notice that, immediately after the Congress of Berlin closed, Bleichroeder had a long interview with Count Schouvaloff, one of Russia's plenipotentiaries, at the end of which the latter promised to work for Jewish emancipation in Russia. See *The Jewish Chronicle, supra,* and *ibid.,* August 16, 1878, and *Israelitische Wochenschrift,* Magdeburg, vol. ix, p. 220, July 3, 1878. Julius Bleichroeder, a cousin of Baron Gerson von Bleichroeder, had signed the call, as a leader of the Berlin Jewish community, for the Brussels Conference of 1874, was in correspondence with the American Board of Delegates, as above noted, and undoubtedly kept his kinsman well-informed as to the developments in the Roumanian Jewish situation. Moreover, Gerson von Bleichroeder had been ennobled because of valuable services rendered by him in 1872 to Roumania, and his name figures frequently in King Charles' diary, *Aus dem Leben König Karls von Rumänien,* often cited herein, as also in Prince Hohenlohe's "Memoirs," London, 1906, and Busch's record of Bismarck's doings, entitled *Tagebuchblätter,* Leipzig, 1899. See the indices of these works, as well as Lucien Wolf's excellent article on anti-

action on this point at the Congress of Berlin, including excerpts from the official protocol, and the assurances given privately by various delegates, is to be found in Leven's valuable history of the *Alliance Israélite Universelle,* which will be freely drawn upon hereinafter, in the account of the Congress of Berlin, supplemented by various references to contemporary Jewish newspapers and other sources."

Semitism, in the " Encyclopedia Britannica," 11th edition, vol. ii, p. 135, where reference is made to the fact that he financed Prussia in the War of 1866 with Austria, when other funds were unobtainable. He was also for twenty-five years, covering this period, British Consul-General at Berlin, and thus closely in touch with English, as well as German, and other officials. The references to him in the text herein, particularly in Baron Henry de Worms' public statement of June 16, and in Netter's letters, show how close and important his relations to this matter were. Copies of telegrams exchanged between him and Sir Moses Montefiore on July 2, 1878, announcing the adoption of the then unpublished religious liberty conditions for Roumania of the Congress the day before, have been preserved, *The Jewish World,* London, July 15, 1878.

¹¹ See also, Oscar S. Straus' article on the Congress of Berlin in " The Jewish Encyclopedia "; George S. Hellman's address before The Judæans on this subject (*The American Hebrew,* January 15, 1909), together with abstract of Prof. Ferrero's address; B. Brunswik's *Le Traité de Berlin annoté et commenté,* Paris, 1878; " Great Britain, Foreign Office: Correspondence relating to the Congress of Berlin, Sessional Papers, 1878," vol. 83, containing English text of the protocol and the treaty; Hanotaux, " Contemporary France," New York, 1909, vol. iv, pp. 323-89, and *Le Congrès de Berlin,* in *Revue des Deux Mondes,* October 1 and 15, 1908; Charles De Mouy's *Récits et Portraits du Congrès de Berlin,* in *ibid.,* October 15 and November 1, 1904; Twiss, " Law of Nations," 2d edition, Oxford, 1884, pt. i, pp. 88-144; Milobar, *Der Berliner Kongress,* Zürich, 1902; *À d'Avril, Negociations Relatives au Traité de Berlin;* French Yellow Book, Paris, 1878, entitled *Le Congrès de Berlin;* Schouvaloff, *Souvenirs inédits du Congrès de Berlin* (quoted in Hanotaux, *supra*); Bluntschli, *Le Congrès de Berlin* in *Revue du droit international public,* Brussels, 1879 and 1880; Carathéodory Pasha, *Souvenirs inédits du Congrès de Berlin* (quoted in Hanotaux, *supra*); T. E. Holland, " European Concert in the East-

In the rearrangement of the countries of the Orient, to which the Congress was called upon to devote itself, it was necessary to obtain the settlement of the situation of the Jews. Russia had pursued the policy of dismembering Turkey to her own gain, by insisting upon the necessity of improving the lot of the Christians, whereas, as England said, in the famous note of her Minister, Lord Salisbury, on April 1, it was necessary only to

give effect to the policy of reforming Turkey under the Ottoman Empire, removing well-grounded grievances, and thus preserving the Empire until the time when it might be able to dispense with protective guarantees. (Reprinted in "Foreign Relations of the United States, 1878," p. 263.)

Russia wanted to secure the welfare of the Christians, but not that of the Jews. In the programme of the Congress, they were not considered. The *Alliance Israélite Universelle* had occupied itself previously with the Conference of Constantinople, and the declarations of Germany, England, France and Italy gave great hope. In case the condition of the Jewish population of Roumania and Serbia should come into the framework of the Congress of Berlin, as Baron Bernhard von Bülow said, in a statement herein cited, it was inadmissible,

---

ern Question," Oxford, 1885, and "Studies in International Law," Oxford, 1898; S. P. Duggan, "The Eastern Question," New York, 1902; *Allgemeine Zeitung des Judentums*, 1878, pp. 357, 387, 435, 451, 469, 484, 499, 535, 545, 548, 563, 567, 596, 627, 659, 674; Hahn, *Bismarck*, Berlin, 1881, vol. iii, pp. 119-315; Martens, *Nouveau Receuil Général*, Göttingen, 1878-9, 2d series, vol. iii, pp. 276-448; Duke of Argyle's "The Eastern Question," London, 1878, vol. ii, pp. 136-214; J. R. Young, "Around the World with General Grant," New York, 1879, vol. i, p. 412 *et seq.;* "Memoirs of M. de Blowitz," New York, 1903; Mary King Waddington, "My First Years as a Frenchwoman," New York, 1914, pp. 133-155; *Bulletin* of the New York Public Library, 1910, entitled "List of Works relating to the Near Eastern Question and the Balkan States." Strangely enough there has been no work in English or German conveniently accessible which gives an account of the debates at the Congress, and there is none in French readily accessible to others than specialists.

not to make regulations for them, since the Jews belonged to Turkey, going with the territory in which they were placed, and passing under a new régime. Could Europe hand over the Jews to Serbia or to Roumania, to have them oppressed? Could not the Congress of Berlin do at last, for all the Jews settled in these countries, that which had been expected of the Conference of Constantinople?

Of the three *Alliance* delegates, Netter, Kann and Veneziani, who went to Berlin to intercede with the plenipotentiaries there assembled, Netter had been in Constantinople at the time of the Conference in 1877, and Kann and Veneziani were well-informed, one regarding the affairs of the *Alliance,* the other concerning those of the Orient.

Before the assembling of the Congress, there had been enlisted, the *Alliance* representatives reported, the support of an influential man in Berlin—von Bleichroeder— who, by his social position, had relations with the plenipotentiaries and a great deal of influence with Bismarck. They began their proceedings; Netter kept a daily account of them in his letters, which are full of interest, as reported in Leven's book.

At first they had apprehensions: would the best disposed Powers be willing to complicate the questions that were so threatening for European peace, with which idea the Congress was permeated, by the Jewish question, where they would clash with Russia? What would Austria do? Her first plenipotentiary was Andrassy, the author of the discriminatory commercial treaty between Austria and Roumania. All the plenipotentiaries had received the memorandum of the *Alliance* with Loeb's book on Serbia and Roumania. The impressions of Netter and the other delegates changed rapidly. After a visit to St. Vallier, Ambassador from France and second French delegate to the Congress, Netter wrote on the 11th of June:

If every one thought as does M. de St. Vallier about our coreligionists, our cause would be won. He knew the matter from the inside.

On the 12: "Lord Beaconsfield is in excellent humor." On the 13th:

> Yesterday Bleichroeder saw Prince Bismarck; he hopes that everything is in favor of the Israelites.

On the 16th:

> To-day we saw Lord Russell; he recalled to us what Lord John Russell had done for the Israelites; he will support our cause.

The same day:

> Fine reception by Baron von Bülow; also assurances on his part. He is a man of vast intelligence and great amenity; he spoke to us about the commercial treaty, about the interpretation that they wanted to give it and of its withdrawal. [It was a discriminatory commercial treaty similar to the one which Austria had made with Roumania; see *supra*, p. 43.]

On the 18th:

> To-day we visited the Prince of Hohenlohe-Schillingsfürst. He began his career by fighting for the cause of the Israelites of Bavaria; he wanted to crown it by defending it at the Congress; he begged us to give him supplementary references, should the opportunity occur.[15] We visited M. de Launay, the Italian plenipotentiary; he was as cordial as could be. He will always fight for the cause of the Israelites, who in all countries where they have equal rights, have always shown themselves equal to them.

The 19th:

> This morning M. Kann saw M. Toizé, secretary to Andrassy, who told him that these gentlemen have agreed to uphold the cause, which, no doubt, will be moved in the order of the day by Lord Beaconsfield; in any case Andrassy will support him.

---

[15] It will be remembered that Prince Hohenlohe, a delegate to the Congress, subsequently was Imperial German Chancellor. His "Memoirs," London, 1906, contain much material of interest confirming the statement in the text, including also the one made while the Congress was in session (vol. ii, p. 219), as follows: "Roggenbach thinks that Bismarck is passionately aroused against Roumania." Again, under date of July 5, 1878 (*ibid.*, p. 221): "I had a visit from an Israelite of Bucharest, who gave me some interesting information as to the position of the Jews in Roumania."

The 21st:

> Baron von Bleichroeder saw Prince Bismarck yesterday and was assured by him that he would bring the question before the Congress, and Baron von Bleichroeder, having insisted that that would be Bulgaria's opportunity, he received the answer that they had not yet reached that question, but he gave his word and said they could be reassured.

The *Alliance* delegates also occupied themselves with the press. They conversed with the correspondents of the important European newspapers; they kept them informed themselves. They were in close proximity to Ristitch, the Serbian representative, and to the representatives of Roumania. Bratiano and Cogalniceanu, who, having come to Berlin to defend their country before the Congress, worked for the press at the same time, to mislead public opinion on the subject of the Israelites of their country. After hesitating, the delegates of the *Alliance* consented to confer with them; Ristitch was less biased against his Israelitish compatriots than Bratiano was. He made a good impression on the delegates. They did not give up hope of getting Ristitch to cheerfully accept the resolutions that they expected from the Congress. He could resign himself to it; Serbia was going to obtain from Congress an extension of her territory. However, the Serbian Minister did not know how to conceal his hostility to the Israelites; his second conference with the delegates ended with a whim of his, which betrayed his project; he hoped for them the reëstablishment of their kingdom in Palestine, which, " the Roumanians say, we also wish them, so as to get rid of them." They had a long talk with Bratiano, but without result; he knew that his country's loss of Bessarabia, determined on by the Congress, would be the cause of his losing his ministry.

The Congress of Berlin had devoted five meetings to the creation of a Bulgaria which would be much smaller in extent than the one Russia wanted in her Treaty of San Stefano, when the French plenipotentiaries proposed, at the fifth meeting, on

June 24, 1878, with M. William Henry Waddington,[76] the first French plenipotentiary, as their spokesman, two additional articles, of which the first introduced into the constitution of Bulgaria, the principles of 1789. The first was worded thus:

All Bulgarian subjects, whatever their religion may be, shall enjoy complete equality of rights. They may hold all public

---

[76] It is often loosely stated that the credit for securing the adoption of the provisions for religious liberty in the Treaty of Berlin belongs to France, and particularly to her senior plenipotentiary, Waddington. This is only superficially true, and it is difficult to justify a conclusion which gives more credit to France than to England, Germany and even Italy. It is true that M. Waddington offered these Balkan resolutions at the Congress, and vigorously supported them throughout its sessions, and the protocol often speaks of them as the French propositions, see *infra*, pp. 60-61, 64, 66; and this is also the view of Hanotaux, *supra*, vol. iv, pp. 367, 376, 479. Naturally, the French Jewish delegates of the *Alliance Israélite Universelle* have claimed the chief credit for France in the matter, as have Jewish writers of other countries, for their own lands. Superficially, Waddington's claims are strengthened by the circumstance that M. de Blowitz, in his "Memoirs," New York, 1903, p. 200, suggests that Bismarck supported the provisions at the Congress in order to oblige France, though it appears from evidence collated in this book (which was unknown to de Blowitz) that Bismarck had given assurances of his support long before France offered them, and that it was at one time apparently intended that Beaconsfield should offer these provisions, and at another time that Bismarck himself should, and that, in any event, already on June 16, Baron Henry de Worms stated in England that adoption of such provisions was quite probable, particularly in view of Bismarck's support. On the other hand, France had long before established a kind of protectorate over certain holy places in the East, and was eager to maintain her concessions from Turkey regarding them and the related matter of protection of the religious, political and civil rights of minorities in various Eastern lands. Accordingly, when the Congress of Berlin was being arranged for, partly in order to secure the maintenance of peace by attempting to limit the deliberations of the Congress to a few points in controversy between Russia, England and Austria, and perhaps also in order to safeguard these

offices, functions and honors, and differences in faith will not be urged against them as a ground for exclusion.

The exercise and public practice of all creeds will be entirely free, and no restrictions will be applied, either on the hierarchical organization of different faiths, or to their relations with their spiritual chiefs.

---

special Turkish "capitulations" of her own, and her own peculiar Eastern interests, France accepted the invitation to attend the Congress only on condition that the Congress should consider solely the questions arising from the war, and not the Egyptian question, for instance, or that of the Lebanons, or the holy places, not affected by the Treaty of San Stefano (Hanotaux, "Contemporary France," vol. iv, p. 343; Hahn, *Bismarck*, vol. iii, pp. 120, 309), and this limitation was acquiesced in by the other powers, despite England's wishes to make the conference more comprehensive. After France had determined to participate in the Congress, however, Waddington stated in the Chamber of Deputies on June 7, 1878, that "France will go to the Congress. In going, she will also remember that there are Christians besides the Bulgarians in the Balkan peninsula; that *there are other races which*, at least in some degree, *merit the interest of Europe.*" (*Annales du Sénat et de la Chambre des Députés*, June 7, 1878; Hanotaux, *supra*, p. 344; Hahn, *supra*, p. 309.) This language was certainly comprehensive enough to include Jewish emancipation in the Balkans, and was so construed in the Jewish press at the time (*Israelitische Wochenschrift*, vol. ix, p. 193). France had, of course, for many years previously interested herself in this cause, and Crémieux, then Waddington's associate in the French Senate, and other Jewish leaders, did not neglect to endeavor to secure Waddington's assistance for the Balkan Jews. Contemporary French history indicates, however, that the French Government was quite undecided about participating in the Congress at all, and Mrs. Waddington reports ("My First Years as a Frenchwoman," New York, 1914, pp. 133-155) that the Ministry gave her husband absolutely no instructions as to the course he should pursue at the Congress, and, before and after, Waddington's associates feared to burn their fingers over the Congress. Unfortunately, Mrs. Waddington reports practically nothing as to what occurred at the Congress, though her husband's correspondence and files must have been full of the subject. Waddington was, however, exceptionally deeply interested in and thoroughly familiar with this subject, as the official protocol shows, particu-

The second article assured entire liberty " to religious orders and to foreign Catholic bishops " for the practice of their faith in Bulgaria and in Eastern Roumelia.

The president decided to defer these propositions to a later session, after ordering them printed.

---

larly because he himself belonged to a minority faith in France, and had written, more than twenty years before, on "The Protestant Church and Religious Liberty in France," in "Cambridge Essays for 1856." Probably the championship of this cause at the Congress was left by the Powers to France for the further reason that England had so many other direct interests there, which required her particular attention, unlike France, and Bismarck preferred ostensibly to play the rôle of disinterested friend between Russian policies and those of her opponents. But the protocol of the Congress and the other facts herein collated leave absolutely no doubt as to the unhesitating and unequivocal support which Bismarck and his German associates gave to the cause of religious liberty at the Congress, and Baron von Bleichroeder's above-quoted statement of July 5, 1878, seems not to be wide of the mark, that it " required the coöperation of all the Powers, and I must here repeat that Prince Bismarck was foremost in the work of humanity, and he has the greatest merit in its accomplishment." It should be remembered that England, France and Italy, in coöperation with the United States, had several times made futile efforts, as has been seen, to secure Balkan Jewish emancipation, but now they secured hearty support for this cause from Germany at an opportune time. In fact, almost the only instance in which Bismarck referred to special German causes was at the beginning of the Congress, when he said on June 22: "His Serene Highness thinks it his duty to add that on this question he cannot, as German Plenipotentiary, remain neutral. The instructions which he has received from the Emperor, his august master, previous to the opening of Congress, enjoin upon him to seek to maintain for the Christians at least the degree of protection which the conference at Contantinople had desired to secure for them, and not to consent to any arrangement which would attenuate the result obtained for that important object." Reference is hereinafter made to the fact (p. 59) that it was largely Bismarck's skillful handling, which enabled the Congress to insert provisions for safeguarding the rights of Christians in Asiatic Turkey, despite the more limited French and

The protocol added only " that Count Schouvaloff and M. Waddington exchanged remarks [without saying what they were] about the import of these two propositions."

Then followed another similar proposition about the application of the treaties of commerce and navigation to Bulgaria and to Eastern Roumelia, made by Austria, France and Italy.

The discussion of these propositions was adjourned after Prince Bismarck observed that they ought first of all consider the questions that might come up, as to which there might be a disagreement between the cabinets:

English propositions on the subject, and despite the understanding that the Congress would deal only with matters presented by the Treaty of San Stefano. Of course, the instructions of Emperor William I., above referred to, were not even represented as applying to any but the Christian victims of religious persecution; and in view of the facts hereinafter narrated (*infra*, p. 75), it seems quite certain that Bismarck acted according to his own independent judgment and sense of justice in the matter. His break with Lasker, Bamberger and other Liberal leaders, did not occur till immediately after the Congress, and was therefore no factor then. Even Lasker, embittered against the powerful enemy who had crushed him politically, did not go further than to say of Bismarck that he was an anti-Semite *because* he did not crush German anti-Semitism, at a time when Lasker thought he could have done so. On Bismarck's relations to the Jews, see "The Jewish Encyclopedia," *s. v.* Bismarck, by Prof. S. Mannheimer, and Anti-Semitism, by Prof. G. Deutsch; Lucien Wolf in the "Encyclopedia Britannica," *supra;* Busch, *Tagebuchblätter*, Leipzig, 1899; and *Fürst Bismarck's Verhältniss zum Glauben, insbesondere zum Judenthum*, Magdeburg, 1877, a pamphlet in which a series of articles with that title was reprinted from the Magdeburg *Israelitische Wochenschrift* of that year. The man on the street is often inclined to attribute the provisions of the treaty regarding Jewish emancipation to Beaconsfield, because of his knowledge of Beaconsfield's Jewish birth, and a comment of Gladstone (*infra*, p. 71) indicates that this was also Gladstone's impression. While no doubt Beaconsfield lent this phase of the cause of religious liberty at the Congress his loyal and hearty support, as did also his associates, particularly the Marquess of Salisbury, he cannot be held primarily responsible for the insertion of these clauses in the treaty.

As to those which have in view an advance in civilization, and against which doubtless no Cabinet will have objections in principle [those were Waddington's propositions], he thought that the authors of such propositions ought to be left free to indicate the time that would seem to them most convenient to bring them before the High Assembly.

One of the French plenipotentiaries, Félix Désprez, on June 25, proposed a slight change in phraseology; he replaced the words "Bulgarian subjects" by those of "inhabitants of the

---

England was compelled to concentrate at the Congress upon other matters, more vital to her, in view of the impending danger of warfare. It is possible that Jewish subjects of Turkey were particularly in the minds of British statesmen when the words "*and other subjects of the Porte*" were inserted in the treaty between England and Turkey, signed just previously, June 4, 1878, by which the Sultan promised "to introduce necessary reforms to be agreed upon later between the two powers, into the government and for the *protection of the Christian and other subjects of the Porte in these territories.*" ("Foreign Relations of the United States, 1878," p. 889.) According to King Charles (*Aus dem Leben König Karls*, vol. iv, p. 233), Bismarck informed Sturdza, the Roumanian envoy, in July, 1879, that France and Italy had initiated these Jewish provisions at the Congress and that Germany could not withhold her support from such fundamentals of civilization. When Beaconsfield's correspondence is made available much light will doubtless be thrown on this and related questions. It is, of course, quite beyond the scope of the present work to consider the question of Beaconsfield's relations to the Jews, and the supposed influence of his Jewish origin upon England's course in the Eastern Question, as to which so much has been written. See Monypenny and Buckle's biography; Lucien Wolf's articles on Disraeli, particularly his notes in the "Centenary Edition" of "Vivian Grey" and "The Young Duke"; Israel Zangwill's "Primrose Sphinx" in "Dreamers of the Ghetto"; Bryce's "Studies in Contemporary Biography," New York, 1903; Froude's "Beaconsfield," New York, 1890; Georg Brandes' "Beaconsfield," London, 1878; Emma Lazarus, "Was the Earl of Beaconsfield a Representative Jew?" in *The Century Magazine*, vol. i, p. 939; "The Jewish Encyclopedia," *s. v.* Benjamin Disraeli; and the writings of Gladstone, Edward A. Freeman, and others.

"Principality of Bulgaria," in Waddington's proposition. This new designation was more comprehensive.

The protocol stated: "This modification is accepted and the proposition unanimously adopted."

Russia voted with the other Powers on the second proposition. Count Schouvaloff proposed to substitute for the words "religious orders and foreign Catholic bishops," the words "foreign ecclesiastics and members of religious orders." Lord Salisbury having expressed the hope that the same legislation would be, in this respect, established in Roumelia and in other provinces of Turkey, the first Turkish plenipotentiary, Carathéodory Pasha, declared

that any proposition concerning the free exercise of worship in the province of Eastern Roumelia seemed altogether superfluous, that province being on the point of being made subject to the authority of the Sultan, and in consequence, to the principles and to laws common to all parts of the Empire, which established equal tolerance for all faiths.

Waddington apparently found justifiable this protest against the so-called oppression of the Christians, which Russia emphasized, so as to excuse before Europe the crushing of Turkey; in view of the declarations of the Turkish plenipotentiary, he asked for an adjournment of the discussion until the following day, so as to revise his proposition before submitting it to the Congress.

The discussion of the next day (June 26) is worth recalling:

M. Waddington stated that in view of the declaration made yesterday by the Turkish plenipotentiary, and from which it appeared that the liberty of the Catholic faith remains guaranteed in Eastern Roumelia by the general laws of the Empire and by treaties and conventions, the French plenipotentiaries felt bound to present the following considerations:

As regards the additional article which they have presented, relating to the foreign Catholic religious orders, the French plenipotentiaries noted the principles of absolute liberty laid down yesterday by the Congress in favor of all communions and all faiths in Bulgaria, as well as of the declaration made, at the same meeting by the first Turkish plenipotentiary, namely, that in Eastern Roumelia no violation of rights secured to foreigners in the Ottoman Empire will take place.

Lord Salisbury regretted that the plenipotentiaries of France do not follow up their proposition by extending their tenor to all Turkey in Europe. In that his Excellency would have seen important progress realized.

M. Waddington answered that the progress of which Lord Salisbury spoke was gained by the acceptance, at yesterday's session, of the first French proposition which secured entire liberty of faith.

Lord Salisbury having remarked that this proposition concerned Bulgaria only, the president said that for his part, he wished that liberty of faith be required for all of Turkey, as much in Europe as in Asia, but he asked if the assent of the Ottoman plenipotentiaries could be obtained.[77]

---

[77] As indicated in the preceding note, both England and France were embarrassed in phrasing this provision by the assurances exacted by France that the Congress of Berlin should confine itself to the changes made by the Treaty of San Stefano in prior treaties. This doubtless accounts for France's limitation of this provision to the Turkish province of Eastern Roumelia, and Lord Salisbury's suggestion that it should be made to embrace all Turkey in Europe. Bismarck's position enabled him, without objection on anyone's part, to secure a more comprehensive provision in the treaty, covering all Turkish dominions, Asiatic, as well as European. By thus playing off Turkey and her voluntary acceptance of the principle of religious liberty against Russia and Roumania, Bismarck greatly strengthened the Jewish cause at the Congress. The various references in the protocol to Turkey's resentment and repudiation of Russia's charges that Turkish persecution of Christians had caused the Russo-Turkish War (see *infra*, p. 67), just concluded by the Treaty of San Stefano, are of great interest to any student of the question of the international safeguarding of religious liberty. They indicate Great Britain's efforts to refute, or at least qualify, Russian charges in this respect. Over a year previously, Baron Henry de Worms had made some interesting contributions to the position of the Tory party on this question. In his book, "England's Policy in the East," pp. 32 to 34 are devoted to a rebuttal of these anti-Turkish charges, including quotations from American missionaries in Turkey in favor of Turkish tolerance toward them and Jewish residents, with which he con-

Bismarck well knew that it would be obtained; he evidently was anxious to accentuate, through the Ottoman plenipotentiaries, their important declarations of the preceding day.

Carathéodory Pasha declared, that in answering M. Waddington yesterday, he referred simply to the general legislation of the Ottoman Empire, as well as to their treaties and conventions. His Excellency added that the tolerance which all faiths in Turkey enjoyed, admitted of no doubt, and that in the absence of a more extended proposition, which would have to be explained, he believed he was right in considering it superfluous to make special mention of Eastern Roumelia.

The president stated that the Congress unanimously adhered to the wishes of France to take action on the declarations made by Turkey in favor of religious liberty. Such was the aim of the French plenipotentiaries, and they attained it. Lord Salisbury would have liked to have gone further and to have extended the

---

trasted (p. 40) Russia's persecution of the Jews. In one of his leading addresses, delivered at the Guildhall in London on the achievements of the Congress of Berlin (*The Times*, London, August 5, 1878; Hahn, *Bismarck*, vol. iii, p. 298), Lord Beaconsfield, in line with these arguments, said: " There was a body of men in Turkey—men of the highest principle, of even a sublime character—men who devoted their lives to the benefit of their fellow creatures, and sought no reward but the convictions of their own consciences—and these were the American missionaries (Cheers). The American missionaries were scattered over every part of Turkey, and when this war commenced—on false pretenses in a great degree—(Cheers) the American missionaries addressed the Emperor of Germany and said it was their duty to tell him that they had lived and labored in every part of the Ottoman Empire, and since the Crimean War and the Treaty of Paris the improvement in the condition of the Christian subjects of the Porte was most remarkable (Cheers). They mention in that document that regard for life and property was now most striking. They mention in that document that education was very largely pursued, and that toleration was almost complete (Cheers); but these changes could only be effected by the influence of the Sultan himself." See also as to protection of missionaries by international law, J. B. Moore's " Digest of International Law," Washington, 1906, vol. iii, § 521; vol. vi, § 922; O. L. Owens' forthcoming Johns Hopkins Study, " The Protection of American Foreign Missionaries by the United States."

original proposition, not only to Bulgaria and Roumelia, but to all the Ottoman Empire. As concerns Germany, Prince Bismarck, who had supported the French proposition, would also gladly have approved that of Lord Salisbury, but the discussion of so complex a question would have diverted the Congress from the purpose of its present session.

Bismarck, in setting forth the declarations of Turkey, in order to support them, challenged those of Russia. In regard to Bulgaria, Count Schouvaloff would have put himself in ill-favor by denying to the Jews, in the Bulgarian provisions, the maintenance of religious liberty which they had enjoyed under the Turkish régime. Therefore he found it more politic to say that

the wish of Lord Salisbury to have religious liberty extended as far as possible in Europe and Asia seemed quite justifiable to him. His Excellency desired that, in the protocol, mention be made of his adherence to the wish of the English plenipotentiary, and he remarked that the Congress having sought to efface the ethnographic frontiers and to replace them by commercial and strategical ones, the Russian plenipotentiaries wished all the more that these borders would not become religious barriers.

Summing up the declaration of Russia, the president resumed the debate by saying:

That it would be entered in the protocol that the Congress unanimously acceded to the French proposition, and that the majority of the plenipotentiaries voted for the extension of liberty of faith.

There was no opposition. The French proposition, applied to Bulgaria, extended logically to all the states for which the Congress was about to make regulations.

At the meeting of June 28, the Congress busied itself with Serbia. The Treaty of San Stefano had declared her to be independent. The president asked if this principle was admitted.

Carathéodory Pasha declared that Turkey would not oppose it,

being persuaded that this independence will be genuine and honest, that it will be assumed by the countries with the full consciousness of the rights, as well as the duties, which it imposes on them, for from thenceforth it must be respected, and Servia will not lessen the security of public European order, which the bond of suzerainty had known how to create and maintain.

It was a good thing to remind Serbia of her duties; she disregarded them for a long time; but that was not enough.

Lord Salisbury intervened to say

that he favored recognizing the independence of Servia, but thought it would be opportune to stipulate, for the Principality, the great principle of religious liberty.

M. Waddington was still more explicit, he

admitted the independence of Servia, but on condition that the vote of the proposition [which he read] be identical with that which the Congress had accepted for Bulgaria.

At this point, the opposition of Prince Gortschakoff, which was as impolitic as it was violent, was heard:

He feared that this text may have special reference to the Israelites, and without manifesting any opposition to the general principles that were laid down in it, his Most Serene Highness would not like to have the Jewish question, which will come up later, prejudged by a previous declaration. If the question was solely one of religious liberty, Prince Gortschakoff declared that it had always been applied in Russia; he, for his part, adhered entirely to this principle and would be ready to extend it in the largest way. But, if it was a question of civil and political rights, his Most Serene Highness asked that the Israelites of Berlin, Paris, London or Vienna, to whom there would be no question of refusing any political and civil rights, be not confounded with the Jews of Servia, of Roumania, and of several Russian provinces, who were, in his opinion, a veritable scourge to the native peoples.[18]

---

[18] In Prince Hohenlohe's "Memoirs," *supra*, vol. ii, p. 218, his diary of this date reads: "On the occasion of the debate over the rights which Servia should acquire, the subject of the Jews was touched upon; Gortschakoff spoke against them, and said that he distinguished *entre juifs et israélites*. The former were a plague; the latter might be excellent people, as could be seen in Berlin and London. *On the whole, his speech was feeble.*"

Prince Gortschakoff wanted religious liberty in Serbia to be such as it is in Russia, with the refusal of civil and political rights to those who practice a religion different from an orthodox religion. His argument did not gain anything by being upheld by an attack on the Jews of Serbia, Roumania and also Russia. Europe remembered that the prince and ministers of Serbia had spoken well of the Jews whom they oppressed. No one needed to defend them, but Bismarck gave himself the sly pleasure of becoming the defender of the Russian Jews against Gortschakoff, whom he did not like:

> The president [the minutes report], remarked that it might be to the purpose to attribute this regrettable condition of the Israelites to the restrictions placed upon their civil and political rights.

This observation put Gortschakoff ill at ease; he found nothing better to do than to continue his attack upon his fellow-countrymen, by saying that in certain Russian provinces, the government—under the impulse of an absolute necessity, justified by experience—had subjected the Israelites to an exceptional rule, in order to safeguard the interests of the population.

There was no better way of testing Waddington's proposition. The Congress understood it, and Waddington said, with that mixture of acuteness and force, with which he distinguished himself in the deliberations of the Congress:

> That it was important to seize this solemn occasion to make the representatives of Europe affirm the principles of religious liberty. His Excellency added that Servia, who wanted to join the European family on the same footing as the other States, ought first acknowledge the principles which form the basis of social organization in all the governments of Europe, and accept them as a necessary condition of the favor which she solicited.

Perhaps the lesson was heeded by Gortschakoff; he weakened his previous declaration by saying that

> civil and political rights could not be assigned to the Jews in Servia in an absolute way.

Count Schouvaloff understood that Gortschakoff had not sufficiently weakened his first remarks; he said that

the remarks of the Prince did not constitute a fundamental opposition to the French proposition;

he considered it impolitic to let it be thought that Russia rejected what Waddington had called

the principles which are the basis of social organization in all the governments of Europe;

he also added that

the Jewish element, which was excessive in certain Russian provinces, had been perforce the object of a special provision; but his Excellency hoped that, in future, it would be feasible to avert the unquestionable inconveniences pointed out by Prince Gortschakoff, without trenching upon religious liberty, which Russia wished to develop.

Then followed the declarations of Germany, Italy, Austria and Turkey.

Prince Bismarck adhered to the French proposition, by declaring that

the assent of Germany is always given for every motion favorable to religious liberty.

Count de Launay, said in Italy's name,

that he was eager to adhere to the principle of religious liberty, which formed one of the essential bases of the institutions of his country, and that he joined in the declarations made by Germany, France and Great Britain.

The protocol stated that

Count Andrassy expressed himself as being of the same opinion and that the Ottoman plenipotentiaries did not raise any objection.

Prince Gortschakoff was completely defeated. Prince Bismarck took pains to emphasize the fact:

After having ascertained the results of the vote, he declared that the Congress admitted the independence of Servia, but on condition that religious liberty will be recognized in the Principality. His Serene Highness added that the Committee on Editing, in formulating this decision, would have to express the connection established by the Congress, between the proclamation of Servian independence and the recognition of religious liberty.

At last Roumania's turn came. The vote on Serbia had not reassured the delegates of the *Alliance*. They feared Russia's opposition; they distrusted Austria. Roumania had just lost Bessarabia; she claimed to have been poorly compensated by having had Dobroudja transferred to her. But could she still hope for success, for two days before the determination, on June 28, von Bülow had said to Netter: "The plenipotentiaries have all agreed to demand of Roumania what they have demanded of Serbia; it is a question of principle." It was, in fact, decided by the clever order of business that the Congress had established.

It had been decided for Bulgaria, without the possible contradiction of the government which constituted it; it was just the same for Serbia, which the Congress had treated so liberally. Could the Congress settle things differently for Roumania?

At the meeting of July 1, the Congress listened to the Roumanian delegates, Cogalniceanu and Bratiano, who strove to gain the favor of Europe, after the quarrel they had had with her in regard to the Jewish question. They did not say a word about it, while they developed their protests, the principal one being against the retrocession of Bessarabia to Russia.

Immediately after their departure, Prince Bismarck asked the Congress

if it thought it proper to recognize the independence of Roumania, under what conditions it would make this important decision, and if the conditions had to be the same as those already established by the Congress for Servia.

M. Waddington declared

that, faithful to the principles that had inspired them so far, the French plenipotentiaries asked that the Congress impose the same conditions on Roumanian independence as on Servian independence. His Excellency did not overlook the local difficulties which exist in Roumania, but, after having carefully examined the arguments that can be turned to account in one way or another, the French plenipotentiaries deemed it preferable not to swerve from the grand rule of equality of rights and liberty of worship. It would be difficult, moreover, for the Roumanian government to reject, in its territory, the principle that Turkey recognized for her own subjects. His Excellency thought that there was no reason to hesitate, that Roumania, asking to join the great European family, ought to accept the obligations, and even the drawbacks of the position, the benefits of which she claimed, and that for a long time there would not be found again an opportunity so solemn and decisive to affirm anew the principles which constitute the honor and security of civilized nations. As for the local difficulties, the first plenipotentiary of France deemed that they would be more easily surmounted when these principles will have been recognized in Roumania, and when the Jewish race shall have learnt that it has nothing to hope for, but from its own efforts, and from the union of its interests with those of the indigenous population. M. Waddington closed by urging that the same conditions of political and religious order determined on for Servia be equally imposed upon the state of Roumania.

Prince Bismarck was the first to support Waddington, making allusion to the principles of public right embodied in the constitution of the German Empire and to the interest attached by public opinion to the application in their foreign policy, of the same principles observed in internal affairs, and he declared his adhesion in the name of Germany, to the French proposition.

All the plenipotentiaries assented to this proposition. Count Andrassy accepted it, as the others did. Lord Beaconsfield's declaration was particularly energetic. He said:

That he gave his complete support in the name of the English Government, to the French proposition. His Excellency could not suppose, for a moment, that the Congress would recognize the independence of Roumania apart from this condition.

The Italian plenipotentiaries made the same declaration.

At last Prince Gortschakoff—who would have believed it?—rallied entirely to this proposition,

referring to the expressions which prompted the French proposition and which gave the greatest latitude to religious liberty. It was true that Russia had not yet obtained the retrocession of Bessarabia. That was another condition of Roumanian independence, of which Count Schouvaloff reminded the Congress.

The Ottoman plenipotentiaries did not raise any objection to the principles laid down by the French plenipotentiaries, and the president stated that the Congress was unanimous in not according independence to Roumania except on the same conditions as were imposed on Serbia.

There was an epilogue to this chapter of the history of the Congress. At the meeting of the 4th of July, M. Ristitch, representing Serbia, advised the Congress that Prince Milan had authorized him to declare that the Serbian Government would seize the first opportunity, after the conclusion of peace, to abolish by legal means the last restriction still existing in Serbia, relative to the position of the Jews.

The president, without wishing to enter into an examination of the question, observed that the words "by legal means" appeared to be a reservation, to which he called the attention of the High Assembly. Prince Bismarck thought it right to declare that in no case can this reservation derogate from the authority of the decisions of the Congress.

At this meeting, another incident in regard to Lord Salisbury's proposition was brought to notice,

to apply to the Ottoman Empire the principles adopted by the Congress for Servia and Roumania.

Was not this proposition made in order to get the first Turkish plenipotentiary to read a communication which he had just received from his government? These were the terms thereof:

In view of the declarations made in the Congress under various circumstances in favor of religious tolerance, you are authorized to state that the sentiments of the Sublime Porte on this point are entirely in harmony with the objects sought by Europe. Its most steadfast traditions, its secular policy, the instinct of its populations, all tend to this result. Throughout the whole Empire, religions widely differing are professed by millions of the Sultan's subjects, and no one has been annoyed in his faith or in the exercise of his creed. The Imperial Government is determined to maintain this principle in all its force, and to give it all the extension it admits of.

This was the protest of Turkey against the Power that had conquered and crushed her. She did not wish that the safety of the Christians should be made the pretext for the war which the Congress ended, and which, without the intervention of Europe, would have resulted in her dismemberment."[79]

Turkey agreed to the proposition of Lord Salisbury, but desired it to appear in the text that the principles in question expressed the legislation of that Empire in contrast to that of Serbia and Roumania, and that the provisions were

in conformity with the declarations of the Porte and with the previous stipulations, which it declared itself willing to maintain.

Lord Salisbury, after having remarked that these provisions have not always been observed in practice, accepted, and the Congress adopted the amendment of the Porte.

After their adoption, the decisions of the Congress were sent back to the Committee on Editing. At the meeting of July 10, the reporter of this committee, M. Désprez, stated that the article dealing with the equality of rights and freedom of religious worship had given rise to some difficulties in drafting; that this article applied equally to Bulgaria, Montenegro, Serbia and Roumania, and that the Drafting Commission had to find a single formula to suit different situations; it was particularly difficult to make it include the Roumanian Jews whose situation was undetermined in point of nationality. He added that Count de Launay

aiming to prevent any mistake, had suggested, in the course of the discussion, the insertion of the following phrase: "The Jews of Roumania, in so far as they do not belong to a foreign nationality, acquire by full right Roumanian nationality."

M. de Launay wanted to prevent the difficulties that Roumania had already raised and which she was about to aggra-

---

[79] See note 77.

vate, concerning the nationality of the Roumanian Jews; this phraseology certainly was better than that which had been adopted and it would have prevented the very subterfuge subsequently resorted to by Roumania to evade the provision as adopted.

But Prince Bismarck pointed out

the inconvenience which would attend the modification of the resolutions adopted by the Congress and which formed the basis of the work of the Committee on Revision. It was necessary that the Congress oppose every attempt to revert to the original question.

M. Désprez added: " That the committee had preserved the original version which seemed to it to be of a nature to conciliate all the interests concerned," and M. de Launay confined himself to asking for the insertion of his proposition in the protocol.

Prince Bismarck was right in fearing a new debate. In fact, Prince Gortschakoff

recalled observations that he had made at a preceding session, in regard to the political and civil rights of the Jews in Roumania. He did not wish to renew his objections, but he desired to state again that he did not, on this point, share in the opinions expressed in the treaty.

The final text of the treaty was more exact than its original version. For each of the four countries it was settled in the following terms:

FOR BULGARIA.

V. The following points shall form the basis of the public law of Bulgaria:

The difference of religious creeds and confessions shall not be alleged against any persons as a ground for exclusion or incapacity in matters relating to the enjoyment of civil and political rights, admission to public employments, functions and honors, or the exercise of various professions and industries in any locality whatever. The freedom and outward exercise of all forms of worship are assured to all persons belonging to Bulgaria, as well as to foreigners, and no hindrance shall be offered either to the hierarchical organization of the different communions or to their relations with their spiritual chiefs.

The same formula was used for Serbia, Montenegro and Roumania, with one difference, that is, for those governments, already existing, it was not said that these provisions should form the basis of their public law, but that their independence was recognized on the same condition. The provision as to Roumania (Article XLIV) added:

The subjects and citizens of all the Powers, traders or others, shall be treated in Roumania without distinction of creed on a footing of perfect equality.

The work of the Congress of Berlin [says M. Leven, p. 230] was considerable: it had introduced into international law the principles which the French Revolution had put into the Declaration of the Rights of Man; united Europe had sanctioned them. Russia would have feared to place herself outside the pale of civilized nations, if she had not ended by doing them homage. She had been about to concede, through one of her plenipotentiaries, the hope that she would make her own law accord with them. The thing achieved was that these principles became, by the wish of Europe, the basis of public law for the new governments, and for the others, the condition of their independence. That was a benefit for all the peoples, and, for Judaism, a unique act in its history, the solemn charter of its enfranchisement. Fifteen years of effort and of persevering strife here found their reward.

The *Alliance* thanked the Congress and the plenipotentiaries, particularly Waddington, who had most valiantly defended its cause. In acknowledging its expression of gratitude the French plenipotentiary, de St. Vallier, defined the rôle of France:

In defending and bringing about the triumph of the cause of the Israelites in Roumania, Servia and Bulgaria before the Congress, we have defended the cause of justice, humanity and civilization. We have done it with the consciousness that we are performing an act of justice, for which it fell to our dear France, the spokesman of all liberal and generous causes, to take the initiative, and we have had the good fortune of meeting with the assent and the unanimous vote of the members of the Congress. Liberty of faith, respect for all religions, equality of civil and political rights without distinction of creed, freedom of the professions, those are the grand principles that we are striving to have recognized all over, and in favor of which we have been fortunate in meeting with a unanimous acceptance. (*Allgemeine Zeitung des Judentums*, 1878, p. 469; Leven, *supra*, p. 230 *et seq.*)

The German Union of Jewish Congregations similarly expressed its appreciation to Bismarck for his services at the Congress, and the British Jewish societies theirs to Beaconsfield and Salisbury.[30]

Our "Foreign Relations,"[31] contains a report by Mr. Kasson, from Vienna, dated August 3, 1878, as to several conclusions of the Congress of Berlin, particularly interesting to our Government; he wrote:

Absolute freedom and equality of religious faith and profession for all forms of faith and worship, and of the persons adhering to these different forms of faith are expressly stipulated in Bulgaria (Article V), in Montenegro, in Servia and in Roumania, in identi-

---

[30] *Allgemeine Zeitung des Judentums*, 1878, p. 467, 469-470; *The Jewish Chronicle*, July 26, 1878. In the official letter of transmittal of the proceedings of the Congress, the Marquess of Salisbury expressly mentioned, as one of its main achievements, those clauses relating to religious liberty. He wrote: "Provisions having for their object to insure entire equality of all religions before the law have been applied to all the territories affected by the Treaty." It is interesting to observe that Gladstone, despite his vigorous opposition to most of the conclusions of the Congress of Berlin, expressly approved in Parliament of the provisions for Jewish emancipation (Hansard's Debates, third series, vol. 242, p. 678). See Gladstone's letters on the subject reprinted in *The Jewish Chronicle*, December 26, 1879. The biographers of both Gladstone and Beaconsfield ought to note the interesting circumstance that, despite the severe attacks exchanged between these two leaders at this period, Gladstone wrote a letter to *The Jewish Chronicle* (published in its issue for August 16, 1878), in answer to an enquiry regarding the above-described address, in which he said: "My words described Lord Beaconsfield's conduct about Jewish disabilities as honorable to him, as I think it, and I was glad of an opportunity of so describing it." Thus both the Conservative and Liberal leaders in England expressly approved of these provisions.

[31] 1878, pp. 50-1.

cal phrases. . . . . By Article LVII religious liberty and the personal equality of the adherents of all the religious rites are stipulated and declared for all the provinces of the Turkish dominions. You will observe in reading the model Article V how completely that equality of religious right is expressed. I wrote you before the meeting of the Congress in respect to the propriety and possibility of ameliorating the condition of the Jews in those principalities, by coming to accord with European governments upon some clause of a treaty in which this could be secured as a condition of the recognition of their independence [*supra*, pp. 41-42]. This result has been attained by the great powers in the Berlin Treaty; but it remains to give effect to it by a change of the laws in the several principalities. Unless and until this is done, it would be wise to incorporate the provisions in substance in the case of a government which is not a party to the Berlin Treaty.

M. Dufaure, the French *premier,* in his official letter of July 13, 1878, to Waddington on the achievements of the Congress of Berlin, singles out these provisions for religious liberty and equality.[52] It is interesting to note that Cardinal Franchi, Papal Secretary of State, sent a special letter of appreciation to Waddington, the Protestant, for the provisions as to religious liberty of the Treaty of Berlin,[53] and the latter emphasized the necessity of inserting these clauses in debates in the French Chamber of Deputies.[54]

After the decisions of the Congress, the delegates of the *Alliance* had nothing more pressing to do than to attempt a reconciliation between the delegates of Serbia and Roumania and the Israelites of these countries.

Netter relates that there was no trouble in making M. Ristitch admit that the decision of the Congress was advantageous for Serbia. Ristitch promised to watch its loyal application. He kept his promise. In a circular of the Minister of Justice, dated May 4, 1884, are found the follow-

[52] French Yellow Book, *Congrès de Berlin*, 1878, p. 297.
[53] *Ibid.*, p. 299.
[54] *Journal Officiel de la République Française*, 1879, p. 7892, August 1.

ing words, indicating the scope of the Treaty of Berlin and the diplomatic agreements that are connected with it:

> These treaties have been ratified by our legislative body, and consequently have become laws of the country, binding for the courts, as they are for the other authorities of Servia. If they are contradictory of the old laws, it goes without saying that these earlier ones should be considered abolished and that the new ones only should be applied.

As for Bulgaria, her constitution of January, 1879 (like that of Eastern Roumelia, adopted in March, 1879), recognized for every one born in Bulgaria, and not subject to foreign protection, the title of Bulgarian subject, and proclaimed all Bulgarians equal before the law. M. Leven says (p. 232):

> For a time it seemed possible to come to an understanding with Bratiano and Cogalniceanu. Cogalniceanu was more politic than Bratiano. Netter called Bratiano a rhetorician, while he praised Cogalniceanu's suppleness. "He tries," says Netter, "to make the best of a situation which cannot be improved, but which he cannot avoid. He foresaw what this association of the pot of earth with the pot of iron would produce, the alliance of Roumania with Russia; it was repugnant to Bratiano also. It would have been arranged long ago, if it had depended only on him. Several months ago he said to his colleagues that the Jewish Question would be settled by others if they would not get the start; the past is past; so much the better, perhaps, but before your enemies excuse this foreign intervention in your favor, secure an extension of your frontier to Dobroudja. Take the map, draw for us in pencil what is offered and what is wanted; state the cost. All this was done in an instant with remarkable brightness."
>
> He was mistaken as to the rôle of the *Alliance*. It went to Berlin only to defend the rights of the Israelites; trading, as proposed by Cogalniceanu, did not enter any more into its designs than it did into its power. This conversation was interrupted by Bratiano, coming to announce that the Congress had established the limits of Roumania. Cogalniceanu accepted more resignedly than Bratiano did the resolutions of the Congress. They were not respected by Roumania; the public authorities had but one purpose, which was to evade them. It is quite a history to relate.

As already pointed out in the passage from Leven's valuable history, Bulgaria, Serbia and Turkey observed the conditions of the Treaty of Berlin, while Roumania resorted to one trick and device after another to violate them and aggravate the condition of the Jews. Much light upon Roumania's course is thrown by extracts from the published journal of King Charles of Roumania, hereinbefore cited, entitled *Aus dem Leben König Karls von Rumänien*. It is recorded there that Jewish emancipation aroused no such opposition in Serbia, as it did in Roumania,[55] and a letter of Prince Alexander of Bulgaria to King Charles of Roumania, dated August 10, 1879,[56] contains the following significant passage regarding Bulgaria:

> While I have been an enemy of the Berlin Treaty [with respect to its provisions in favor of the Jews], I have nevertheless completely adopted it in my new position; I have shaped my mission in the most pronouncedly European spirit possible, and require equal rights to be accorded to all.

On the other hand, in Roumania these provisions aroused vehement and continuous opposition, even to the point of a proposal to reject independence on these terms. Prince Karl Anton, the father and chief adviser of the ruler of Roumania, wrote to him as early as July 26, 1878,[57] regarding the Jewish provisions of the Treaty of Berlin, that they are merely

> humane generalities. It is left for the legislative body alone to phrase them, and I am convinced that later on, with the exception of the *Alliance Israélite*, no rooster will crow over the form in which these provisions will be phrased.

For some time, however, the Powers declined to accept the constitutional provisions adopted by Roumania to carry out, or rather to evade, these provisions, England, France and Germany being particularly emphatic regarding their inadequacy, but they were finally misled into accepting Roumanian assur-

---

[55] Vol. iv, p. 86.

[56] *Ibid.*, p. 245. Official Serbian announcements and assurances were similar. *The Jewish Chronicle*, October 4 and December 20, 1878.

[57] *Aus dem Leben König Karls*, vol. iv, p. 87.

ances that they would be liberally enforced and extended;[88] and the United States seems to have been the last great power to enter into a treaty with Roumania for this reason,[89] just as she was the first power, not excepting France, to establish absolute religious liberty. King Charles' journal contains, under date of July 25, 1879,[90] a transcript of a letter from Emperor Wilhelm I., of Germany, to the Empress, which the Emperor suggested might be shown to King Charles' father, a kinsman of the Imperial Hohenzollerns, in which the Emperor said:

With regard to Roumania, I have, as you know, from the outset most strongly disapproved of the resolution of the Congress concerning the Jewish question, though only after the blow had fallen, since I was not then at the helm. Since then I have of course only had to support the strict execution of the resolutions of the Congress, but I have demanded at every opportunity that no pressure be used in this matter.

Elsewhere, Prince Karl Anton informed his son that the Emperor told him that, if he had not been suffering from his wounds during the Berlin Congress, he would never have consented to that extension of the Jewish question, and the Prince added that he was convinced that Bismarck did not consult the Emperor in the matter at all, or at least did not report it to him fully, and that the Emperor was surprised to learn that Germany was even more insistent than England upon strict Roumanian enforcement of the religious rights provisions of the treaty.[91]

[88] See *infra*, pp. 123 *et seq.*, 141 *et seq.*
[89] "Foreign Relations of the United States, 1880," pp. xii, 35-6, 42-3, 51-3, 818.
[90] *Aus dem Leben König Karls, supra*, p. 236.
[91] *Ibid.*, p. 224. Princess Radziwill, "My Recollections," New York, 1904, p. 91, says that Emperor William I. made the same comment to her. But where the interests of a Hohenzollern were not directly involved William was more liberal. Prince Hohenlohe records in his "Memoirs" (vol. ii, p. 273) a private conversation which he had with William I. on November 29, 1880, at the time of Stöcker's anti-Semitic crusade: "We then came to the question of the Jews. The *Kaiser* does not approve of the action of *Pfarrer*

On the other hand, Bluntschli, the distinguished publicist, in his pamphlet " Roumania and the Legal Status of the Jews in Roumania," written in 1879, well says:

The opinion that the Jews were a foreign nation, interpolated among the Christian people, was certainly held in the early

---

Stöcker, but he thinks that the affair will come to nothing, and considers that the noise is of use in making the Jews more modest." In " The Jewish Encyclopedia," *s. v. Verein zur Abwehr des Antisemitismus*, it is stated that William I., and also Frederick III., subsequently denounced Stöcker. There is reason to believe that the personal leaning of the Emperor towards his kinsman, Prince Charles, notwithstanding Bismarck's prior, reiterated assurances to Bleichroeder in November, 1878, that Roumania would not be recognized by Germany until she had emancipated her Jews fully (see *The Jewish Chronicle*, November 22, 1878), and two additional circumstances presently to be noted, were somewhat responsible for the course of the Powers in accepting assurances from Roumania, instead of accomplishments, in the matter of Jewish emancipation. Of these additional factors, one was the course of Austria and Italy in meantime unconditionally recognizing Roumania for personal considerations of their own, without awaiting the result of the negotiations conducted by England, France and Germany, making recognition conditioned on Jewish emancipation, which continued until February, 1880. The other was that Germany desired Roumania to purchase some Roumanian railways, the securities of which were held by Germans, before recognition was accorded, and Roumania now deemed it good policy to accede to Germany's wishes in this respect, so as to make her more amenable to her views on the Jewish question. When it appeared that Austria, Italy and Germany were recognizing Roumania anyhow (and of course Russia was not interested in effecting Jewish emancipation), France and even England preferred not to continue the contest alone and accepted Roumania's promises, only partially performed, in a carefully phrased identical note (*infra*, p. 126). See, besides, the English Blue Book and the French Yellow Books on the recognition of Roumania; Waddington's statement in the French Chamber of Deputies on July 31, 1879; *Journal Officiel de la République Française, supra; Aus dem Leben König Karls;* " Foreign Relations, 1880," p. 52, and a very recent biased and unreliable booklet, entitled *Ces ques les Juifs roumains doivent à la Prusse*, Paris, 1916.

middle ages, but it has been rejected ever since the formation and consolidation of territorial and national States. Throughout Europe the native Jews, in the different countries and States in which they are found, are included amongst the other subjects as belonging to the country, and as constituents of those States. Only those Jews who are subject to foreign States are considered strangers, just as is the case with Christian strangers. The Roumanian Jews are in no other sense distinguished from non-Roumanian Jews living in Roumania, than Roumanian Christians are to be distinguished from foreign Christians living in Roumania. . . . . . By international law they are distinguished from aliens."[92]

Lord Salisbury's remarks on July 24, 1879, as Secretary of State for Foreign Affairs, about the applicability to the Jews of Roumania of these provisions of the Treaty of Berlin, to a delegation led by Baron Henry de Worms, of representatives of British Jews, are particularly apt:[93]

I do not think that Baron de Worms has in the least degree exaggerated the evils of the state of things which has hitherto existed in Roumania. These evils attracted the attention of the Powers at Berlin and *they adopted the somewhat unusual, if not unprecedented course of making their recognition of a great political change dependent upon certain modifications of the internal laws of the country. It was a great homage to the principles which all the civilized nations of Europe now recognize, and it was a very solemn international act from which I do not think the Powers will recede.* . . . . The fact that she [Roumania] came under the guardianship of the Powers of Europe as a whole, and that her practical internal independence was secured to her by a diplomatic act was, as Baron de Worms says, the result of the blood which England and France and Italy shed in the Crimea.

The history of the Roumanian failure to carry out these conditions, which she ostensibly accepted, and of her constantly

---

[92] See, accordingly, L. de Bar, *Observations concernant la preuve de la nationalité et l'expulsion par le gouvernement roumains d'Israélites nés et domiciliés en Roumanie*, in *Revue du droit international*, II, vol. ix, pp. 711-716; Stambler, *L'histoire des Israélites roumains et le droit d'intervention*, Paris, 1913. See also, *infra*, pp. 150-1.

[93] *The Jewish Chronicle*, August 1, 1879.

increased anti-Jewish measures, is too far removed from the scope of this paper for fuller consideration here.[94]

Bulgaria, in her constitution promulgated April 16, 1879, unreservedly inserted clauses establishing civil and religious liberty, regardless of race or creed.

M. Franco, principal of the *Alliance* school at Shumla, Bulgaria, well says in the article on Bulgaria in "*The Jewish Encyclopedia*":

> They [the Jews] are electors, are eligible to office, and are to be represented in every municipality by one or two members. They may become members of the Sobranje [Chamber of Deputies]. They are subject to military service, and have the right of military promotion. . . . . The liberality of the new constitution was at once received with enthusiasm by the Jews. Three graduates of the military school at Sofia attained the rank of major.

He further notes that

> in 1877, when the Turks set fire to the city of Sofia, it was the Jews and Jewesses, according to Bianconi (*Carte Commérciale de*

---

[94] See, however, Appendices IV, V, and VI, *infra*, pp. 108, 114, 137 *et seq.*; "The Jewish Encyclopedia," *s. v.* Roumania; "Sincerus," *Les Juifs en Roumanie*, London, 1901; E. Schwarzfeld, "The Situation of the Jews in Roumania since the Treaty of Berlin," in *The American Jewish Year Book* for 1901-1902; Stambler, *L'histoire des Israélites roumains et le droit d'intervention;* Rey, *La question israélite en Roumanie*, Paris, 1903; Lazare, *Die Juden in Rumänien;* Plotke, *Die rumänischen Juden unter dem Fürsten und König Karl*, Frankfurt, a.M., 1901; French Yellow Book, 1879 and 1880 (*Affaires Etrangères: Documents diplomatiques: Question de la réconnaisance de la Roumanie*); "Great Britain, Parliamentary Papers, 1880," vol. 79, "Correspondence Relative to the Recognition of Roumania," and vol. 81, "Correspondence Respecting the Condition of the Mussulman, Greek and Jewish Populations in Eastern Roumelia"; Edwards, "Career and Correspondence of Sir William White," London, 1902; Israel Davis, "The Jews in Roumania," London, 1872, and D. F. Schloss, "The Persecutions of the Jews in Roumania," London, 1885; "An American in Roumania," in "Memoirs of David Blaustein," New York, 1913, pp. 65-79; F. C. Conybeare, "Roumania as a Persecuting Power," in *National Review*, 1901, vol. xxxvi, p. 818.

la Bulgarie, p. 12, published by Chaix, Paris), who fought the flame and armed with whatever weapons came to hand beat off the soldiers employed in setting fire to the buildings. Thus the Bulgarian capital owed its preservation to its Jewish inhabitants, and, in recognition of their bravery, Prince Alexander decreed in 1879 that the fire brigade should be chosen exclusively from Jewish citizens, and on all occasions of reviews, processions, etc., the Jewish firemen have the place of honor next to the picked troops of the Bulgarian army. When, in 1885, Bulgaria was waging war against Servia, the Bulgarian Jews distinguished themselves so highly in the battles of Pirot and Slivnitza that Prince Alexander publicly thanked them, calling them true descendants of the ancient Maccabees.

Similar views were expressed more recently by W. S. Monroe, in his work " Bulgaria and Her People."[95] who says:

The Moslems and the Jews in Bulgaria have known nothing of the bitter race antogonisms that their compatriots in the other Balkan States have had to face. Jews and Turks are not only represented in the national assembly, but they occupy posts of honor in the civil service of the country.

As Eastern Roumelia was annexed to Bulgaria in 1885, this description is applicable to the Jews who resided there also, though even previously, in 1879, Eastern Roumelia had loyally complied with the requirements of the Treaty of Berlin in her constitution. So also had Montenegro.

Although Serbian persecution of the Jews had aroused international protests even before Roumanian discriminations, particularly on the part of England and the United States, Serbia also fully complied with the terms of the Treaty of Berlin, and her new constitution expressly abolished the anti-Jewish laws of 1856 and 1861.[96]

---

[95] Boston, 1914, p. 189; see, also, Segall, *Juden in Bulgarien*, in *Zeitschrift für Demographie und Statistik der Juden*, vol. vii, 1911, pp. 6-10, 17-21; Chaunier, *La Bulgarie*, Paris, 1909; M. Philippson, *Neueste Geschichte des jüdischen Volkes*, Leipzig, 1910, vol. ii, pp. 340-3, 356.

[96] M. Franco in " The Jewish Encyclopedia," *s. v.* Servia; *supra*, p. 74; Philippson, *supra*, pp. 343-5, 356; Razhichich, *Das kirchlich-religiöse Leben bei den Serben*, Göttingen, 1896; Rachic, *Le*

IV.

Secretary Hay's Roumanian Note of 1902 and the Peace Conference of Bucharest of 1913.

In Secretary John Hay's famous Roumanian Note of July 17, 1902, a new ground for American intermediation in case of religious persecution is outlined, in addition to those previously presented. This arises from the circumstance that foreign immigration to the United States is unduly and vexatiously artificially stimulated, when religious persecution forces thousands, suddenly and precipitately, to seek refuge on our shores under our sacred American principle of asylum for the persecuted. The heavy increase in Roumanian Jewish immigration, just prior to the writing of Secretary Hay's note, was ascribed to the persecutions resulting from a disregard of the provisions of the Treaty of Berlin, above referred to. Our protest was voiced

not alone because it [our Government] has unimpeachable ground to remonstrate against the resultant injury to itself, but in the name of humanity.[97]

Royaume de Serbie, Paris, 1901; Sloane's "The Balkans," New York, 1914; Jiriček, *Geschichte der Serben*, Gotha, 1911; "The Balkan Wars and the Jews," in *American Jewish Year Book* for 1913-1914, pp. 188-206; *ibid.*, for 1914-1915, pp. 382-388; Stead, "Servia and the Servians," London, 1909, p. 156; Kanitz, *Serbien und das Serbenvolk*, Leipzig, 1904-9, vol. ii, p. 208; "A Diplomatist," "Nationalism and the War in the Near East," Oxford, 1915 (Carnegie Endowment for International Peace).

[97] For fuller quotation and able analysis of this note by Congressman Chandler, see *infra*. p. 133; the full text is printed in "Foreign Relations of the United States for 1902," p. 1910; Adler, in *Publications. supra*. No. 15, p. 54; Wiernik, "History of the Jews in America," New York, 1912, p. 447. See paper on the Hay Note and its significance, by W. Maitland Abell, in *Gunton's Magazine*. vol. xxiii, pp. 476-87; also, addresses by Hons. Oscar S. Straus, Elihu Root and Andrew D. White, and by Rev. Dr. Joseph Krauskopf at the "Unveiling and Consecration of the John Hay Memorial Window at the Temple of the Reform Congregation Keneseth Israel, Philadelphia," December 2, 1906.

Copies of this note were sent to our representatives in France, Germany, Great Britain, Italy, Russia and Turkey, to call to the attention of the governments that had signed the Treaty of Berlin.

Mr. Jacob H. Schiff, shortly before this Hay Roumanian note was written, called the attention of President Theodore Roosevelt to the shocking persecutions which caused this Roumanian emigration, and immediately found him to be a most sympathetic auditor, eager to aid in alleviating these conditions, and the President himself immediately afterwards joined Mr. Schiff in urging Secretary Hay to find a way to aid in ameliorating this situation, despite possible diplomatic difficulties. The result has been an important and conspicuous advance in international endeavors to secure liberty of conscience the world over. Hons. Lucius N. Littauer and Oscar S. Straus also coöperated in securing such aid, and Hon. Simon Wolf, Chairman of the Board of Delegates on Civil Rights of the Union of American Hebrew Congregations, both before and afterwards, was untiring in acquainting Secretary Hay with the urgency of governmental action on our part. Mr. Oscar S. Straus prepared two memoranda on this subject for President Roosevelt, the first of which was presented to the President by Mr. Schiff in his original interview with him, and both are hereto annexed as Appendix IV.[28] After the Hay Roumanian note was published, Mr. Straus wrote letters of appreciation to President Roosevelt and Secretary Hay, and in the course of his letter to President Roosevelt, said, under date of October 1, 1902:

> Secretary Hay has formulated with a logic and force as has never been done before, *the ethical principle that where wrongs extend beyond national boundaries, so also does the right for their redress,*

which is a most cogent and convincing statement for international action in such cases as this. In the course of his

---

[28] See *infra*, pp. 108-114.

answer to Mr. Straus, Secretary Hay wrote, under date of October 4, 1902:

> I agree with you in hoping that some good may result from what we have done, even if for the moment Roumania seems obdurate, and some of the great Powers indifferent, to the moral question involved.

The President acknowledged Mr. Straus' letter through Secretary George B. Cortelyou, under date of October 2, 1902, in a letter which established President Roosevelt's personal activity in the matter of the dispatch of this Roumanian note, stating with respect to Mr. Straus' appreciation:

> It gives him [the President] great pleasure, as the Roumanian note was prepared under his personal supervision.[99]

The conditions, economic and political, leading to Roumanian Jewish immigration to the United States, are admirably treated, both historically and in a descriptive manner in Samuel Joseph's "Jewish Immigration to the United States from 1881 to 1910,[100] as also the fortunes of these immigrants in the United States, showing that, under new conditions and laws, and with the idea of a wholesale exodus eliminated, we are now able satisfactorily to assimilate Roumanian Jews here in much larger numbers than in Peixotto's day. When we remember that Roumania has in our own day produced such distinguished Jewish sons as the late Solomon Schechter, of New York, the *Haham,* Dr. Moses Gaster, of London, the late Élie Schwarzfeld, of Paris, Dr. C. Lippe, Dr. M. Beck and Adolf Stern, we can see how unjust and unwarranted are the attempted distinctions, drawn by Roumanian officials and reëchoed by Gortschakoff at the Congress of Berlin,

---

[99] Compare an appeal by the *Alliance Israélite Universelle* to the French Government on behalf of the Roumanian Jews, soon after the Hay note was despatched, translated in *The American Hebrew,* November 14, 1902. Efforts were made in a number of other European countries to coöperate with Secretary Hay's plans. See *Publications, supra,* No. 15, pp. 61-73, and *American Jewish Year Book* for 1903-1904, pp. 17-18.

[100] *Columbia University Studies,* New York, 1914.

between the Jews of Roumania and those of London, Paris, Berlin and New York.

Since Secretary Hay's Roumanian note was written, an excellent, forcible, and humane plea for American intermediation with Roumania was delivered before the House of Representatives on October 10, 1913, by Congressman Walter M. Chandler of New York, entitled "The Jews of Roumania, and the Treaty of Berlin," [101] the Roumanian Jewish section of which is reprinted as Appendix V (pp. 114-137), and "hearings" before the Committee on Foreign Affairs of the House of Representatives on "The Jews of Roumania" were also held December 10, 19 and 22, 1912, and issued in pamphlet form, including arguments by Congressmen Chandler, Henry M. Goldfogle and William S. Bennet. Congressman J. Hampton Moore and Senators Moses E. Clapp and Miles Poindexter have also interested themselves in the subject by means of public addresses.

At the close of the Balkan Wars of 1912-1913 the United States Government intervened on behalf of the Jews of that section, urging that the treaty of peace should make specific provisions, guaranteeing full civil and religious rights to the Jews whose allegiance was about to be transferred, by reason of cessions resulting from the wars. Important correspondence [102] took place in this connection in 1913 between Mr. Louis

---

[101] *Congressional Record*, vol. 50, p. 5541; *infra*, p. 115. See also, U. S. Senate Document No. 611, 63d Congress, 2d Session, "Jewish Immigrants—Report of a Special Committee of the National Jewish Immigration Council, appointed to examine into the question of illiteracy among Jewish immigrants and its causes," showing the practical working of Russian and Roumanian laws and regulations and their administration in discriminating against Jews of these lands in the matter of educational opportunities. Conybeare's excellent study of Roumanian Jewish disabilities, in the *National Review*, *supra*, contains valuable material on Roumania's attempts to deny educational opportunities to her Jewish "stepchildren." See *infra*, pp. 130-1, 146-7, 149.

[102] *Cf. American Jewish Year Book* for 1913-1914, pp. 240-241; *ibid.*, for 1914-1915, pp. 382-388.

Marshall, Dr. Cyrus Adler and Dr. Herbert Friedenwald, representing the American Jewish Committee, on the one hand, and Presidents William H. Taft and Woodrow Wilson and the Hon. John Bassett Moore, Acting Secretary of State, on the other, reading as follows:

I.

New York, January 14, 1913.

DEAR MR. PRESIDENT:

On behalf of the American Jewish Committee, of which I have the honor to be president, I venture to urge that the American Embassy at London may be instructed to bring to the attention of the delegates now assembled in London to arrange terms of peace between the Allied States and the Ottoman Empire, to the British Foreign Office and to the Ambassadors in London, the satisfaction with which the United States would regard the insertion in any such treaty of peace of a clause which will effectively secure to all people of every race and religion whatsoever, now domiciled in the conquered territory, ample protection for their lives, their liberty and their property, equality of citizenship and the right to worship God according to the dictates of their conscience.

There are now in the Ottoman Empire approximately a half million Jewish subjects, probably more than half of whom live in European Turkey. Of this number a considerable proportion resides in the territory now occupied by the Greek, Bulgarian, Servian and Montenegrin armies. There is, therefore, a reasonable presumption that the occupied area will, to a large extent, pass from Turkish rule to that of the conquering Powers. Important consequences from the change in sovereignty are inevitable. Thus in Salonica, to which Greece lays claim, of a total population of 120,000 there are 75,000 Jews, who have hitherto been measurably free from harsh discrimination. A great proportion of the Jews of that part of the Ottoman Empire to be affected by the impending treaty are the descendants of the Jews who were exiled from Spain in 1492. They have resided in Turkey for more than four hundred years and constitute an integral part of her population.

There are two grounds upon which, it seems to me, the United States is justified in making known its view to the participants in the negotiations now in progress, and to the representatives of the Powers in London:

(1) The Orthodox Greek Church is practically the established Church of the allied states to whom this part of the Ottoman Empire is to be ceded. For the last thirty years that Church as now constituted in Russia and the Balkan States has been notoriously hostile to the Jews. The facts are so well known and the results so patent in our own population that it is unnecessary to dwell upon this painful fact. If the Jews of Turkey who have hitherto lived there under favorable conditions should be oppressed, persecuted or harried by the new sovereignty by reason of their faith, a new influx of immigrants to the United States will be inevitable. While in no manner unfriendly to such immigration it is nevertheless evident that it should not be forced upon the United States, as it unquestionably would, if no action is taken at the London Conference which would preclude the possibility of discrimination against the Turkish Jews by the successors in sovereignty to the Ottoman Empire. Though the United States is not a party to the Conference and is supposed to have no standing in the proceeding now in progress, I venture to remind you in this connection of a passage employed by President Harrison in his message to Congress of December 9, 1891, which reads as follows:

"The banishment, whether by direct decree or by not less certain indirect methods, of so large a number of men and women is not a local question. A decree to leave one country is, in the nature of things, an order to enter another—some other. This consideration as well as the suggestions of humanity, furnish ample ground for the remonstrances which we have presented to Russia."

The peace conference in London is similar to the Congress held in Berlin to consider the terms upon which the consequences of the Russo-Turkish War were arranged. When that Congress was in contemplation, our Minister to Vienna, Mr. Kasson, under date of June 5, 1878, called attention to the attitude of the Roumanian Government to the Jews, and urged that our Government interest itself in securing for them equal rights and freedom from persecution. The Foreign Relations of 1878, 1879 and 1880 contain a number of dispatches indicating that our Government in fact interested itself to this end. Unhappily the conditions which were imposed by Article XLIV of the Treaty of Berlin to guarantee the equality of the Jews, were not fulfilled by Roumania, with the result that thousands of Roumanian Jews were compelled to emigrate to this country. In spite of the fact that the United States was not a party to the treaty, Secretary Hay in 1902 addressed the Powers who were signatories to the Berlin treaty, urging fulfilment of that clause of the treaty which was designed to protect the Jews of Roumania, and giving abundant reason for such action by our Government.

(2) Though these facts have been adverted to as affording technical warrant for the action requested by the American Jewish Committee, I believe that independently of the considerations thus far discussed, the exercise of the good offices of our Government with the Conferees and the Powers is in keeping with the policy which the United States has for more than seventy years pursued, of acting in the name and at the behest of humanity, whether American interests are involved or not.

Believing that at the present juncture both humanitarian and American interests are involved, I am confident that this plea will not have been made in vain.

Permit me also to suggest that in view of the fact that the death of our late Ambassador at the Court of St. James has created a vacancy in the American Embassy at London, present conditions might justify a designation by you of one or more special commissioners, who are familiar with the problems arising in the Balkan States and the Ottoman Empire, to make the necessary representations to the Conferees and to the Ambassadors of the Powers at London, by means of which the desired relief in this exigency may possibly be attained.

Your obedient servant,
LOUIS MARSHALL,
President American Jewish Committee.

The President,[103]
White House,
Washington, D. C.

II.

Washington, D. C., March 28, 1913.

THE PRESIDENT:[104]

Supplementing our interview of this morning on behalf of the American Jewish Committee and the statements contained in the letter of Mr. Louis Marshall, president of that committee, to President Taft, a copy of which was left with you, we beg, in

---

[103] Mr. Taft.
[104] Mr. Wilson.

accordance with your request for additional information, to submit the following:

The Jews in European Turkey have, under the Ottoman rule, been allowed the free exercise of their religion and have been secure in their civil rights. Their Chief Rabbi has been on a plane of equality with the heads of other religious denominations. They represent in the main an old stratum of the population, partly from remote antiquity and partly the people who sought refuge from Turkey when they were exiled from Spain in 1492. A quarter of a million or more of Jews will in all likelihood be incorporated into the Balkan States which will result from the present unhappy war. In a single town, Salonika, between seventy and eighty thousand of a population of one hundred and forty thousand inhabitants are Jews who represent a very high state of civilization. The prevailing church of the Balkan States is the Greek Catholic Church, which, to our profound regret, we are obliged to say has been and is notoriously hostile to the Jews. The churches permit the promulgation of the wicked slander of the use of Christian blood for ritual purposes, which inflames the minds of the populace, and hardly a year passes but there are attacks upon the Jews at the time of the Greek Easter. Immediately upon the capture of Salonika by the Greeks, the Jews were singled out, a number murdered, their houses and shops pillaged and their women outraged and maltreated.

We would cite also Roumania, which is understood to desire to secure a portion of the territory now belonging to Bulgaria in and about Silistria in compensation for additional territory which Bulgaria may secure. The attitude of Roumania towards its Jewish population has always been extremely hostile and in such flagrant defiance of the very constitution of that state, that although the United States was not a signatory to the conference which established Roumania, Secretary Hay, in 1902, was moved to address an identical note to our ambassadors and ministers residing in the countries of Europe, instructing them to present the views of our Government to the signatory powers upon this point. If Roumania, for example, is to secure more territory, the interests of humanity entitle every nation to take whatever steps can be taken, to see that Roumania gives rights to the Jews, who have been on the soil longer than the present Roumanians themselves, but are nevertheless treated as aliens and outcasts. The Bulgarian Jews residing in the nearest Roumanian territory have appealed to their government and have declared that the transfer suggested would be tantamount to a deprivation of their political freedom and equality and to their moral degradation. Signor Luzzatti, at one time Prime Minister of Italy, has publicly endorsed this statement.

In view of these dreadful possibilities we earnestly petition the President to lend the powerful aid of the United States, to the end that before the conclusion of the treaties of peace which will result in the increase of the territory of the existing Balkan States and in the possible formation of new states, guarantees shall be obtained that all the inhabitants shall be secure in their lives and property, shall have equal rights and be permitted to worship God according to the dictates of their conscience.

Our suggested means for carrying out these proposals, about the propriety of which we feel there can be no disagreement, is the appointment of a special commissioner on the part of the United States, to proceed to London or to whatever other point the conference of the powers will be held, to settle upon terms of peace in the Balkan States, with authority to present the views of this Government to the representatives of the Balkan States and of the powers participating in the conference.

For the interposition of such friendly offices of the United States there is ample precedent, and we here only refer to the action of the United States on behalf of the Jews at Damascus in 1840, at Morocco in 1880 and at the Algeciras Conference in 1906.

We venture to urge a speedy consideration of the matter, because the war seems to have drawn to a close and the conference which will inevitably ensue is not likely to be long delayed. We ask for the appointment of an experienced person to be on the spot, which is especially urgent in view of the change in ambassadorships now taking place and the likelihood that for several months, and during the period of this conference, a number of our important posts may be without ambassadors. We believe that it would be dangerous to delay action until such time as the question of the frontier and other important political matters which will be brought up in the conference are settled, because new states will be formed or existing states will acquire additional territory upon the terms laid down by the European Conference. We have more reason to hope for better treatment of minority populations at a time when the Balkan States can secure some advantage for the majority populations than on any other occasion.

We most respectfully urge your favorable and speedy action upon this petition. We believe that the United States would have a stronger moral influence in this action than any other power. The appointment of a commissioner would show the profound interest of the government and the people of the United States in this righteous cause, and no suspicion of any desire of territorial or other aggrandizement would lie against the United States.

In partial support of this communication we submit such documents as we have at hand:

(1) A memorandum of the important instances in which the United States has interposed its good offices on behalf of the Jews.

(2) A memorandum prepared by the Jews of England and submitted to Sir Edward Grey on the treaty rights of the Jews of Roumania.

(3) A copy of a memorial presented by the Roumanian Jews to their parliament.

(4) The correspondence with respect to the part taken by the United States on behalf of the Jews at the Algeciras Conference.

(5) Volume 15 of the *Publications* of the American Jewish Historical Society, published in 1906, which contains extracts of the diplomatic correspondence of the United States relating to the Jews, and which is but a small fraction of a much larger correspondence which could be furnished.

We have the honor to be,
Your most obedient servants,
CYRUS ADLER,
HERBERT FRIEDENWALD.

III.

DEPARTMENT OF STATE,
Washington, July 24, 1913.

MR. CYRUS ADLER.

SIR: Referring to your recent call on the Secretary of State in the course of which you left with him copies of the American Jewish Committee's letters to President Taft, under the date of January 14th, and to President Wilson, under date of March 28th last, I have to inform you that the Department has given careful consideration to the question of the status and rights of such of your coreligionists as may be transferred from the jurisdiction of the Ottoman Empire to that of any of the several Balkan States. The Department has now found it possible to instruct the American Ambassador in London, that, understanding that the questions involved in the settlement of affairs in the Balkan Peninsula continue to be considered by the Conference of Ambassadors of the European Powers in London, under the Chairmanship of the British Secretary of State for Foreign Affairs, it desires the Ambassador to take occasion to express to the British Foreign Office the satisfaction with which the United States would regard the inclusion, in any such agreement as may ultimately be concluded in regard to these questions, of a provision assuring the full enjoyment of civil and religious liberty to the inhabitants of the territories in question, without distinction of creed.

      I am, Sir,
       Your obedient servant,
         J. B. MOORE,
        Acting Secretary of State.

IV.

       DEPARTMENT OF STATE,
        Washington, July 30, 1913.

CYRUS ADLER, ESQUIRE.

 SIR: Referring to the recent letter in which you were advised of the action taken by the Department in instructing the American Ambassador at London to make known to the British Secretary of State for Foreign Affairs, as Chairman of the Ambassadorial Conference in London, the satisfaction with which this Government would regard an assurance of full civil and religious liberty to the inhabitants of former Turkish territories which may pass under the jurisdiction of any of the several Balkan States, I have to inform you that there has now been received from the Ambassador a telegram reporting that it is the purpose of the Conference of Ambassadors to deal only with such questions as the delimitation of certain boundaries, and the determination of the mutual relationships of the interested European Powers with reference to the questions incidental to the Balkan War; that the Conference is not expected to deal with the domestic questions of the several Balkan States; but that the British Secretary of State for Foreign Affairs has expressed his willingness to lay before the Conference, in the event that it should undertake the consideration of the question, the views made known to him by the Ambassador in behalf of this Government.

      I am, Sir,
       Your obedient servant,
        for the Secretary of State,
          J. B. MOORE,
           Counselor.

V.

Department of State,
Washington, August 6, 1913.

Cyrus Adler, Esquire.

Sir: Adverting to the letter of July 24th in which you were advised of the action taken by this Department in instructing the American Ambassador at London to make known to the British Secretary of State for Foreign Affairs, as Chairman of the Ambassadorial Conference in London, the satisfaction with which this Government would regard an assurance of full civil and religious liberty to the inhabitants of former Turkish territories which may pass under the jurisdiction of any of the several Balkan States, I have to advise you that the American Ministers accredited to Greece and Montenegro, and to Bulgaria, Roumania and Servia, have subsequently been instructed to make to those Governments a communication similar to that which had been made to the British Foreign Secretary by the American Embassy in London.

I am, Sir,
Your obedient servant,
for the Secretary of State,
J. B. Moore,
Counselor.

VI.

Department of State,
Washington, August 9, 1913.

Cyrus Adler, Esquire.

Sir: In further reference to the Department's letter of July 24th advising you of its action in instructing the American Ambassador at London to make known to the British Secretary of State for Foreign Affairs, as the Chairman of the Ambassadorial Conference in London, the satisfaction with which this Government would regard an assurance of full civil and religious liberty to the inhabitants of former Turkish territories which may pass under the jurisdiction of any of the several Balkan States, I have to inform you that there has now been received from the American Minister at Bucharest (to whom the action thus taken was communicated by telegraph) a despatch reporting that it is to be anticipated that the Jewish inhabitants of the territory about to be transferred from Bulgarian to Roumanian sovereignty will be accorded the same rights and privileges as are given to persons of other races and religions, as was the case when the Dobrudja was acquired in 1878. This dispatch further reports that Jews in Bulgaria and Servia enjoy the full rights and privileges of citizenship and are not discriminated against in any way; and that under the circumstances it is not probable that any discrimination will be made with regard to newly acquired territory.

Referring to the Department's letter of the 6th instant advising you that the American Ministers accredited to the several nations in the Balkan Peninsula had been instructed to make communication similar to that which had been made to the British Foreign Office by the American Embassy in London, I have now to inform you that the views of this Government were at once communicated to the delegates of the five States participating in the Peace Conference at Bucharest. At this conference, the Bulgarian Government is represented by its Minister of Finance, with full powers, and Greece, Montenegro, Roumania and Servia are represented by their Prime Ministers who, in the case of the latter two countries, are also Ministers for Foreign Affairs. The American Minister at Bucharest now reports that on the 5th instant the views presented in behalf of this Government were taken up by the Conference, which unanimously decided that it would be superfluous to include in the Treaty of Peace a special provision of the nature contemplated, inasmuch as the Constitutions of all the States involved guarantee civil and religious liberty and the Minister for Foreign Affairs of Roumania took occasion to declare the view that in accordance with the principles of international law all citizens of annexed territory without distinction of race or religion, become citizens of the annexing State.

      I am, Sir,
       Your obedient servant,
        for the Secretary of State,
         J. B. MOORE,
          Counselor.

The official protocol of the Bucharest Conference fully bears out the advices of our State Department as to the nature of the guarantees given at this Peace Conference. On August 5, 1913, the question was raised at the Peace Conference by a communication from the United States Government, expressing the hope that a provision would be introduced into the treaty, according full civil and religious liberty to the inhabitants of any territory subject to the sovereignty of any of the five Powers, or which might be transferred from the jurisdiction of any one of them to that of another.

M. Majoresco, the chief Roumanian plenipotentiary, expressed the opinion that such a provision was unnecessary
as the principle inspiring it had long been recognized, in fact and in law, by the public law of the Constitutional States represented at the Conference,

but he added that he was willing to declare, on behalf of the plenipotentiaries, that
the inhabitants of any territory newly acquired will have, without distinction of religion, the same full civil and religious liberty as all the other inhabitants of the state.

In this view the other plenipotentiaries concurred.[105]

On October 13, 1913, the London Board of Deputies of British Jews and the Anglo-Jewish Association, addressed a Joint Memorial to Sir Edward Grey [106] urging that affirmative guarantees be secured,[107] and pointing out that Roumania had repeatedly ignored and repudiated similar assurances, as in fact she has done since then, also, in this particular instance. This memorial expressly conceded, however, that
in four of the annexing States, namely, Greece, Bulgaria, Servia and Montenegro, the Constitutions provide for the equal rights of all religious denominations, and they gratefully acknowledge that for may years past, the Jews in those countries have had no reason to complain.

Sir Edward Grey directed this memorial to be answered by an important letter, reading: [108]
The articles of the Treaty of Berlin to which you refer, are in no way abrogated by the territorial changes in the Near East, and remain as binding as they have been hitherto, as regards all

---

[105] Protocol No. 6.

[106] *The Jewish Chronicle*, October 31, 1913, prints the full text.

[107] *Cf.* their earlier Memorial of 1908, printed as Appendix VI, *infra*, pp. 137-153.

[108] *The Jewish Chronicle*, November 7, 1913.

territories covered by these articles at the time when the treaty was signed. Her Majesty's Government will, however, consult with the other Powers as to the policy of reaffirming in some way the provisions of the Treaty of Berlin for the protection of the religious and other liberties of the minorities in the territories referred to, when the question of giving formal recognition by the Powers to the recent territorial changes in the Balkan peninsula is raised.

Such guarantees have not, however, thus far been secured, and will become all the more necessary, in view of probable territorial changes at the close of the present war.

It is interesting to observe that in a work just published on "The Doctrine of Intervention" by H. C. Hodges,[109] probably the first on the subject written in the United States, the author makes a strong plea for such American intervention on behalf of persecuted foreign Jews, though without specific reference to our American precedents of intercession on behalf of the victims of religious persecution, which Charles Sumner in 1870, as seen, described in the Senate, with reference to Roumanian Jewish persecution, as "the guardianship of humanity, which belongs to the great Republic," and which Secretary Forsyth in 1840, in connection with the Damascus blood accusations, had emphasized as following from our mission as the pioneer exponent of religious liberty, which distinctive characteristic of our Government invests with a peculiar propriety and right the interposition of our good offices in behalf of an oppressed and persecuted race.

As seen, Secretary Hay and Acting Secretary Moore, in 1902 and 1913, followed the same precedents. Mr. Hodges says:

---

[109] Princeton, 1915. See similar views in Oscar S. Straus' address, "The Humanitarian Diplomacy of the United States," in his "The American Spirit," New York, 1913, p. 19 *et seq.;* and see Stambler, *supra;* Wheaton, "Elements of International Law," 5th English edition (Phillipson), London, 1916, pp. 90-130, regarding the right of intervention and interference; T. J. Lawrence, "The Primacy of the Great Powers," in his "Essays on Some Disputed Questions in Modern International Law," Cambridge, 1884.

The case of an intervention in the interest of persecuted Jews presents several distinct peculiarities. In the first place, the race has no direct protecting governmental authority. In the second place, due to their scattered condition, they are unable to unite in sufficient numbers for their own adequate protection. These two facts are sufficient to explain the peculiarity of the present situation of the Jews in Roumania.

At the Berlin Conference in 1878, the Powers agreed to recognize the Balkan States on the condition that they should not impose any religious disabilities on their subjects. This was the spirit and letter of Article 44 of that Agreement. Recognition was granted with the understanding that this stipulation would be fulfilled. Hence it follows from the spirit of Article 44 that should this article be violated, the Powers signing that agreement had the right, and even more the duty, of intervention. Nevertheless, in accordance with the municipal law in Roumania, the Jews are, with a few exceptions, considered as foreigners, so that they may not come under the provisions of the article just mentioned. On the other hand, the authorities argue that since these Jews are not subjects of any other state, Roumania may compel them to render military service. The authorities treat them, in respect to many other matters, as their discretion may direct. It would seem that the parties to this Berlin Conference are lax in the fulfilment of their obligations so long as they allow such actions to continue. For them intervention for the correction of the present anomalous condition of the Roumanian Jew, is legally justifiable. For other states the cause is very weak. It must be admitted that the so-called rights of mankind are not absolutely assured.

If Oppenheim's history of the development of the mutual ascendancy of the Christian religion and the principles of international law [110] is a true one, it is hard to see upon what grounds an

---

[110] Mr. Hodges, on p. 94 of his work, quotes the following passage from Oppenheim's "International Law" (2d edition, London, 1912, vol. i, p. 368):

"The Law of Nations is a product of Christian civilization and represents a legal order which binds states, chiefly Christian, into a community. It is therefore no wonder that ethical ideas which are some of them the basis of, others a development from, Christian morals, have a tendency to require the help of international law for their realization. When the Powers stipulated at the Berlin

intervention for the suppression of such conditions as exist in Roumania in respect to the Jewish population can be denied.

The development of the "hands off" policy is nullifying sympathy in a similar case, where no agreement exists to justify an intervention. The case of the Jews in Russia is known to the civilized world. The reports cannot all be false. The condition of these people arouses pity, but, although deplorable conditions exist there, they are not existing in violation of any international agreement. The Jews in Roumania have a much stronger case than the Jews in Russia, but the only legitimate authority for taking up their cause from a strictly legal standpoint has failed to act.

One of the strongest views in opposition to an intervention based on religious oppression is expressed by Hall, from whose writings Oppenheim says many of his opinions are formed. Evidently this opinion came from a different source. There are

---

Conference of 1878 that the Balkan States should be recognized only under the condition that they did not impose any religious disabilities on their subjects, they lent their arm to the realization of such an idea. Again, when the Powers after the beginning of the nineteenth century agreed to several international arrangements in the interest of the abolition of the slave trade, they fostered the realization of another of these ideas."

On the same page, he also quotes Phillimore as follows:

" Phillimore in his work on International Law states that one of the just causes of intervention is 'to protect persons, subjects of another state, from persecution on account of professing another religion not recognized by that state, but identical with the religion of the intervening state.' (I, p. 468.)"

In his interesting historical discussion of intervention, Mr. Hodges points out (p. 8), that the religious principle was one of the earliest causes of intervention, the best example of this being the Crusades and the wars instituted " in the effort to keep open the road, that their countrymen might make pilgrimages to the shrines of the Holy Land," and he also mentions, as another early justification, intervention based on the theory of " barbarity," which was invoked as an added incentive and justification for the Crusades on account of Turkish cruelties, and which ground found a recent application in England's course in Egypt, culminating in her annexation of that country in 1914 (p. 9). These causes were also marked as grounds for intervention in the religious wars of

several writers who maintain that the Law of Nations guarantees to every individual, wherever he might be, the so-called rights of mankind, no matter what may be his status; that is, even though he may be stateless. Among these writers are Bluntschli, de Martens, Bonfils and others.[111]

We may conclude that, although the opinions of the writers just mentioned can hardly be said to obtain at the present time, nevertheless there is a tendency to depart from that very strict construction given to the principle by Hall. As in the case of humanity it seems that the tendency of an ever increasing pressure of public opinion, combined with a more universal demand for justice, is to push the claim for legality of this cause ever nearer that point where it will be recognized by the majority. Religious toleration will be one of the accomplishments of an advanced international community just as surely as it is of the more enlightened states of the present time.

---

the sixteenth and seventeenth centuries (p. 10). He also recognizes protection of missionaries as an established ground for intervention (pp. 74-80), as also "the cause of humanity" (pp. 87-92), examples of which were intervention by the great Powers of Europe in 1827 on behalf of Greek independence, and again in 1860 to put a stop to the massacre of Christians in the district of Mount Lebanon, which Lawrence has justified. See, also, Hodges' study of American precedents (pp. 13-16, 36-37, 39-40, 61-79, 101-102, 118-146, etc.). Of course, self-protection justifies intervention (pp. 6-7, 23-28, 104-105, 215), and where treaties or conventions affirmatively grant the right, or intervention is called for to enforce such treaties or guarantees, as in the case of the Balkan States, an additional ground for intervention exists according to his classification (p. 36), he, in this case, citing Hershey's "Essentials of International Public Law" (*ibid.*) to this effect; and Oppenheim (*supra,* vol. i, p. 190) writes to the same effect and gives a particularly lucid treatment of the whole subject of intervention, with numerous citations (*ibid,* pp. 118-119, 188-189).

[111] See quotations in Stambler, *supra,* pp. 200-203; Oppenheim, "International Law," 2d edition, London, 1912, vol. i, p. 188.

APPENDIX I.

PETITION OF THE ROUMANIAN JEWS TO THE CHAMBER OF DEPUTIES; 1872.

Mr. President, Gentlemen, Deputies of the Chamber of Roumania:

In true fealty to the land of our birth, we, the undersigned Roumanians of Mosaic faith, descendants of those who shared in the days of national reverses all burdens and sufferings alike with our countrymen of other faiths, approach to ask in most respectful but earnest terms the extension of those rights which have so long been withheld from us.

Driven from other lands where intolerance and persecution had made their lives bitter and hopeless, the children of Israel found in Roumania refuge and asylum. Cultivating the arts of peace, industry and commerce, they lived in harmony with their Christian brethren, and contributed to the wealth and progress of the nation. Only with the introduction of those notions of political economy which have sought to raise false distinctions between one class of the population and the other, have we come to be overwhelmed with the monstrous charges of long buried ages, and to be considered and treated as pariahs in our fatherland. We deem it superfluous to refute these charges. To contend that because of our religious differences we cherish other than patriotic feeling, would be to refute the whole history of the past and the action of the most advanced nations of the present.

Almost every civilized government of the present day has admitted the Hebrew to complete civil and political liberty. Roumania, too, regenerating herself, has been led by these priciples in stipulating, in an accord with the guaranteeing Powers, by Article 46 of the Convention of Paris, July 19, 1858, that all Moldavians and Wallachians should be equal before the law, irrespective of religion, making this distinction with reference to political rights whose extension was left to the Legislative Chamber, because all Europe supposed that the liberal Roumanians would accomplish of their own volition this act of justice, confirming thereby their just title to be admitted into the family of the most enlightened nations.

We are pained to see that, after waiting more than fourteen years since the promulgation of the Convention of Paris, not only have we not been admitted to those rights, but even those rights which we formerly enjoyed under old laws have been taken from us by an erroneous interpretation of the new organic law.

We ask you, gentlemen deputies, to consider our position in the present moment. We are denied almost every right which man cherishes as dear as life itself. We have no political rights, no civil liberty. We cannot hold property in or till the soil. We cannot purchase even the dwellings sheltering our families. We are shut out from the learned professions, excluded from several industrial and commercial pursuits, and in the army where several thousand soldiers of Jewish faith serve in the ranks, all hope of promotion is denied. Nor is this all; the public mind of the country is continually excited against us by misrepresentations and invectives, while general and systematic persecution has its apologists.

We must respectfully submit that all this has been contrary to the spirit of past and existing treaties and opposed to the spirit and letter of the Constitution. Article 21 of that instrument declares liberty of conscience to be unrestricted and guarantees the freedom of all religions. There is then no distinction between Roumanians born in Christian or Jewish faith. Nor in the support to be rendered to the country is any discrimination made, both being subject to the same taxes and required to fulfill the same obligations. Both should therefore be equal before the law, and it should not be for a moment insisted that of those born in the country only one part should enjoy all rights and prerogatives, while the other part should have only duties, no rights.

In the only clause referring to religious distinction in the Constitution, it is said, Article 8: "Only strangers of Christian religion can acquire naturalization." This clause cannot be applied to us, we are no strangers. Here our fathers made their homes in the early days of history. More than five centuries have passed since our ancestors first came to this land.

Can we, who have here buried our fathers, be destitute of love for the country which holds within the bosom of her soil their sacred ashes? Should we not be pained to the depths of our souls, we, who are bound to this country by thousands of ties, to see our birthright given to foreigners, while we, children of the soil, are treated as strangers, and oftentimes forced to seek foreign protection?

The youth of the Mosaic faith, educated on the benches of the national schools, together with the Christian youth, can they be less accessible to the sentiments of patriotism, the spirit of Roumanianism? We most solemnly declare in spite of all our sufferings that we love Roumania, the land of our birth, we recognize no other country, we have no other home!

We come then, gentlemen deputies, to pray that by virtue of the high authority with which the sacred obligations of international treaties have invested you, you declare our rights as Roumanians. We address ourselves to you, venerable deputies, you who, by living traditions and long experience, have been in a position to convince yourselves that your brethren of the Jewish faith now, as of old, are peaceable, loyal and industrious, contributing to the national wealth, without ever thinking or profiting by agitations and disturbances.

Convince your colleagues that all the arguments brought forward against us are slanders drawn from the dark ages, unworthy of modern thought, inconsistent with the teachings of history and logic, and opposed to the broad principles upon which rests our national edifice. Persuade them to be in our favor. We address ourselves to you, young deputies, who have been brought up in the most civilized countries of Europe, who have been nourished at the springs of the most enlightened universities, and who have had frequent occasion to witness that in those countries, where the Israelite is equal with his Christian brother, there exists no jealousy, no religious hatred. There the Hebrew does not remain behind his companion of other faiths, either in the sciences, the arts, or patriotism. Tell this to your colleagues, that they shall follow the example of those prosperous, enlightened states, and revive the ancient spirit of generosity which once fired the soul of every Roumanian. With you rest the proudest hopes which the age builds for the future. We shall not plead with you in vain.

We address ourselves to you, gentlemen professors, deputies in the Chamber. You, who have the noble and beautiful mission of familiarizing youth with the history of the fatherland. Tell them and tell the world that the Jews are no strangers in Roumania. Their presence in this country dates back to the remotest periods of history. That they came into Dacia with the Roumanians, that Decebalus received them and gave them homes in the valley which they then called Talmus, and which to this day is called Talmaci. That under the reign of Dan II, in 1376, the Hebrews, driven out from Hungary by King Ludwig, found refuge in Roumania. Tell them that the Jews had to suffer equally with the Christians from the cruelties of Stefan III, and others who demolished their synagogues. Explain to them that if the Jews engage principally in commerce, this cannot be imputed as a failing, but rather as an honor; for idleness begets sin, and labor alone dignifies. Tell them, too, that because of long centuries of oppression, which forbade us to follow the pursuits of our patriarchal fathers, we have been compelled to adopt commercial and mechanical pursuits, in which alone we were permitted to gain a livelihood. Tell them that a people, who in every age have preserved their faith in the one Living God, who have survived the fall of empires, the crash of thrones, and whose matchless code of laws forms the basis upon which all other religious systems are founded, may well claim to be considered a part of the body politic of any nation.

We address ourselves finally to all the Deputies of the Chambers, of whatsoever shade. We believe that the time has come when every son of the soil, every native-born son of the country should be declared, without distinction of religion, a Roumanian. We believe that the time has come of which M. Cogalniceanu spoke in his discourse delivered in the Divan-ad-hos, on the 15th of November, 1857. "I believe," said he, "that soon the time will come when religion will be no title of exclusion for any citizen; the time will come when all will be Roumanians in beloved Roumania. For we must be just to all the sons of Roumania, because only by justice can we secure tranquility in the country, and only by the ties of mutual love can we unite all the powers of our nation, in order to have a beautiful and true Roumanian fatherland."

Gentlemen Deputies, when all civilized nations of modern times have established the civil and political rights of the Hebrew, shall only the Roumanian Jew be kept in bondage? Shall Roumania alone among the nations make so unjust an exception? No; our country, young in its new institutions, needs the hands of all her sons to develop her resources. Our cause not only involves principles of justice and humanity, but the internal peace and future welfare of the nation.

Gentlemen Deputies: We rely upon your sense of justice and confide our cause in your keeping, confident that you will meet this our petition in that broad spirit which is characteristic of the age, and upon which all permanent progress is founded. We look alone to you and our fatherland, we ask no other help. With prayers for the health of our august Sovereign, invoking the wisdom of Almighty God upon your labors,

      We are Your Humble Petitioners, &c.

APPENDIX II.

MEMORIAL submitted to the Conference of the European Powers at Constantinople by the Conference of Israelites held at Paris (1876).

Paris, December, 1876.
To the President and Members of the Conference at Constantinople:

GENTLEMEN: You are called upon to deliberate upon the interests of a numerous population in the East, and to achieve a work of peace and justice.

In coming before you to-day, we do not appeal to your liberality in behalf of ourselves. The privileges which we solicit from your powerful authority we already enjoy in the different countries of our birth, and among the populations of which we constitute a portion. We are sent to you by the Israelites of Germany, America, England, Austria, Belgium, France, Holland, Italy and Switzerland.

Bound together by the same religious belief, we solicit through you the accomplishment of the work of humanity with which you are charged, and which seems full of important results.

You are assembled to regulate the civil and political condition of various Eastern nations. We, as Israelites, citizens of free nations, ask you not to make any distinction between the different religions, and to guarantee to our coreligionists the same rights as are enjoyed by other inhabitants of those countries.

A bitter experience in the Danubian Principalities has demonstrated the danger of unequal civil rights between the different populations of the same country, and the same fact was made obvious by the Treaty of Paris in 1856, and the Convention of Paris in 1858. Every privilege denied to a race or religion gives rise to persecutions, such as those which Roumania and Servia have for many years presented to Europe, and which we trust are drawing nigh to a close.

It cannot, therefore, be the intention of any of the great nations participating in the Conference at Constantinople to secure any rights for Christians from which the Ottoman subjects of other creeds would be debarred.

From time immemorial, Turkey has treated her non-Mussulman subjects without any distinction. In the present country, the Israelites have been included in all laws for the organization of the Empire, and to ameliorate the condition of the *rayas*, such as the *hatti-sherif* of Gulhave, of the 13th of November, 1839, and the *hatti-humayun* of 1856.

The civil law of Turkey establishes equality between all persons, without any distinction of race or creed. These legislative precedents hold out to the Israelites, as well as to all non-Mussulman subjects, an equal share in the improvements and reform which may be brought about in the administration and political Government of Turkey.

In the Principalities, on the contrary, the condition of the Israelites, instead of being improved, has never ceased to grow worse since those provinces have been governing themselves. Servia banishes them from their homes, and forbids them to settle in every portion of her territory, except Belgrade, and by a strange irony it leaves their political rights intact, while it refuses them their civil rights. Who is there that does not know of the shocking persecutions which they have endured in Roumania? They are in the memories of all men, and have, on several occasions, deeply stirred the emotion of Europe.

The Convention of Paris in its 46th Article, had secured all civil rights to Israelites, by extending them to all Moldo-Wallachians who were non-Christian, and thus left to the liberality of the section the concession of political rights.

The Moldo-Wallachian Christians' and non-Christians' rights were soon enlarged by the laws of the country.

In order to prevent the Jews from enjoying the advantages accorded to them by their possession of civil rights, they denied that the Israelites, in spite of their birthplace, had been Moldo-Wallachians. Afterwards, to keep them from becoming such, the Constitution of 1866 reserved to foreign Christians only the right of being naturalized.

Deprived by these expedients of the protection of the Convention of 1858, the Israelites were simultaneously delivered over to the despotism of the law-makers of the country, and the fury of the populace. Every one knows the long list of crimes, riots, and banishments which, from 1863 to 1872, roused the indignation of every civilized people, the destruction of the synagogue at Bucharest in 1866, the wholesale expulsion in 1867, the drowning of Galatz, the renewed banishments from the districts of Bajan and Vaslui in 1868, followed by the protests of all the consuls, the banishment on a great scale from the districts of Bajan, Galatz and Vaslui in 1869, the riots of Tecuh and Battosehan in 1870, the riot at Ismael, Cahul and Vilcow in 1872, the acquittal of the rioters by the jury and renewed threats of expulsion at Dorshoi, Tolschan, and other places this very year.

When the consuls interfered to put a stop to these atrocities, the most wicked schemes were broached in the Legislature of Roumania, with the idea of expelling the Jews from the rural districts, and at the same time of making their living in the cities an impossible matter.

To stave off the protests of European representatives, they henceforward desisted from mentioning the Israelites by name in laws legislating against strangers, and the Jews, treated as such notwithstanding their long residence in the country, notwithstanding the old laws of Moldavia-Wallachia and the international treaties, which recognize them as native-born, and, finally, in spite of their attachment to their home, have lost, during the last few years, by a series of laws more murderous than the violence of the riots, the right to settle in the rural districts, and to purchase even or lease country property, to own real estate in the cities, to attend auction sales, to manufacture and sell tobacco, to retail liquors in the country districts. The freedom of going and coming, of engaging in trade, the right of holding property, being taken away from them, are they not already outlaws?

But every public charge or obligation is, nevertheless, imposed on them; even military duty, which, by a refinement of cruelty, they perform not as Roumanians, a capacity on which they might base their claim to the rights of non-Christian Moldo-Wallachians; they perform this last duty as strangers born or residing in Roumania, and are shut out from promotion from the lowest grade.

The Roumanians go even further. They wish to exclude Israelites of all countries. In their treaties of commerce with other nations, they ask that the Israelites of the country which enters into the treaty with them, be subject to the same laws which govern their coreligionists in Roumania. As early as 1868, Lord Stanley, now Earl of Derby, Minister of Foreign Affairs of Great Britain, expressed himself in the following language in the House of Commons: "I really think it is a question which concerns Christians even more than Jews, because if the suffering falls upon the Jew, the disgrace falls upon the Christian. I know of no instance in our time of a series of oppressive acts which were committed so completely—I will not say merely without any provocation, but so far as I can see, without any reasonable and intelligible motive whatever." (Hansard's Debates, *supra*, vol. 191, p. 1267.)

Can this very deplorable state of things be tolerated in Europe, in a country which owes its existence to Europe itself? The leading Powers have never ceased to complain of them. Their protests have too frequently remained without effect. Assembled for the first time since the Treaty of 1858, they now have a splendid opportunity to make known their will to cause Roumania and Servia to respect the Treaty, for the performance of which all the inhabitants of those nations are bound, and to give to Israelites the rights of which they are deprived. Europe cannot be silent; while it demands, in a unanimous voice, the social and political equality of the Christians of the East, will it suffer, in Roumania, a population of 250,000 souls to be the victims of an unheard-of persecution?

By protecting the Jews in Roumania, as well as non-Mussulmans in Turkey, it will proclaim that it upholds everywhere religious liberty, which towers above all faiths and religions.

The Israelitish delegates, representing the different countries mentioned in this Memorial, have therefore the honor to respectfully submit to the Conference the two following requests:

1st. To grant complete civil, religious and political equality to all non-Mussulmans in the provinces of Turkey, the condition of which is now under the consideration of the Conference, and in the principality of Servia.

2nd. To revise and complete the Paris Convention of 1858, in all matters concerning the Jews of Roumania, in order that they may have the full enjoyment of civil and political rights.

Accept, gentlemen, the assurance of our profound respects, etc., etc.

APPENDIX III.

MEMORIAL OF ALLIANCE ISRAÉLITE UNIVERSELLE OF PARIS TO THE CONGRESS OF BERLIN.[112]

To the President and Members of the European Congress:

Sixteen months ago, Israelitish delegates from all countries addressed the European Conference at Constantinople and asked it to put an end to the oppressive rule to which the Jews in Roumania and Servia are subjected, and to secure to those provinces of Turkey, whose fate was to be regulated by the Conference, the civil and political equality claimed for all non-Mussulmans. You meet to-day in order to resume the work of the Conference of Constantinople. Representatives of the Great Powers of Europe, you are called upon to establish in Eastern Europe a government under which populations of different races and beliefs may live peacefully with each other. Europe would not approve of a peace

---

[112] *The Jewish Chronicle,* June 28, 1878.

which was not based upon respect for the great principles of public right; the equality of men among themselves, freedom of religious belief. The necessity of writing in the constitutions of Oriental countries, that religious belief cannot be for anyone a cause of social or political inferiority, is imposed by the law of civilization. It is still more so by the necessity for suppressing the danger of permanent conflicts between populations of different races and religions.

The Treaties of 1856 and 1858 ended by enacting the application of these principles in Roumania and in Servia; but the insufficiency of the stipulations of these Treaties was the cause of breaking the spirit of them and rendering possible a series of restrictive laws against the Jews of these two countries. In Servia they were successively hunted from the country and the villages, excluded from every employment and from every function, and reduced to misery. The deprivation of their most precious rights did not free them from any burdens, however. They were subjected, like all Servians, to the blood tax; like them, they were bound to military service.

In the last war they thought to conquer the ill-feeling of the country towards them by dint of patriotism. They fought bravely and mingled on the fields of battle their blood with that of their compatriots. If their sacrifices brought them some kind words from the Minister of the Interior at the great Skupschtina in 1877, their condition did not at all change. It was in vain that at the time of the Convention concluded between Servia and Turkey in 1877, Turkey claimed for them the rights stubbornly refused. Under such rule their number has long since diminished to half. They are constantly in certain villages threatened with edicts of expulsion.

In Roumania the condition of the Jews, who are there more numerous, is still more frightful. For two years they have been subject to the most cruel persecutions. Almost every year Europe is moved by the recital of the riots, murders, pillage or expulsions *en masse*, of which they are the victims. To these acts of violence legal persecution has been added by a set of laws excluding the Jews from all employments, from all liberal careers, from every public function, and from numerous branches of commerce, fettering them even in the free exercise of religious practices, and seeking by every possible means to reduce them to misery, and to disparage them. In vain the Guaranteeing Powers, supported by Article 46 of the Convention of Paris, which granted to the Roumanian Jews at least civil rights, remonstrated against this fatal and barbarous policy. No heed was given either to their advice, or their remonstrance. Roumania, without pity for the Jews, has, however, in them subjects devoted to work useful to the development of commerce and of industry, capable of raising themselves and of doing honor to their country in liberal careers. In the last war the services which they rendered with the ambulances and in the hospitals, and their conduct on the battle-field, have brought them public marks of recognition from their Prince; but nevertheless, a thing unheard of, some laws, and more recently a decree of a court of justice declared that these Jews who shed their blood for the glory of their country did not belong to any nationality or to any country.

If such is the conduct of Servia and Roumania with regard to the Jews, what have they not to fear from other emancipated provinces of Turkey? Is it necessary to recall the sad episode of Eska-Zagra and Kezanlik, in order to show the dangers which menace the Jews in Bulgaria and part of Roumania? Thousands of them still wander about without shelter and without any resources, far from their country.

In the name of the Israelites, in the name of humanity, we respectfully address Europe in favour of our unhappy coreligionists of Bulgaria, Servia, Roumelia and Roumania. We wait with her for the end of their sufferings. Her protection to them is indispensable in the present and in the future. May Europe cause her powerful voice to be heard, may she proclaim the equality of men, independent of all religious beliefs, and may she enforce the insertion of this principle in the constitutions! May she at length be a vigilant guardian over them!

Such is the work which the world looks for from the Congress of 1878. It is demanded by the traditions of European policy, by the wishes of enlightened men of all nations. It will give peace to Europe and prosperity to countries cruelly tried by the war. It will be pregnant with happy results for all nations, glorious for our epoch, and the remembrance of this Congress will remain indelible in the memory of future generations.

APPENDIX IV.

Hon. Oscar S. Straus' Memoranda Preceding Dispatch of the Hay Roumanian Note.

I.

New York, April 2, 1902.

Mr. Jacob H. Schiff.

My dear Sir: Following the conversation I had with you yesterday regarding the terrible persecutions of our co-religionists by the Roumanian Government, and as you informed me that you intended going to Washington to-morrow and have a conversation with the President respecting some matters, I trust that you will lay before him a statement regarding the inhuman treatment of the Jews by the Roumanian Government.

If the matter were of concern to the Government and people of the United States, and especially to the Jews of our country, from only a humanitarian standpoint, I would not have the President's noble heart disturbed with its recital, but as it is one of practically international bearing, I think it but proper and just that we should get the President's advice upon the subject.

By the Treaty of Berlin (13th of July, 1878) between England, France, Germany, Austria, Russia, Italy and Turkey, Roumania was made an independent kingdom and by the forty-fourth article of that treaty it was provided that difference of religion shall not be ground for exclusion or incapacity in matters relating to civil and political rights or the exercising of the various professions or industries. This clause was put in there specially to protect the Jews.

Notwithstanding this express provision of the treaty, the Jews are not only excluded from civil rights, excepting that they are compelled to serve in the army, but not permitted to become officers therein. They are subject to exceptional taxes, they are practically excluded from all professions and from owning and cultivating land, and new laws are being promulgated practically shutting them out from every avenue of self-support. They are not permitted to become citizens, excepting in rare instances. Now what is the result?

These people are emigrating *en masse*, that is, all who have or can borrow enough money to pay for their transportation. As is well known, the obstacles to immigration in Western European countries are so great, that few find resting places there and they are by force of circumstances driven to our shores.

I am sure that every American familiar with our history will ever approve of the doctrine laid down by the famous divine Jonathan Mayhew, who suggested to James Otis the idea of a Commission of Correspondence prior to our Revolution, when he said "and if any miserable people of the Continent or Isles of Europe be driven in their extremity to seek a safe retreat from slavery in some far distant clime, oh, let them find one in America."

Yet, when any country with whom we are on terms of amity and friendship, subjects a portion of its population to such persecutions as to force them in large numbers, and many of them in a pauperized condition, upon our shores, that in itself is an unfriendly act, and aside from any question of sentiment, gives our government the right, not only to protest, but to remonstrate against such inhuman laws, that discredit the age in which we are living.

As you know, Mr. Schiff, reliable information has reached us lately that new laws and additional restrictions have recently been placed upon the Jews in Roumania, and, as a result, emigration from Roumania and immigration into the United States of this persecuted people will be and is being augmented.

The facts regarding this persecution are now on file in the office of the Commissioner General of Immigration, being the reports made by Special Immigrant Inspector Robert Watchorn to T. V. Powderly, Commissioner General of Immigration, during the month of September, 1900.

Inspector Watchorn, on July 28, 1900, was instructed to report "as to the causes leading to the exodus of the Roumanian Jews, the number and character of those likely to come to the United States and the conditions which surround the people there generally, and which contribute to their leaving their native land." Following these instructions he made a series of reports, from which I extract a few passages:

That the Jewish population in Roumania numbers 400,000.

That a Jew may not secure, hold or work land in a rural district, he may not reside in a rural district, he may only reside in one of seventy-one towns designated as abiding places for the Jews.

He may not follow the occupation of an apothecary, a lawyer, stock broker, a member of the Bourse or Stock Exchange, a pedlar or regular dealer. These are only a few of the callings denied him.

To be deprived of the right to own, rent or labor on a farm or garden in a peculiarly agricultural country must be recognized as a tremendous handicap in the race of life, but to follow that up with the closing of the greater part of the avenues of endeavor in urban countries greatly intensifies the hardships to which he is subjected. And, as though the foregoing category was not considered sufficient, a still further impediment is found in the regulation which forbids employers of labor to employ Jews, until they have first employed two Christians.

This was the condition at the time the report was made. Within the past few months additional restrictions have been placed, so that not only are the schools closed to the children of the Jews, and the special taxes increased, but they are forbidden to trade in many articles of commerce and to dispose of their wares after they have manufactured them.

During the administration of President Grant, in 1872, when the persecutions first attracted our attention in Roumania, our government made a strong remonstrance, both in its own behalf and through its Consul at Bucharest in conjunction with Germany, Austria, France, Great Britain, Greece and Italy. (See Foreign Relations of the United States, 1872, pp. 688-690.)

Secretary Fish in his Instructions says:

This government heartily sympathizes with the popular instinct. . . . It is deemed to be due to humanity to remonstrate against any license or impunity which may have attended the outrages in that country . . . and you will also do anything which you discreetly can with a reasonable prospect of success, toward preventing the reöccurrence or continuance of the persecution adverted to.

The action taken by the United States at that time had a marked effect in moderating the action of the Roumanian Government, so that the persecutions abated and so did the emigration from Roumania to the United States, until these persecutions were again renewed in intensity within the last few years, and consequently within the past two years the immigration of Roumanian Jews into this country has grown inordinately.

While not wishing to suggest for the consideration of the President any specific line of action, it appears to me that it would not be contrary to precedent if a strong resolution were introduced into each House of Congress by the Chairman of the Committee of Foreign Affairs, expressive of sympathy and protesting against the inhuman treatment on the part of Roumania of unoffending people, who are driven by the hand of persecution to seek refuge in our country.

The President might deem it proper, upon his own motion or following such a resolution of Congress, to send a Minister or Special Commissioner with diplomatic rank to Roumania to remonstrate against this action on the part of Roumania. The passage of such a resolution authorizing the appointment of a Special Commissioner would of itself have a prompt and far-reaching effect, not only in Roumania, but would awaken action by the more enlightened European nations who were parties to the treaty.

The fact that the far greater number of Roumanian Jewish refugees seek an asylum in this country is reason why, in my judgment, our Government is justified in initiating such a remonstrance as I have referred to.

Very truly yours,
OSCAR S. STRAUS.

II.

New York, May 15, 1902.

PRESIDENT ROOSEVELT.

SIR: On April 4th last, through the mediation of Mr. Jacob H. Schiff, of this city, I had the honor of laying before you a statement regarding the terrible persecutions of the Jews by the Roumanian Government, and the consequent forced emigration to this country of a large number of these unfortunate people. This statement having been referred by you to Secretary Hay, I had a conference with him at the Department of State, and I was requested by the Secretary to present a further statement giving some additional facts, for the consideration of the Government.

Since the date above referred to, the conditions in Roumania have become still more alarming, as appears from the public press and a series of reports made by the agent of the *Alliance Israélite Universelle* from Bucharest, the last under date of the 30th of April, now before me.

In my last statement I referred to the official reports made to the Commissioner General of Immigration of the United States by Special Immigrant Inspector Robert Watchorn (September 9, 1900), detailing the repressive laws that up to that date had been passed to drive the Jews of Roumania from every avenue of earning a livelihood. These laws, and others since enacted, are now being rigorously enforced, and the recent cable dispatches report that some 12,000 able-bodied artisans, and others, with their families, are preparing to emigrate and seek a refuge in this country. I refer to this fact, not with a view of intimating any protest on the part of American Jews against receiving these refugees in this country, which from the day that the Pilgrim Fathers set foot upon our shores, has been the haven of refuge for the persecuted in all lands, but on the contrary, to call your attention more specifically to the circumstances, so that our Government may take such action as it has taken in the past under circumstances even less aggravating, and perhaps less rigorous and inhuman, than under the laws now being enforced in Roumania.

Lord Stanley, the British Minister in 1868, in protesting against an outbreak of persecution in Roumania, said:

If the suffering falls upon the Jew the disgrace falls upon the Christian. . . . I can only explain the action of the Roumanian Minister as the tendency of a weak and not very scrupulous government to trade on the worst popular passions. (See *supra*, pp. 3, 104.)

Lord Shaftesbury, at a later period, said:

The records of this principality have been stained by a series of bloodthirsty actions that would have been a disgrace to the wildest savages in the remotest parts of Africa, and we can hardly hold it to be credible that they were committed by the inhabitants of Roumania in Europe. (See *supra*, p. 16.)

Under the Treaty of Berlin (1878) it was provided that religious and political freedom should be guaranteed to all Roumanian subjects, irrespective of creed or race, but no sooner had Roumania obtained her independence than by subterfuge she evaded the provisions of that Treaty by classifying the Jews as "Aliens," although they and their forbears for generations were born and have lived in that country.

Without entering upon the international aspect of the question, which gives to our country the right to remonstrate against the action of another country with which it is at peace, from persecuting a portion of its population, so that they are driven *en masse* to seek a refuge in this country, permit me to refer to the action taken by our Government under the administrations of President Grant and President Harrison. In 1872, when the persecutions became marked in Roumania (then known as the principalities of Moldavia and Wallachia), Mr. Fish instructed our Ministers accredited to the principal European powers as follows (I quote from the instructions sent to Minister Curtin at St. Petersburg, Foreign Relations, 1872):

It has been suggested to this Department, and the suggestion is concurred in, that if the sympathy which we entertain for the inhumanly persecuted Hebrews in the principalities of Moldavia and Wallachia were made known to the Government to which you are accredited it might quicken and encourage the efforts of that Government to discharge its duty as a protecting power pursuant to the obligations of the Treaty between certain European States. Although we are not a party to that instrument, and, as a rule, scrupulously abstain from interfering directly or indirectly in the public affairs of that quarter, the grievance adverted to is so enormous as to impart to it, as it were, a cosmopolitan character, in the redress of which all countries, governments, and creeds are alike interested. You will consequently communicate on this subject with the Minister for Foreign Affairs of Russia in such a way as you may suppose might be most likely to compass the object in view.

(See also as to instructions sent to other Ministers of the United States in Europe, Foreign Relations, 1872, page 698.)

In 1891 Secretary Blaine instructed Charles Emory Smith, United States Minister to Russia, as follows:

The mutual duties of nations require that each should use its power with due regard for the results which its exercise produces on the rest of the world. It is in this respect that the condition of the Jews in Russia is now brought to the attention of the United States, upon whose shores are cast daily evidences of the sufferings and destitution wrought by the enforcement of the edicts against these unhappy people. (Foreign Relations, 1891, p. 739.)

Permit me also to refer in this connection to President Harrison's third annual message to Congress wherein he refers more in detail to the action that was taken by our Government, and to the bases of our remonstrances.

From a statement before me, made by the United Hebrew Charities of this city, it appears that by reason largely, if not entirely, of the increased persecution of the Jews in Roumania, the number of Roumanian Jewish immigrants that have arrived at the port of New York since October 1, 1899, to October 1, 1901, is in round numbers some 16,000. Since then the law of March, 1902, has been passed, prohibiting the employment of Jewish workingmen in any trade. It is quite evident that the enforcement of this law will cause all of these persecuted people who can by the sale of their effects, or otherwise, secure the means of transportation, to leave the country, and that many of them thus forced to abandon their homes and to sacrifice their effects, will be driven in an impoverished condition to seek a refuge in this country.

Mr. President, I am voicing the sentiment and earnest appeal of the Jews of the United States in petitioning you to make the protest and remonstrances of our Government known to the King and the Government of Roumania, and to instruct our Ambassadors and Ministers to confer with the Governments to which they are accredited, with a view that similar action may be taken by the chief European powers who are parties to the Treaty of Berlin.

The remonstrance of our Government in behalf of oppressed humanity which has time and again had so much effect in the past, cannot fail to have great influence at this present crisis impending over the Jews of Roumania. The Government of no country has a better right to make such a remonstrance than the United States, which will in all probability receive the largest number of those oppressed people who are forced by these restrictive and repressive laws to seek a refuge in foreign lands.

I have the honor to be,
Your most obedient servant,
OSCAR S. STRAUS.

APPENDIX V.

THE JEWS OF ROUMANIA AND THE TREATY OF BERLIN.

Extracts from an address delivered by the Hon. Walter M. Chandler, in the House of Representatives, Washington, October 10, 1913.[113]

Mr. Speaker, I wish now to address myself to the subject of Roumanian persecution of the Jews in defiance of the Treaty of Berlin, and I preface my remarks by reciting a joint resolution which I have introduced this afternoon.

The joint resolution is as follows:

House joint resolution 138.

Whereas the following is the literal text of Articles XLIII and XLIV of the Treaty of Berlin of July 13, 1878:

"XLIII. The high contracting parties recognize the independence of Roumania, subject to the conditions set forth in the two following articles.

"XLIV. In Roumania the difference of religious creeds and confessions shall not be alleged against any person as a ground for exclusion or incapacity in matters relating to the enjoyment of civil and political rights, admission to public employments, functions, and honors, or the exercise of the various professions and industries in any locality whatsoever.

"The freedom and outward exercise of all forms of worship shall be assured to all persons belonging to the Roumanian state, as well as to foreigners, and no hindrance shall be offered either to the hierarchical organization of the different communions or to their relations with their spiritual chiefs.

"The subjects and citizens of all the powers, traders or others, shall be treated in Roumania, without distinction of creed, on a footing of perfect equality."

Whereas the Government of Roumania accepted the terms of said articles of said treaty as a condition precedent to the recognition of her independence; and

---

[113] See *Congressional Record*, vol. 50, p. 5541, *et seq.*; see *supra*, p. 83.

Whereas it is a matter of certain knowledge that the Jews of Roumania, numbering about 250,000, have been the barbarized and impoverished victims of Roumanian discriminatory legislation and of Roumanian riots and massacres for a period of more than 30 years in violation of both the letter and the spirit of the treaty of Berlin: Therefore be it

Resolved by the Senate and House of Representatives of the United States of America in Congress assembled, That it is the sense of the American Congress that the interests of civilization, the rights of humanity, the principles of eternal justice, and the dignity and sanctity of international law demand that the signatory Powers of the Treaty of Berlin compel Roumania to observe the stipulations of the Treaty of Berlin in the matter of the treatment of the Jews.

Resolved, That the Secretary of State be requested to transmit a copy of this resolution to the Governments of Great Britain, Germany, Austria, Russia, France, Italy, and Turkey. . . . .

The modern Kingdom of Roumania was formed by the union of the ancient Principalities of Moldavia and Wallachia, provinces situated near the mouth of the Danube, having an area of about 50,000 square miles, and occupying an extent of territory some 350 miles in length and 160 miles in breadth. The shape of the country is an irregular half-moon, touching the Black Sea near the center of the crescent.

The people of Roumania proudly boast a classic antiquity in their supposed descent from the Romans who conquered the ancient Scythian Kingdom of Dacia, which was practically the modern territory of Roumania.

If not classic in history the country of Roumania is at least classic and historic in soil, for the legions of Rome, the hordes of Attilla, the crusaders of Richard and Barbarossa, and the Cossacks of Peter the Great, have crossed its borders and traversed its plains.

The language of Roumania has a groundwork of Latin and Slavonic, with a superstructure of Turkish, Greek, and French.

The social, political, religious, and intellectual life of the people is a strange, weird blending of the cruder forms of occidental and oriental civilizations.

The population of Roumania in 1910 was about 6,850,000. Fully 6,000,000 of these were Roumans or Vlachs; the rest were Jews, Armenians, Gypsies, Greeks, Germans, Turks, Magyars, Servians, and Bulgarians.

Of the total population of Roumania the Jews number about 250,000. And it is with the Jews of Roumania, in their relationship as citizens and subjects to the Government of Roumania, and with the Government of Roumania in its relationship to its Jewish population, under binding treaty obligations entered into by Roumania with the great Powers of Europe, that I shall hereafter in this address deal particularly and pointedly.

I desire especially to discuss the persecution of the Jews by Roumania, in defiance of the Treaty of Berlin of July 13, 1878. I shall, however, in the first place, as a foundation for that discussion, submit for your consideration a classified list of Roumanian laws, passed during the half century preceding the assembling of the Congress of Berlin, which were intended to discriminate against the Jews. This list, though short, may be tedious and tiresome to study and contemplate, but it will be decidedly illuminating and enlightening when we come to consider the motive and conduct of the great Powers in forcing Roumania, through treaty stipulations, to accord better treatment to her Jewish subjects. The following is a résumé, with authorities cited, of the leading Roumanian legal enactments against the Jews between the years 1802 and 1876:

1803. Alexander Monize forbids Jews to rent farms. ("American Jewish Year Book," 1901, p. 48.)

May 18, 1804. Alexander Monize, of Moldavia, forbids Jews to buy farm products. (Loeb, "La Situation des Israélites en Turquie, en Serbie et en Roumanie," p. 212, Paris, 1877, hereafter cited as "Loeb.")

1817. Code Cahmachi, section 1430, forbids Jews of Roumania to acquire real property. (Loeb, p. 213.)

By 1818. Code of John Caradja, of Wallachia, repeats the ancient church laws against allowing Jews to be witnesses against Christians. (American Jewish Year Book, 1901, p. 50.)

By 1819. Code of Kallimachor of Moldavia gives civil rights to Jews, who, however, may not own land. (American Jewish Year Book, 1901, p. 50.)

1831. Fundamental law of Moldavia, chapter 3, section 94, orders all Jews and their occupations to be registered; Jews not of proved usefulness are to be expelled; others of same class shall not be allowed to enter. (Loeb, p. 214.)

March 11, 1839. Tax of 60 piasters per annum placed on Jews of Moldavia. (Loeb, p. 215.)

December 12, 1850. No Jew allowed to enter Roumania unless possessed of 5,000 piasters and of known occupation. (Loeb, p. 216.)

May 5, 1851. Appointment of commission of vagabondage at Jassy to determine right of entry of foreign Jews. (Loeb, p. 216.)

June 17, 1861. Circular of Roumanian ministry preventing Jews from being innkeepers in rural districts. (Loeb, p. 217.)

April 12, 1864. Communal law of Roumania permits only those Jews to be naturalized who (1) have reached the grade of non-commissioned officers in the army (2) or have passed through college (3) or have a recognized foreign degree (4) or have founded a factory. (Loeb, pp. 107-108.)

December 4, 1864. Jews excluded from being advocates. (Loeb, p. 124.)

December 7, 1864. Elementary education obligatory for all children between the ages of 8 and 12. (Sincerus, " Les Juifs en Roumanie," p. 119, hereafter cited as " Sincerus.")

April 14, 1866. Ghika, Roumanian Minister of Interior, permits Jews already settled in rural districts to keep farms till leases run out, but they must not renew them. (Loeb, p. 218.)

March, 1868. Law submitted to chamber preventing Jews from holding land, settling in the country, selling food, keeping inns, holding public office, trading without special permits. Jews already settled in rural districts were to be driven therefrom. This was withdrawn April 5 in fear of the intervention of the Powers. (Loeb, pp. 169, 311-312.)

June 23, 1868. All Roumanians forced to serve in Army, "but not strangers" (Loeb, p. 109); therefore Jews who served were for this purpose regarded as Roumanians.

December 27, 1868. Jews excluded from medical profession in Roumania. (Loeb, p. 124.) Clause omitted in decree of June, 1871.

January 15, 1869. Jews not allowed to be tax farmers in rural communes. (Loeb, p. 112.)

July, 1869. Note of M. Cogalniceanu to French consul at Bucharest refuses to consider Jews as Roumanians. (Loeb, p. 102.)

October, 1869. Extra tax put on kosher meat at Roman and Focsan. (Loeb, p. 127.)

October 25, 1869. Jews prevented from being apothecaries in Roumania, except where there are no Roumanian apothecaries. (Loeb, p. 125; Sincerus, p. 102.)

November 10, 1870. Servian Jews obliged to serve in Army. (Loeb, p. 57.)

February 15, 1872. All dealers in tobacco in Roumania must be "Roumanians." (Loeb, p. 120.)

April 1, 1873. Law forbidding Jews to sell spirituous liquors in rural districts. (Loeb, p. 188.) A license may be given only to an elector. (Sincerus, p. 19.)

These enactments show the legal disabilities of the Jews. But they do not tell the full story of shame and humiliation of a long-suffering and wretched people. Written in the calm and dignified phraseology of the law they cannot and do not recount the bloody details of riot and massacre, whose occurrence was the disgrace of civilization and whose horrors compose the blackest chapters of Roumanian history. I will not harrow your feelings with a recital of the details. I shall content myself with a simple and dispassionate discussion of legal rights and treaty obligations in the matter of Roumania and the Jews.

It was at the close of the War of the Crimea that the great Governments of Europe first gave serious attention to the oppressions of the Jews by the rulers of the principalities of Moldavia and Wallachia, the provinces from which the kingdom of Roumania was afterwards formed. At that time the first decisive effort was made to relieve the legal disabilities of the Jews.

The following articles of the protocol of the conference of Constantinople of the 11th of February, 1856, imposed, it must be admitted, rather exacting terms upon Moldavia and Wallachia:

XIII. All the religions and those who profess them shall enjoy equal liberty and equal protection in the two Principalities.

XV. Foreigners may possess landed property in Moldavia and Wallachia on discharging the same liabilities as natives and on submitting to the laws.

XVI. All Moldavians and Wallachians, without exception, shall be admissible to public employments.

XVIII. All classes of the population, without any distinction of birth or religion, shall enjoy equality of civil rights and particularly of the right of property in every shape, but the exercise of political rights shall be suspended in the case of natives placed under a foreign protection.

The language of these articles was an emphatic and unequivocal declaration in favor of civil and religious liberty for all the inhabitants of Roumania. A complete realization of the protection afforded by these articles would have been all that the Jews could reasonably have asked. But such a thing was not to be. No such blessing was in store for them. The reigning Prince of Moldavia, Gregory Ghika, began at once a course of subterfuge and evasion for the purpose of rendering abortive the intentions and efforts of the Powers. He contended that a strict application of the provisions of these articles was impracticable, if not impossible, on account of the great number of unassimilated Jews in the Principalities; and two years later he presented a memorial to the Congress of Paris asking that the realization of the principle embodied in the articles of the protocol of the Conference of Constantinople, which he admitted to be excellent within itself, should be left to the discretion of the local Government, which alone, he contended, knew how to apply the principle. His arguments were plausible, if not sound and righteous, and at last, out of deference to the wishes and pledges of Ghika, the Powers modified their intentions by the adoption of Article XLVI of the Convention of Paris, which runs as follows:

All Moldavians and Wallachians shall be equal in the eye of the law and with regard to taxation, and shall be equally admissible to public employments in both principalities.

Their individual liberty shall be guaranteed. No one can be detained or prosecuted but in conformity with the law. No one can be deprived of his property unless legally for causes of public interest and on payment of indemnification.

Moldavians and Wallachians of all Christian confessions shall equally enjoy political rights. The enjoyment of these rights may be extended to other religions by legislative arrangements.

Indeed, the pledge of Ghika and the expectations of the Powers based upon this pledge, were that the Jews would be gradually enfranchised and emancipated politically by legislative arrangements. But Roumanian legislation during the past 50 years shows how badly founded were those expectations and how complete has been the evasion of that pledge.

Instead of relieving their legal disabilities, the efforts of the Powers to help the Jews through stipulations of the Conventions of Constantinople and Paris proved to be a positive misfortune. "So far," says a modern writer, "from ameliorating the condition of the Jews, the Convention of Paris by a regrettable accident led to more burdensome disabilities and more barbarous persecution than they had ever before endured. Under the old organic laws, by which the Principalities were governed previously to 1859, the people had no effective voice in the government. Hence there was little cause for jealousy between Christians and Jews, and with the exception of occasional explosions of religious fanaticism, they lived together in harmony. The new order of things established in 1858 destroyed this equality. It gave to the Christian population a monopoly of political power which they were not slow to use against their trade rivals among the unenfranchised Jews. This unfortunate incidence of the Convention of Paris was aggravated by the new electoral law under which a preponderating franchise was reserved for the mercantile classes, with whom the Jews, being chiefly of the same classes, most directly competed. The result was that not only was the fulfillment of Article XLVI of the Convention of Paris rendered impossible, but the whole influence of the mercantile electorate was employed to obtain the imposition of fresh disabilities upon the Jews and to inflame the religious and racial prejudices of the populace against them. Instead of gradually emancipating them in accordance with the provisions of the Convention of Paris, even their status as 'non-Christian Moldo-Wallachs,' acknowledged in that instrument, was denied them. They were assimilated by the civil code of 1864 to aliens, though admitted by the code to be 'indigenes,' and were made dependent on a difficult and tedious process of naturalization for their acquisition of political rights (Arts. VIII, IX, and XVI). Even this privilege was withdrawn from them by the constitution of 1866, which declared (Art. VII) 'that only Christians may obtain naturalization.' Consequently Article XLVI of the Convention of Paris remained a dead letter."

In the meantime the Jews of Roumania were more bitterly oppressed than ever. New laws discriminating against them were passed; riots and massacres were renewed with greater fury. They were languishing in a bondage worse than that endured by their fathers in ancient Egypt when hope was revived again among them by the adoption of Article XLIV of the Treaty of Berlin of July 13, 1878.

The Berlin Congress of 1878 was a gathering at the German national capital of the brainiest and most brilliant statesmen of Europe. The purpose of the Congress was to settle the questions growing out of the Russo-Turkish war of 1877-78.

On the 24th of April, 1877, Russia declared war against Turkey with the avowed object of protecting the Christian inhabitants of the Ottoman Empire. Bulgaria, Roumania, Servia, and Montenegro were either tacitly or openly the allies of the Czar. After varying successes the fortunes of war finally favored the Russians, and the fall of Plevna opened the way to Constantinople. The Turks sued for peace, and on March 3, 1878, the Treaty of San Stefano was signed. Some of the terms of this treaty were displeasing to several of the Governments of Europe. Austria and England were decidedly dissatisfied. The political changes made and the territorial readjustments provided for in the Treaty, together with the exaction of 1,400,000,000 rubles war indemnity, which promised to cripple most seriously the resources of the Turkish Empire for years to come, practically made the Czar permanent arbiter of Balkan affairs. To avert such a catastrophe had been the traditional policy of Austria, and to prevent a result so disastrous to her interests, England had waged the war of the Crimea.

Assuming the initiative in the matter Count Andrassy, in the name of the Austrian Government, dispatched a circular note to the signatory Powers of the Treaty of Paris of 1856 and the London protocol of 1871 suggesting an international congress for the purpose of establishing "the agreement of Europe on the modifications which it might become necessary to introduce into the above-mentioned Treaties," in view of the provisions of the Treaty of San Stefano. The suggestion of Count Andrassy met with a ready response. Germany was especially willing to cooperate with England and with Austria, her ally, in the assembling of a congress of which her own great statesman, Bismarck, was sure to be the dominating figure. Russia was naturally displeased with the turn events had taken. She felt intuitively that she would lose all that she had gained in the war with Turkey if she consented to the revision of the articles of the Treaty of San Stefano by an international conference dominated by her enemies.

But she was powerless to resist. She demanded, however, as a condition of giving her consent to the assembling of the proposed congress and of her participation in its proceedings, that the scope of its powers be limited by the exclusion of certain clauses of the Treaty of San Stefano from its consideration. The reply of Disraeli, on behalf of England, to this demand was to mobilize the militia and to bring Indian troops to the Mediterranean. Finding that the diplomatic support which she had hoped to receive from Bismarck had failed her, she took the hint, and finally consented to submit the whole question of the Balkan situation to the determinations of a new international conference.

On the 3d of June, 1878, Count Münster, in the name of the German Emperor, invited the delegates of the signatory Powers of the Treaty of Paris of 1856 to assemble at Berlin. The invitation was accepted. Great Britain was represented by Lord Beaconsfield, Lord Salisbury, and Lord Russell; Germany by Prince Bismarck, Prince Hohenlohe-Schillingsfürst, and Baron von Bülow; Austria by Count Andrassy, Baron Karolyi, and Baron von Haymerle; Italy by Count Corti and Count Launay; France by William H. Waddington, Félix Désprez, and Le Comte de St. Vallier; Russia by her imperial chancellor, Prince Gorchakov, Count Shuvalov, and Paul D'Oubril; Turkey by Alexander Pasha, Ali Pasha, and Sadullah Bey.

These distinguished representatives of the leading nations of the world—lords, princes, barons, counts, ambassadors, and prime ministers—men renowned in statesmanship, diplomacy, law, and letters, convened, and organized the Congress of Berlin, on the 13th day of June, 1878, under the presidency of Prince Bismarck.

On the 13th of July, a month after the assembling of the congress, the Treaty of Berlin was signed. It consists of 64 articles.

Two great purposes of the delegates of the congress are revealed in the terms of the Treaty:

(1) The reconstruction, upon an equitable basis, of the map of southeastern Europe;

(2) The establishment of the independence of certain Balkan States upon a foundation of civil and religious liberty.

The first great purpose was achieved, in the main, by certain territorial changes. Bulgaria was divided into two parts—Bulgaria proper and Eastern Rumelia. Parts of Armenia were given to Russia and Persia. Bosnia and Herzegovina were transferred to Austria, and Bessarabia was restored to Russia.

The second great purpose was accomplished by the recognition of the independence of Roumania, Servia, and Montenegro under terms of guaranty by them of civil and religious liberty to all the inhabitants of their territories.

In the archives of history are few more important documents than the Treaty of Berlin. It readjusted the boundaries of kingdoms and empires. It proclaimed the independence of states and the freedom of races. It was, above all, a grand proclamation of religious emancipation.

The conditions of life among the Jews of Roumania were far more pitiable and their political situation was infinitely worse when the Berlin Congress convened in 1878 than they had been 20 years before when the Conferences of Constantinople and Paris met. In 1858 the legal status of the Jews was admitted to be that of unenfranchised Roumanians. In 1878 they had been declared to be outcasts and aliens, and were cruelly treated as such. A succession of barbarous persecutions, culminating in riots and massacres had reduced them to such a state of misery and degradation that the pity of mankind was excited and the indignation of the civilized world found vigorous expression in official protests to the great powers of Europe. This was the state of affairs when Roumania asked the delegates to the Congress of Berlin to recognize her independence as a kingdom.

The representatives of the powers knew well the cunning character of Roumanian statesmanship. They remembered distinctly the subterfuge and chicanery employed to evade the pledges given at the time of the Conferences of Constantinople and Paris. They recalled that discretion had been allowed and that it had been abused in the matter of the promise of Ghika to emancipate the Jews gradually by legislative enactment. They now resolved to withdraw all discretion from the Government of Bucharest in the matter of the emancipation of its non-Christian subjects. And to the demand of Roumania that her independence be recognized the Powers responded with Articles XLIII and XLIV of the Treaty of Berlin of July 13, 1878, which imposed as a condition of recognition the absolute equality of all religious creeds and confessions in the Kingdom. The following is the text of those articles:

XLIII. The high contracting parties recognize the independence of Roumania, subject to the conditions set forth in the two following articles:

XLIV. In Roumania the difference of religious creeds and confessions shall not be alleged against any person as a ground for exclusion or incapacity in matters relating to the enjoyment of civil and political rights, admission to public employments, functions, and honors, or the exercise of the various professions and industries in any locality whatsoever.

The freedom and outward exercise of all forms of worship shall be assured to all persons belonging to the Roumanian State, as well as to foreigners, and no hindrance shall be offered either to the hierarchical organization of the different communions or to their relations with their spiritual chiefs.

The subjects and citizens of all the powers, traders or others, shall be treated in Roumania without distinction of creed on a footing of perfect equality.

Such were the terms offered by the Congress of Berlin to Roumania as a condition of the recognition of her independence.

Strangely and unfortunately the Powers were once again persuaded to agree to a compromise. "That only Christians may obtain naturalization" was a provision of Article VII of the Roumanian constitution of 1866. Acting upon the arbitrary and illegal assumption that all Jews were aliens, Roumania contended that the only disability imposed upon them was exclusion from naturalization under this article, and she consequently proposed to revise Article VII of her constitution as a satisfaction of Article XLIV of the Treaty of Berlin. The offer of Roumania, in other words, was to open the door of naturalization to the Jews, the inference then being, of course, that all other blessings would flow from citizenship.

The Powers pointed out in reply that by the Roumanian naturalization law the "equality of citizen" could only be obtained after a probation of 10 years, and then by individual act of Parliament, which was liable to be defeated by the Chambers; and the offer of compromise was consequently declined.

Roumania then changed her ground by deserting her legal position and urging a plea of expediency. She insisted that if the Jews were not aliens in law, they were aliens in fact, "not only by their religion, but by language, custom, manners, aspirations—in a word, by all that constitutes distinctive character in a man as a member of society." She contended, further, that the Jews were "illiterate and fanatical," and that they were "peculiarly accessible to foreign influences, and that, owing to their large numbers, they were calculated to strike a fatal blow at the homogeneity of the Roumanian national character." And as a final plea it was urged that "the nation was strongly opposed to an immediate and wholesale emancipation, and that if the Powers insisted upon it the effect would be that the cause of religious liberty in Roumania would be endangered rather than promoted."

The Powers seem to have been somewhat impressed by the force of these contentions, but, nevertheless, they still declined to admit that a revision of Article VII of the Roumanian constitution would, in full measure, meet the requirements of Article XLIV of the Treaty of Berlin.

It was then that Roumania, fearing the shipwreck of her hopes to become an independent nation, gave the most solemn assurances that if the proposed solution was accepted, it would be made to apply at once to all assimilated Jews, and that the naturalization of unassimilated Jews would be provided for and accomplished within a reasonable time.

Sir William White was told by Boeresco, the Roumanian Foreign Minister, "that if the present bill could only become a law, a more complete measure of emancipation would be accepted by the electorate later on when the present agitations had subsided."

But more specific and emphatic than this were the promises contained in a circular dispatch sent out by Boeresco under date of August 31, 1879, a document that he himself described as "a sort of exposé des motifs of the measure we are about to submit to the Chambers." The essential passages of this dispatch are the following:

Will the Jews who do not immediately obtain naturalization remain foreigners? No; they will remain what they always have been—Roumanian. But in the measure that they identify themselves with the population of the country, in the measure that by schools and other means of preparation they become enlightened men and attached to the country, they will be able to obtain and exercise political rights.

* * * * * * * *

There will be three categories of Jews—foreigners, Roumanian subjects, and citizens. Hitherto both the foreign and native Jews have been the objects of certain prohibitions, but in their quality of Jew alone. From the moment that article 7 of the constitution shall be suppressed all these prohibitions will disappear, and no distinction will be made between the foreign Jew and the foreign Christian. It will be the same with the Jews who are Roumanian subjects. Hitherto certain civil rights have been denied them. Thus they could not be advocates, professors, State engineers; they could not serve on juries, etc. Under the new régime they will have, in the first place, all the rights enjoyed by foreigners in general. Then, as Roumanian subjects they will have the right of serving in the army and the national guard, the right of acquiring real estate, the right to be advocates, to serve on juries, to exercise freely every profession and every trade; they will, in short, have the same civil rights as Roumanians and will be protected in the same way by the same law and by the authorities. (Official documents extracted from the diplomatic correspondence of 2/14 September, 1878; 17/29 July, 1880. Bucharest, 1880, pp. 121-123.)

The Governments of Austria and Italy were somewhat inclined to accept these assurances, but England, France, and Germany still demanded that legislative guaranties be given for the faithful observance of the Treaty and that this be done within a reasonable time, if not immediately.

The negotiations between Boeresco and the Powers were still in progress when the Roumanian Parliament passed an act revising Article VII of the constitution, which was soon afterwards promulgated by the Prince in the following terms:

In room of Article VII, which is revised, the following shall be placed:

"ART. VII. The difference of religious creeds and confessions does not constitute in Roumania an obstacle to the acquirement of civil and political rights and their exercise.

"1. Every foreigner, without distinction of creed, whether enjoying any foreign protection or not, can acquire naturalization under the following conditions:

"(a) By addressing to the Government an application for naturalization, in which must be declared the capital he possesses, his profession, and his wish to establish his domicile in Roumania.

"(b) By residing in the country for 10 years after having made this application and by proving by his acts that he is useful to the country.

"2. The following may be exempted from this delay of residence (10 years):

"(a) All who shall have introduced into the country industries, useful inventions, or distinguished talents, or who shall have founded large commercial or industrial establishments.

"(b) All who have been born and educated in Roumania of parents domiciled in the country and have, neither in their own case nor that of their parents, at any time been in the enjoyment of any foreign protection.

"(c) All who have served with the colors during the war of independence, and these can be naturalized collectively on the proposition of the Government by a single law, without further formalities.

"3. Naturalization can only be granted by a law, and individually.

"4. A special law will determine the manner in which foreigners can establish their domicile on Roumanian territory.

"5. Roumanian and naturalized Roumanian citizens can alone acquire rural estates in Roumania.

"Rights acquired up to the present time are respected."
The international conventions existing at present remain in force, with all their clauses and for the term mentioned therein.

This decisive action of the Parliament of Bucharest, bold in design and prompt in execution, seems to have changed the notions of the Powers, for they soon afterwards consented, though reluctantly, to the Roumanian solution. But before giving their final consent, they required the Roumanian Government to make a formal declaration of acceptance of the principle of Article XLIV of the Treaty of Berlin and of its resolution to act upon it " loyally and sincerely." The required obligation was expressed in the following note:

Article 7 of the Roumanian constitution, sanctioning the principle of article 44 of the treaty of Berlin, has opened to the Jews access to citizenship and has abrogated all existing laws. That principle will continue to be observed sincerely and loyally. The organic powers will devote themselves to assuring its respect and will pursue its application with the view of securing a more complete assimilation of the Jews. . . . . Meanwhile all Jews residing in the country will possess, from the point of view of private civil law, an assured juridical position, and will have no cause to fear arbitrary administrative measures or exceptional laws aimed at confessions or religions. (Statement by Signor Cairoli in the Italian Parliament, Dec. 9, 1879.)

Upon the receipt of this note Austria and Italy signified their willingness to recognize the independence of the new Kingdom.

After considerable hesitation Great Britain, France, and Germany did the same, but not before they had made it perfectly clear to the Roumanian Government that they were well aware that the conditions of the treaty of Berlin had not been fulfilled and that they relied upon the solemn pledges of the principalities " to observe them in the spirit and to execute them gradually in the letter."

That there might be a clear understanding of the situation the three last-mentioned powers presented an identic note to M. Boeresco on the 20th of February, 1880. The following are the essential paragraphs of that note:

Her Majesty's Government cannot consider the new constitutional provisions which have been brought to their cognizance—and particularly those by which persons belonging to a nonchristian creed domiciled in Roumania, and not belonging to any foreign nationality, are required to submit to the formalities of individual naturalization—as being a complete fulfillment of the views of the Powers signatories of the Treaty of Berlin.

Trusting, however, to the determination of the prince's Government to approximate more and more in the execution of these provisions, to the liberal intentions entertained by the Powers, and taking note of the positive assurances to that effect which have been conveyed to them, the Government of her Britannic Majesty, being desirous of giving to the Roumanian Nation a proof of their friendly sentiments, have decided to recognize the principality of Roumania as an independent State. Her Majesty's Government consequently declare themselves ready to enter into regular diplomatic relations with the prince's Government.

Such was the result of the diplomatic negotiations of nearly two years in which the great Powers of Europe had again been cajoled and hoodwinked by a contemptible little Balkan principality. Roumania had secured the recognition of her sovereignty and, in return, had given promises and pledges which the developments of the last 30 years show she never intended to fulfil.

The Congress of Berlin of 1878 accomplished nothing more in fact than did the Convention of Paris of 1858. The illusory pledges of Prince Gregory Ghika remained unfulfilled for 20 years. The promises of the Government of King Charles have been equally false and hypocritical, for more than three decades have passed and yet nothing has been done to meet the just expectations of the Powers. A new generation of Roumanian Jews have been born in the land, and yet they are as far from emancipation as were their fathers. The night of oppression and persecution still hovers over them and the day of freedom and regeneration still seems far away. They are still held to be aliens and outcasts in the land of their birth; naturalization is still practically inaccessible to them; and the sufferings of persecution are still as great and painful as ever.

Roumanian statesmanship triumphed in the matter of the compromise of 1880, not by honest methods of skillful diplomacy, but by craft and cunning and through the negligence of the Powers themselves.

It was a regrettable mistake that the Governments of Europe should have overlooked two fatal defects in the compromise. In the first place they should by all means have forced from the Roumanian Parliament a legislative acknowledgment that Jews " belonging to no other nationality and enjoying no foreign protection were Roumanian nationals in the sense of article 46 of the convention of Paris and of the admission of M. Boeresco in his dispatch of August 31, 1879."

Again the Roumanian Parliament consists of two chambers. All naturalization bills are individual and must pass each chamber by a two-thirds majority. Paragraph 3 of the revised Article VII of the constitution left Jewish petitions for naturalization at the absolute mercy of the Parliament. This was the second fatal defect of the compromise which should not have been overlooked by the Powers.

These defects are all the more to be lamented because they furnish loopholes of escape to Roumania in the matter of keeping her naturalization pledges under the Treaty. They gave ground for the practice of rank hypocrisy, and at the same time for a plea of seeming justification in terms of law.

The unfortunate result has been that in the matter of naturalization, so far from keeping her pledges, Roumania has almost completely ignored them, for the Roumanian chambers have in nearly every case refused to pass bills intended to confer citizenship upon the Jews. Since 1880, the date of the recognition of the new Kingdom, only 176 Jews have been naturalized out of a total population of 100,000 adult males, the greater part of whom are natives, and many thousands of whom have bravely and patriotically performed military service for the Roumanian fatherland.

When arraigned at the bar of the nations and charged with bad faith in the matter of broken pledges, the defense of Roumania is at once astonishingly simple and amazingly cynical. She simply revives her ancient argument that the Jews are now and have always been strangers and aliens in the land, and that the Treaties of 1858 and 1878, under strict interpretation, did not alter their status. When pointed to the formal and categorical pledges of 1880, and the admission of M. Boeresco in 1879, which directly contradicted and repudiated her contentions in this regard, and, moreover, when reminded that Great Britain, France, and Germany had recognized her independence only after she had specifically and emphatically renounced such a theory, she simply points to the equivocal revision of Article VII of her constitution, which Europe had accepted under pressure and protest, and declares that she is bound by that alone.

Strange to say, no attempt is ever made by Roumania to conceal the hypocrisy or to hide the bad faith of her astonishing defense. Indeed, eminent writers of Roumania have frequently boasted of the trick which was successfully played on Europe. One of these, M. Suliotis, writes in this manner:

The Treaty of Berlin was thought to work wonders in favor of the strangers, but Roumania has been wise enough to escape the inconveniences which might have resulted from the application of article 7 in the sense of the Treaty of Berlin, which has had no other effect than to render more difficult the situation of the aliens.

Again, writing in the *Romanul* of December 25, 1881, M. Rosetti, an ex-minister and one of the leading statesmen of the Kingdom, has this to say:

We may congratulate ourselves to-day on having solved the Jewish question in a national sense, and that—we may now avow loudly—contrary to the manifest will of the Powers and even contrary to the spirit of the Treaty of Berlin.

The solution of "the Jewish question" in "a national sense," it will be readily seen, was by the simple method of having the Roumanian Parliament pass laws antagonistic to "strangers," and then have all public officials of Roumania regard the Jews as "strangers," in the application of those laws.

Nothing can better illustrate the determined efforts of the Roumanian Government to evade its pledges in the matter of the Treaty of Berlin than its systematic legislation against "strangers," which was, in fact, intended to apply only to the Jews. The following classified list of laws, discriminating against the Jews, will prove conclusively that Roumania, from the very beginning, never had any intention of fulfilling her obligations under Article XLIV of that Treaty:

October 21, 1879. Roumanian Senate passes law stating that distinction of religion shall not be a bar to civil or political rights, but that "strangers" may obtain naturalization only by special law on individual demand and after 10 years' residence. (Art. VII of constitution; Sincerus, pp. 3-4.)

June 6, 1880. The directors and auditors of the National Bank of Roumania must be Roumanians. (Sincerus, p. 77.)

March 18, 1881. Law of expulsion passed, authorizing minister of interior to expel or order from place to place, without giving reason, any "stranger" likely to disturb public tranquility. (Sincerus, p. 146.) (Originally intended against Nihilists after murder of Czar, but afterwards applied to Jews.)

July 16, 1881. Law promulgated declaring that all "agents de change" or "courtiers de merchandise" must be Roumanians or naturalized, except in the ports (where there are Christian "strangers"). (Sincerus, p. 45.)

October 21, 1881. Ministerial council extends the law excluding Jews from the sale of liquors in rural districts to cities and towns included in such districts. (Sincerus, pp. 22-23.)

November 11, 1881. All "strangers" in Roumania required to obtain a permit of residence before they may pass from place to place. (Sincerus, p. 163.)

February 26, 1882. Jews forbidden to be custom-house officers (Sincerus, p. 53.)

November 3, 1882. Roumanian Senate passes law declaring all "inhabitants" liable to military service, except subjects of alien States. (Sincerus, p. 35.) See above, June 23, 1868.

January 31, 1884. Roumanian Senate decides that "strangers" have no right of petition to Parliament. (Sincerus, p. 197.)

March 19, 1884. Law passes prohibiting hawkers from trading in rural districts. (Sincerus, p. 65.)

April 15, 1885. Pharmacy law permits minister of interior to close any pharmacy not under direction of a recognized person;

pharmacies may be acquired only by Roumanians or by naturalized citizens; permission to employ "strangers" extended to 1886. (Sincerus, p. 104.)

March 13, 1886. Electors of chambers of commerce must be persons having political rights. (Sincerus, p. 75.)

June 16, 1886. Druggists must be Roumanians or naturalized citizens. (Sincerus, p. 84.)

December 7, 1886. Account books must be kept in Roumanian or in a modern European language. (Sincerus, p. 81.) (The object was to keep out Yiddish.)

February 28, 1887. All employees of the "regie" must be Roumanians or naturalized. (Sincerus, p. 29.)

April 28, 1887. Farmers of taxes in Roumania must be persons capable of being public officers. (Sincerus, p. 89.)

May 22, 1887. Majority of administrators of private companies must be Roumanians. (Sincerus, p. 78.)

May 24, 1887. Five years after the foundation of a factory two-thirds of its workmen must be Roumanians. (Sincerus, p. 94.)

August 4, 1887. Ministerial circular orders preference to be given to children of Roumanians in the order of admission to public schools. (Sincerus, p. 123.)

1889. Of 1,307 permits issued to hawkers, only 123 went to Jews; of these, only 6 were held in Wallachia. (Sincerus, p. 70.)

August 31, 1892. Retired Jewish soldiers are not allowed to serve as rural gendarmes. (Sincerus, p. 40.)

April 21, 1893. Professional education permitted to "strangers" only when places are available and on payment of fees. The number of "strangers" on the roll of such an educational institution must not exceed one-fifth of the total roll, and these may not compete for scholarships. "Strangers" are not admitted at all to schools of agriculture. (Sincerus, p. 138.)

May 20, 1893. Roumanian Senate passes law giving preference to children of Roumanians in elementary public schools and placing a tax on children of "strangers" admitted. (Sincerus, p. 129.) This tax amounted to 15 francs for rural and 30 francs for urban schools. (*Ib.*, 127.)

June 26, 1893. Royal decree declaring all functionaries in the sanitary service must be Roumanians except in rural districts. "Stranger" invalids may be admitted to free public hospital only on payment of fees, and they may not in any case occupy more than 10 per cent of the beds. A "stranger" may be taken as an apprentice by an apothecary only where there is a Roumanian apprentice. (Sincerus, pp. 106, 110, 115.)

January 26, 1894. Farmers may be represented in law courts by their stewards if the latter be Roumanians, not Jews. (Sincerus, p. 44.)

May 22, 1895. Students in the military hospitals and army doctors must be either Roumanians or naturalized citizens. (Sincerus, p. 117.)

April 13, 1896. Jews may not act as intermediaries at the customs in Roumania. (Sincerus, p. 54.)

June, 1896. A ministerial order declares that letters on school business—excuses for absence, etc.—need not be stamped except in the case of "strangers"; only children of "strangers" are required to pay entrance fees at examinations. (Sincerus, p. 130.)

June 26, 1896. Ministerial order instructs rural council that permission to remain in a rural district may be revoked at any moment. (Sincerus, p. 185.)

April 4, 1898. Law permitting secondary instruction of children of "strangers" only where places are available and on payment of fees, though to Roumanians tuition is free. (Sincerus, p. 133.)

October, 1898. Admission to public schools in Roumania refused to 11,200 Jewish children. (Sincerus.)

February 18, 1899. Only Roumanians henceforth admitted as employees on State railways. (Sincerus, p. 97.)

October 21, 1899. Ministerial order closes private Jewish schools in Roumania on Sundays. (Sincerus, p. 141.)

1900. Number of Jewish children in elementary public schools in Roumania reduced to 5½ per cent; in secondary schools, from 10½ per cent (in 1895) to 7½ per cent. (Sincerus, p. 133.)

February 27, 1900. Ministerial circular orders pupils to receive instructions in Jewish private schools with heads uncovered. (Sincerus, p. 143.)

March 28, 1900. On private railways 60 per cent of the employees must be Roumanians. (Sincerus, p. 99.)

April 17, 1900. Ministerial circular orders Jewish private schools to open on Saturdays. (Sincerus, p. 142.)

March 16, 1902. Artisans' bill requires special authorization from the authorities to carry on any trade, only to be obtained by "strangers"—$i.\ e.$, Jews—on production of foreign passports, and proof that in their "respective countries" reciprocal rights are accorded to Roumanians. (American Jewish Year Book, 1902-3, p. 30.)

The culmination of Roumanian meanness and malignity was reached in the passage of the artisans' bill. Other measures had been designed to cripple and harass, to degrade and humiliate them, but this bill was evidently intended to starve the Jews to death, for it inevitably deprived many thousands of Jewish artisans of the only means of earning their daily bread. The ludicrous absurdity as well as the fiendish cruelty of such a law are shown by the fact that, under its provisions, no "foreigner" was permitted to exercise a handicraft in Roumania unless "he could show reciprocity for Roumanians in his own country." The Jews being "foreigners not under any foreign protection" were unable to prove this reciprocity. They were therefore unable to carry on any trade without violating the law.

Another characteristic illustration of the ingenious method employed by the Roumanian Parliament in framing laws to evade the spirit, if not the letter, of the Treaty of Berlin is afforded by the military law of November 3, 1882. By Article I of this law "all the inhabitants" of the country are liable to military service.

By Article II "subjects of foreign States" are declared ineligible for entrance into the army. The Jews being "inhabitants" of the country, but not "subjects of foreign States," are required to perform military service, although deprived of all civil and political rights, because of their status as "strangers." Although forced to risk the dangers and bear the burdens of war as privates in the ranks they are denied promotion on the ground that "service in the army is a duty, while the rank of officer is a public function reserved for Roumanian citizens." These distinctions and the reasons for them were all solemnly declared in a speech by M. Bratiano in the Roumanian Senate May 27, 1882. But it is needless to elaborate the question at greater length.

The hideous result of long years of persecution and oppression, of riot and massacre, has been that the Jews of Roumania have been barbarized and impoverished and that life for most of them has been rendered an intolerable burden. Within the last 10 years 60,000 of them have been forced to emigrate and 100,000 others have been reduced to a state approaching vagabondage.

Shall these frightful conditions continue to exist? Shall the barbarous practices of a semicivilized people forever violate the precepts and shock the sentiments of civilization? Shall Article XLIV of the Treaty of Berlin become as dead a letter upon the statute books of nations as did Article XLVI of the Conference of Paris? What says old England, the land of Magna Charta, of the Bill of Rights, the petition of rights, and habeas corpus, the birthplace of Hampden, Pym, and Cromwell, the grandest and most majestic among the commonwealths of the earth? What says she, a party to the Treaty of Berlin? Shall the mighty power that conquered Napoleon and preserved the liberties of Europe be forever defied and mocked by a petty and contemptible little Balkan State? What says France, the brilliant and beautiful among the nations, whose chivalric sympathies sent Rochambeau and Lafayette as ambassadors of freedom to our shores? What says she, a party to the Treaty of Berlin? Shall the bad faith and insolence of Roumania go forever unpunished and unrebuked while France, the dauntless and eternal champion of the rights of man, stands mute and motionless? And last, but not least, what says America, the country of Washington, the Republic of Jefferson, the Union of Lincoln, whose Goddess of Liberty in the harbor of New York brandishes forever a torch of freedom as a beacon light to the oppressed and distressed of all the world? What says America, the protagonist of republican virtue and the model of newborn republics throughout the earth? Shall she give no response and make no protest when a suffering and helpless people ask for sympathy and aid?

But it is contended that America was no party to the Treaty of Berlin and that it would be improper therefore for her to seek to interfere in the local affairs of Roumania. There is a grain of truth in this contention, but only a grain. The fatal defect in the argument is that the barbarous persecution and merciless oppression of any race within the borders of any country causing wholesale emigration of the members of that race to other countries as a means of preserving life are not the internal affairs of the state guilty of the persecution and oppression with which other countries have no concern and in which they should not interfere. Such a contention wrongfully assumes that the intercessory and intervening powers of civilized nations are suspended and paralyzed when the laws of humanity and the rights of races happen to conflict with the local arrangements of some small despotic government.

Whether rightfully or wrongfully, America has already protested, in vigorous and solemn terms, against Roumanian oppression of the Jews; and this protest was not born of the hurry and heat of a political convention or of any other voluntary association of irresponsible persons. It was a calm and deliberate act of American diplomacy, the product of one of the noblest and finest of American intellects.

Following the passage of the artisans' bill of March 16, 1902, which was designed to prevent the Jews from earning a livelihood by any form of handicraft or trade, Mr. Secretary Hay, on August 11, 1902, addressed a ministerial note of protest to the Roumanian Government, pointing out the tendency of such legislation to produce an abnormal stream of emigration to the United States. The following is the essential passage of that note:

The teachings of history and the experience of our own Nation show that the Jews possess in a high degree the mental and moral qualifications of conscientious citizenhood. No class of immigrants is more welcome to our shores when coming equipped in mind and body for entrance upon the struggle for bread and inspired with the high purpose to give the best service of heart and brain to the land they adopt of their own free will; but when they come as outcasts, made doubly paupers by physical and moral oppression in their native land and thrown upon the long-suffering generosity of a more favored community, their migration lacks the essential conditions which make alien immigration either acceptable or beneficial. So well is this appreciated on the Continent that even in the countries where anti-Semitism has no foothold it is difficult for these fleeing Jews to obtain any lodgment. America is their only goal.

The United States offers asylum to the oppressed of all lands, but its sympathy with them in no wise impairs its just liberty and right to weigh the acts of the oppressor in the light of their effects upon this country and to judge accordingly.

Putting together the facts now plainly brought home to this Government during the past few years, that many of the inhabitants of Roumania are being forced by artificially adverse discriminations to quit their native country, that the hospitable asylum offered by this country is almost the only refuge left to them, that they come hither unfitted by the conditions of their exile to take part in the new life of this land under circumstances either profitable to themselves or beneficial to the community, and that they are objects of charity from the outset and for a long time, the right of remonstrance against the acts of the Roumanian Government is clearly established in favor of this Government. Whether consciously and of purpose or not, these helpless people, burdened and spurned by their native land, are forced by the sovereign power of Roumania upon the charity of the United States. This Government cannot be a tacit party to such an international wrong. It is constrained to protest against the treatment to which the Jews of Roumania are subjected, not alone because it has unimpeachable ground to remonstrate against the resultant injury to itself, but in the name of humanity. The United States may not authoritatively appeal to the stipulations of the Treaty of Berlin, to which it was not and cannot become a signatory, but it does earnestly appeal to the principles consigned therein because they are the principles of international law and eternal justice, advocating the broad toleration which that solemn compact enjoins and standing ready to lend its moral support to the fulfillment thereof by its cosignatories, for the act of Roumania itself has effectively joined the United States to them as an interested party in this regard.

It might be well to add that a copy of this note of Mr. Hay, American Secretary of State, to the Government of Roumania was simultaneously sent to the Governments of Great Britain, France, Germany, Italy, Russia, and Turkey, the signatory Powers of the Treaty of Berlin. By this act the United States served notice upon Roumania and upon the great powers of Europe that she considered herself a party to that Treaty, if not by direct signature, then at least by the laws of humanity, by the principles of eternal justice, by the binding obligations of international law in which all civilized peoples have a common interest, and by the right of self-preservation involved in the necessity of protecting her own population and her own civilization against the barbarized and impoverished victims of Roumanian persecution.

This authoritative action of our State Department some 10 years ago is still a landmark and a precedent. No one will question the righteousness of the motive or the soundness of the political principle involved in this action. No one can effectively contend that this diplomatic step should not have been taken. The only regret that can be expressed is that the results accomplished were not greater.

Historical considerations affecting the discussion of the present question are these: A great Balkan war has just been terminated. Roumania was involved indirectly in the struggle. Changes in territory, similar to those brought about at the close of the Russo-Turkish War of 1877-78, will probably be made. The Roumanians, it is said, contemplate revising their present constitution in view of changed conditions. It is more than probable that the great Powers of Europe will again be called upon to adjust, in international conference, various questions growing out of the recent war.

Now, after the lapse of 10 years, Roumanian persecution of the Jews exists in more acute and malignant form than when Mr. Hay dispatched his note of diplomatic protest. Roumanian laws against the Jews have become more stringent and oppressive. Social discrimination and ostracism have become more pitiless and humiliating. Riot and massacre are still as imminent as ever.

In view of the approaching conference of the Powers, what shall be done, what can be done to compel Roumania to act justly and humanely by the Jews within her borders? The Powers will have no difficulty, in the matter of the Jews, with any other Balkan State. At the same time and in exactly the same language as that employed in the case of Roumania, Servia and Montenegro promised the Congress of Berlin to guarantee civil and religious freedom to the Jews within their territories in consideration of the recognition of their independence. Both Servia and Montenegro have faithfully kept these pledges, which demonstrates conclusively that there was no inherent difficulty, no insuperable obstacle in the way of Roumania's doing the same thing.

My own opinion is that the United States should accept the invitation of the European Powers to become a member of the approaching international congress, if such an invitation is extended. I have been reliably informed that our Government was invited to participate in the proceedings of the Berlin Congress, but declined. If we are not invited we should ask that the United States be permitted to be a party to the next conference of the

Powers. We should then join with other nations in reminding Roumania of existing obligations, and in imposing fresh ones upon her in a manner that will preclude any possibility of violating them in the future. If no new conference of the Powers is called, or if the United States for any reason should not be a party to it, if one is called, then let us again, and repeatedly if need be, in the language of Mr. Hay, lend our "moral support" to the great cause of civil liberty and religious emancipation, by such representations to the great Governments of Europe as will secure prompt and vigorous action on their part, in compelling Roumania, even at this late date, to perform her pledges under Article XLVI of the Conference of Paris and Article XLIV of the Treaty of Berlin. If her sense of national honor and international obligation does not incline Roumania to deeds of justice and righteousness, then let the strong arm of force be used and the wrath of the nations be visited upon her.

But why should we do all these things for the Jews, you ask? The reply is that these things are not to be done primarily for the Jews. They are to be done to promote and maintain civil liberty and religious freedom among men; to prevent offenses against international morality and to uphold the dignity and sanctity of international law; and, above all things, to compel respect for the laws of humanity and regard for the principles of eternal justice. These are the primary objects of action to be taken against Roumania.

But if you challenge me to open declaration I will candidly say to you that I am in favor of doing all manner of good things at all times for the Jews simply because they are Jews. And in this declaration is no sickly sentimentality, no maudlin sentiment. I am well aware that the Jewish race is not a perfect one. The Jews, along with all the balance of us, have inherited the curse of Eden. The stamp of sin is upon the Jewish as well as upon the gentile brow. From the records of the courts we gather that there are Jewish as well as Christian criminals. And undoubtedly the sons of Abraham are afflicted at times with all the faults and frailties to which human flesh is heir.

And, again, it should be cheerfully admitted that individual Jews are not entitled to receive and should not receive any particular consideration, any special clemency in the exigencies and crises of life. If Jews steal, they should be sent to prison along with gentile thieves. If they murder, the death penalty should be administered to them as in the case of others. If Jews are physically, mentally, or morally unclean, they should be socially ostracized and banished, as should gentiles who are similarly afflicted. If Jews are guilty of unpardoned sins against the laws of God, they should be consigned to the same place and for the same length of time in the hereafter as in the case of gentile sinners. These statements and concessions I gladly and cheerfully make. But having said these things, I must be permitted to repeat the declaration that where the Jewish race as such is concerned and its rights are involved in terms of religious persecution, all doubts should be resolved in favor of the Jews.

The marvelous contributions of the Jewish people to the spiritual and intellectual wealth of the world entitle them to the gratitude and homage, not the hatred and persecution of mankind. If gratitude were a supreme virtue of nations, as it should be of individuals, there would never be any organized governmental persecution of the Jews. The civilized nations of this earth are too deeply and everlastingly indebted to the Jews to be able ever to cancel the obligation. They should at least treat them with humanity and accord them those considerations which are the absolute essentials of happiness in a civilized state. . . . .

APPENDIX VI.

MEMORANDUM ON THE TREATY RIGHTS OF THE JEWS OF ROUMANIA.

Presented to the Right Hon. Sir Edward Grey, Bart., M. P., etc., H. M. Principal Secretary of State for Foreign Affairs, by the London Committee of Deputies of the British Jews and the Council of the Anglo-Jewish Association, in November, 1908.

The London Committee of Deputies of British Jews (representing the several Jewish Congregations in the British Empire) and the Council of the Anglo-Jewish Association (on its own behalf and on behalf of its Branches throughout the British Empire) desire to bring to the notice of His Majesty's Principal Secretary of State for Foreign Affairs the oppressive disabilities under which their coreligionists of the Kingdom of Roumania labour, in violation of Article XLVI of the Convention of Paris of 19th August, 1858, and of Article XLIV of the Treaty of Berlin of 13th July, 1878. They further beg that these disabilities may be submitted to the judgment of the Conference of the Powers, which it is understood will shortly be summoned to deliberate upon other infractions of the Treaty of Berlin. They make this appeal on grounds of humanity and public law, and in the confidence that the Powers will welcome this opportunity of vindicating the great act of religious emancipation to which they set their signatures thirty years ago, and which the Kingdom of Roumania, alone of the states of the Near East, has refused to obey.

The Convention of Paris (1858).

The oppression of the Jews of Roumania, who now number more than 200,000 souls, first attracted the serious attention of the Great Powers at the close of the Crimean War. In connection with the measures then adopted for the organization of the autonomy of the Principalities of Moldavia and Wallachia, "under the suzerainty of the Porte and the guarantee of the Contracting Powers," steps were taken to relieve the Jews of their legal disabilities. These were embodied in Article XLVI of the Convention of Paris, which runs as follows:

All Moldavians and Wallachians shall be equal in the eye of the law and with regard to taxation, and shall be equally admissible to public employments in both Principalities.

Their individual liberty shall be guaranteed. No one can be detained, arrested, or prosecuted but in conformity with the law. No one can be deprived of his property unless legally for causes of public interest and on payment of indemnification.

Moldavians and Wallachians of all Christian confessions shall equally enjoy political rights. The enjoyment of these rights may be extended to other religions by legislative arrangements.

It is important to observe that while this Article left to the Principalities a discretion in regard to the complete emancipation of their non-Christian nationals, it distinctly recognised the existence of such nationals—"Moldavians and Wallachians of .... other religions"—and accorded them civil rights. This is borne out by the Protocols of the Paris and Constantinople Conferences, and by the correspondence on the subject with the Prince of Moldavia, to be referred to presently. The discretion in regard to political rights was, however, not quite absolute, but was the result of a compromise, in which the Powers were led to believe that it would be exercised in an affirmative sense. Originally it was intended to impose much more exacting terms, as is shown by the following Articles of the Protocol of the Conference of Constantinople of 11th February, 1856, which prepared the bases of the Paris Convention:

XIII. All the religions and those who profess them shall enjoy equal liberty and equal protection in the two Principalities.

XV. Foreigners may possess landed property in Moldavia and Wallachia on discharging the same liabilities as natives and on submitting to the laws.

XVI. All Moldavians and Wallachians, without exception, shall be admissible to public employments.

XVIII. All classes of the population, without any distinction of birth or religion, shall enjoy equality of civil rights, and particularly of the right of property, in every shape; but the exercise of political rights shall be suspended in the cases of natives placed under a foreign protection.

These intentions of the Powers were modified in deference to the wishes and pledges of the reigning Prince of Moldavia, Gregory Ghika, who, in a memorial presented to the Congress of Paris, asked that in view of the large number of unassimilated Jews in the Principalities, the realisation of the principle laid down by the Conference of Constantinople, "*excellente en elle-même*," should be reserved for the local government "qui seul peut l'appliquer utilement." (Sturdza: *Acte si documente relative la Istoria Renascerei Romaniei*, vol. ii, pp. 980, 986.) Nevertheless, as Lord Enfield stated in the House of Commons on 19th April, 1872, the Powers regarded the acceptance of Article XLVI by the Principalities as a binding pledge to accord political liberty gradually to the Jews.

ORIGIN OF THE PERSECUTIONS.

The evasion of this pledge has been the chief preoccupation of the Roumanian legislature during the past fifty years. So far from ameliorating the condition of the Jews, the Convention of Paris by a regrettable accident led to more burdensome disabilities and a more barbarous persecution than they had ever before endured. Under the old Organic Laws, by which the Principalities were governed previously to 1859, the people had no effective voice in the Government. Hence there was little cause for jealousy between Christians and Jews, and with the exception of occasional explosions of religious fanaticism, they lived together in harmony. The new order of things established in 1858 destroyed this equality. It gave to the Christian population a monopoly of political power, which they were not slow to use against their trade rivals among the unenfranchised Jews. This unfortunate incidence of the Convention of Paris was aggravated by the new electoral law under which a preponderating franchise was reserved for the mercantile classes, with whom the Jews, being chiefly of the same classes, most directly competed. The result was that not only was the fulfilment of Article XLVI of the Convention of Paris rendered impossible, but the whole influence of the mercantile electorate was employed to obtain the imposition of fresh disabilities upon the Jews, and to inflame the religious and racial prejudices of the populace against them. Instead of gradually emancipating them in accordance with the provisions of the Convention of Paris, even their status as "non-Christian Moldo-Wallachs," acknowledged in that instrument, was denied them. They were assimilated by the Civil Code of 1864 to aliens—though admitted by the Code to be "indigenes"—and were made dependent on a difficult and tedious process of naturalisation for their acquisition of political rights (Articles VIII, IX and XVI). Even this privilege was withdrawn from them by the Constitution of 1866, which declared (Article VII) that only Christians may obtain naturalisation. Consequently Article XLVI of the Convention of Paris remained a dead letter.

THE TREATY OF BERLIN (1878).

The situation of the Jews, when the Berlin Congress met in 1878, was infinitely worse than it had been twenty years before, when it was first considered and dealt with by the Conferences of Constantinople and Paris. In 1858 their status was at least that of unenfranchised Roumanians. In 1878 they had been declared aliens and outcasts. Their civil rights had been withdrawn from them, and political rights had been placed beyond their reach. They were the pitiable objects of a mass of legal disabilities and police restrictions of the cruellest description. Besides this, they had suffered for ten years from a succession of barbarous persecutions and mob outrages, which had reduced them to the utmost misery and had excited the official protests of the Great Powers, and the outspoken indignation of the civilised world. It was in these circumstances that the Congress of Berlin found itself called upon to recognise Roumania as an independent Kingdom. It responded with Articles XLIII and XLIV of the Treaty of 13th July, 1878, which withdrew from the Government of Bucharest all discretion in the matter of the emancipation of its non-Christian subjects, and imposed upon it as a condition of recognition the absolute equality of all religious creeds and confessions in the Kingdom. The following is the text of these Articles:

XLIII. The High Contracting Parties recognise the independence of Roumania, subject to the conditions set forth in the two following Articles.

XLIV. In Roumania the difference of religious creeds and confessions shall not be alleged against any person as a ground for exclusion or incapacity in matters relating to the enjoyment of civil and political rights, admission to public employments, functions, and honours, or the exercise of the various professions and industries in any locality whatsoever.

The freedom and outward exercise of all forms of worship shall be assured to all persons belonging to the Roumanian State, as well as to foreigners, and no hindrance shall be offered either to the hierarchical organisation of the different communions, or to their relations with their spiritual chiefs.

The subjects and citizens of all the Powers, traders or others, shall be treated in Roumania, without distinction of creed, on a footing of perfect equality.

Unfortunately the Powers were once again persuaded to agree to a compromise.

THE NEGOTIATIONS OF 1879-1880.

Acting on the arbitrary and illegal assumption that all Jews were aliens, Roumania contended that the only disability imposed upon them was exclusion from naturalisation under Article VII of the Constitution, and she consequently proposed to revise this Article in satisfaction of Article XLVI of the Treaty. (*State Papers*, vol. lxxi, p. 1138.) This offer was declined by the Powers. (*Ibid.*, pp. 1140, 1158, 1163.) Its effect would have been—unhappily, it has been—not merely to leave the grievances of the Jews unremedied—for by the Roumanian Naturalisation Law the "quality of citizen" could only be obtained by individual Act of Parliament after a probation of ten years, and then was liable to be refused by the Chambers—but to extinguish the national status of the Jews and their civil rights as acknowledged by the Convention of Paris of 1858. Roumania then shifted her ground. Abandoning the pseudo-legal argument, she adopted a plea of expediency. She protested that if the Jews were not aliens in law they were aliens in fact—"*non seulement par leur religion, mais par la langue, le côutûme, les moêurs, et les aspirations, en un mot, par tout ce qui constitué le caractère distinctif d'un homme dans la société.*" (*Ibid.*, p. 1154.) They were "*incultes et fanatiques,*" peculiarly accessible to foreign influences and, owing to their large numbers, calculated to strike "a fatal blow" at the homogeneity of the Roumanian national character. Finally, it was urged that the nation was strongly opposed to an immediate and wholesale emancipation, and that if the Powers insisted upon it, the effect would be that the cause of religious liberty in Roumania would be endangered rather than promoted. (*Ibid.*, pp. 1136, 1161, 1165.) The force of these arguments was not denied by the Powers, but they still declined to admit that a revision of Article VII would in any way meet the requirements of the Treaty of Berlin.

The Roumanian Government then offered solemn assurances that if the proposed solution was accepted, it would be made to apply at once to assimilated Jews, and that the naturalisation of the remainder would be generously facilitated. M. Boeresco, the Roumanian Foreign Minister, even stated to Sir William White, " that if the present Bill could only become a law, a more complete measure of emancipation would be accepted by the electorate later on, when the present agitations had subsided." (*Ibid.*, pp. 1162, 1168-1169.) The most specific, however, of all the pledges given to the Powers was contained in a circular dispatch of M. Boeresco, dated 31st August, 1879, which he himself described as "a sort of *exposé des motifs* of the measure we are about to submit to the Chambers." The following are the essential passages in this important document:

Will the Jews who do not immediately obtain naturalisation remain foreigners? *No, they will remain what they have always been—Roumanian subjects.* But in the measure that they identify themselves with the population of the country, in the measure that by schools and other means of preparation they become enlightened men and attached to the country, they will be able to obtain and exercise political rights.

* * * * * * * *

There will be three categories of Jews: Foreigners, *Roumanian subjects*, and Citizens. Hitherto both the foreign and native Jews have been the objects of certain prohibitions, but in their quality of Jews alone. From the moment that Article VII of the Constitution shall be suppressed *all these prohibitions will disappear*, and no distinction will be made between the foreign Jew and the foreign Christian. *It will be the same with Jews who are Roumanian subjects.* Hitherto certain civil rights have been denied them. Thus they could not be advocates, professors, State engineers, they could not serve on juries, etc. Under the new *régime* they will have in the first place all the rights enjoyed by foreigners in general. *Then, as Roumanian subjects they will have the right of serving in the army and the national guard, the right of acquiring real estate, the right to be advocates, to serve on juries, to exercise freely every profession and every trade; they will, in short, have the same civil rights as Roumanians, and will be protected in the same way by the law and by the authorities.* (*Official Documents extracted from the Diplomatic Correspondence of 2/14 September, 1878, 17/29 July, 1880*, Bucharest, 1880, pp. 121-123.)

To these assurances the Austrian and Italian Governments were disposed to lend a favourable ear, but Great Britain, France and Germany still demanded legislative guarantees for the execution of the Treaty, if not immediately, at any rate within a reasonable time.

THE COMPROMISE OF 1880.

While the negotiations were still in progress, the revision of Article VII was adopted by the Roumanian Parliament, and promulgated by the Prince in the following terms:

In room of Article VII, which is revised, the following shall be placed:

Article VII. The difference of religious creeds and confessions does not constitute in Roumania an obstacle to the acquirement of civil and political rights and their exercise.

1. Every foreigner, without distinction of creed, whether enjoying any foreign protection or not, can acquire naturalisation under the following conditions:

(a) By addressing to the Government an application for naturalisation, in which must be declared the capital he possesses, his profession, and his wish to establish his domicile in Roumania.

(b) By residing in the country for ten years after having made this application, and by proving by his acts that he is useful to the country.

2. The following may be exempted from this delay of residence (ten years):

(a) All who shall have introduced into the country industries, useful inventions, or distinguished talents, or who shall have founded large commercial or industrial establishments.

(b) All who have been born and educated in Roumania of parents domiciled in the country, and have, neither in their own case nor in that of their parents, at any time been in the enjoyment of any foreign protection.

(c) All who have served with the colours during the war of independence, and these can be naturalised collectively on the proposition of the Government by a single Law without further formalities.

3. Naturalisation can only be granted by a Law, and individually.

4. A special Law will determine the manner in which foreigners can establish their domicile on Roumanian territory.

5. Roumanians, and naturalised Roumanian citizens, can alone acquire rural estates in Roumania.

Rights acquired up to the present time are respected.

The International Conventions existing at present remain in force, with all their clauses, and for the term mentioned therein.

At the same time a Bill was passed naturalising 883 Jews who had served with the colours during the war of Liberation.

Wearied by the long negotiations and sundered by their varying interests in the question, the Powers now reluctantly consented to accept the Roumanian solution. Before doing so, however, they extracted from the Roumanian Government a formal declaration of the acceptance of the principle of Article XLIV of the Treaty of Berlin, and of its determination to act upon it "loyally and sincerely." This was given in the following note:

Article VII of the Roumanian Constitution, sanctioning the principle of Article XLIV of the Treaty of Berlin, has opened to the Jews access to citizenship, and has abrogated all existing laws contrary to that principle. That principle will continue to be observed sincerely and loyally. The organic powers will devote themselves to assuring its respect, and will pursue its application with the view of securing a more and more complete assimilation of the Jews.

. . . . Meanwhile, all Jews residing in the country will possess, from the point of view of private civil law, an assured juridical position, and will have no cause to fear arbitrary administrative measures or exceptional laws aimed at confessions or religions. (Statement by Signor Cairoli in the Italian Parliament, 9th December, 1879.)

On the receipt of this note, Austria and Italy at once notified their recognition of the new Kingdom. Their example was followed, after considerable hesitation, by Great Britain, France, and Germany. The latter Powers, however, took the precaution to formulate in precise terms the view they took of the transaction with the Roumanian Government, pointing out that the conditions of the Treaty of Berlin had admittedly not been fulfilled, and that they relied on the solemn pledges of the Principalities to observe them in the spirit, and to execute them gradually in the letter. These important reservations were contained in the following paragraphs of the identic note presented to M. Boeresco by the three Powers on 20th February, 1880:

Her Majesty's Government cannot consider the new Constitutional provisions which have been brought to their cognizance—and particularly those by which persons belonging to a non-Christian creed domiciled in Roumania, and not belonging to any foreign nationality, are required to submit to the formalities of individual naturalisation—as being a complete fulfilment of the views of the Powers signatories of the Treaty of Berlin.

Trusting, however, to the determination of the Prince's Government to approximate more and more, in the execution of these provisions, to the liberal intentions entertained by the Powers, and taking note of the positive assurances to that effect which have been conveyed to them, the Government of Her Britannic Majesty, being desirous of giving to the Roumanian nation a proof of their friendly sentiments, have decided to recognise the Principality of Roumania as an independent State. Her Majesty's Government consequently declare themselves ready to enter into regular diplomatic relations with the Prince's Government.

ROUMANIAN PLEDGES REPUDIATED.

Except that the rights of the Roumanian Jews had been restated by the Powers in a more categorical form than in 1858, nothing was changed by the Treaty of Berlin. The illusory pledges of

Prince Gregory Ghika, unfulfilled for twenty years, had been repeated by the Government of King Charles with more emphasis and circumstantiality, but with just as little intention of fulfilling them. Thirty more years have now passed, and a new generation of Jews has been born in the land. They, however, are still as far from emancipation as were their fathers, when their sad lot first engaged the sympathy of Europe and the good offices of the Great Powers. They are still held to be aliens; naturalisation is still practically inaccessible to them, and their persecution, legal and otherwise, has been in no way relaxed.

These evasions of the Treaty have been facilitated by two defects in the compromise arrived at in February, 1880. One was the omission to secure a legislative acknowledgment from the Roumanian Parliament that Jews belonging to no other nationality and enjoying no foreign protection were Roumanian nationals in the sense of Article XLVI of the Convention of Paris, and the admission of M. Boeresco in his dispatch of 31st August, 1879. The second defect was contained in paragraph 3 of the revised Article VII of the Constitution, which virtually left the Roumanian Parliament free to deal with Jewish petitions for naturalisation as it pleased.

In the case of naturalisations the result has been this. So far from facilitating the extension of political rights to the Jews in accordance with the solemn pledges given to the Powers, the Roumanian Chambers have placed every possible impediment in the way of granting them. Since the recognition of the Kingdom in 1880, the total number of Jews for whom naturalisation Bills have been passed is 176 out of an adult male population of about 100,000, almost all of whom are natives, and more than 20,000 of whom have duly performed their military service under the Conscription law.

In the case of the national status of the Jews, the result has been to enable the Roumanian Government to reaffirm their alien status, and to re-enact all the old persecuting laws under the guise of laws relating to foreigners. It is true that these laws apply ostensibly to all foreigners alike, but in regard to foreigners with a determined nationality, their persecuting incidence is either not felt by reason of the floating character and limited interests of that class of the population, or is defeated by the protection of their respective Governments. The Jews, on the other hand, having no foreign Governments to appeal to, are subjected to the full force of those laws which usually apply to peculiar circumstances of their social life, differentiating them from authentic aliens. Moreover, the persecuting possibilities of such laws are often accentuated by administrative circulars, and almost invariably by the anti-Semitic zeal of the local authorities, to whom their execution is confided, and who enjoy a perfect immunity for their harsh and often illegal action.

DISABILITIES RENEWED.

The following is a synopsis of the persecuting legislation above referred to:

In the first place, attention must be directed to a class of laws ostensibly aimed at foreigners, but bearing harshly on Jews, which were passed previously to 1878. In accordance with the Declaration of the Roumanian Government made to the Powers on the eve of the recognition of the Kingdom, these laws, so far as they apply to native Jews, should have been abrogated, as being " contrary to the principle of Article XLIV of the Treaty of Berlin." To this day they remain on the Statute Book. They comprise the Decree of 4th December, 1864, reserving the profession of advocates to Roumanians born or naturalised; that of 25th October, 1869, placing the same restriction on the trade of pharmacists; the Law of 3d February, 1868, requiring that tenders for public works should only be accepted from persons possessing civil rights; that of 3d February, 1872, limiting the bonding, manufacture, and sale of tobacco to Roumanian citizens; and the Law of 13th February, 1873, placing a similar restriction on the retail sale of spirituous liquors. The latter law reduced thousands of Jews to beggary without affecting a single authentic foreigner, and led Lord Granville to propose an intervention of the Powers, which was only defeated by the non-adhesion of Russia.

Since 1878 these restrictions have been multiplied with the cruellest ingenuity.

A Law of 1868, which forbade the settlement of Jews in rural communes, was renewed in 1881 and 1887, and in order to concentrate them in a comparatively few towns, where they could be more easily persecuted by the police, a large number of urban communes were transformed into rural communes, and the Jews expelled from them under circumstances of great hardship.

Jewish children are not admitted to the national schools on the same footing as Christian children. Although the Law of 12th May, 1896, declares primary instruction obligatory and gratuitous for all Roumanians, a heavy fee is imposed upon " foreigners," and even then they can only be admitted when the requirements of the Christian population have been fully satisfied. The result is that in many cases the primary schools are closed to Jews. Similar restrictions apply to secondary, superior, technical, agricultural and normal schools. (Laws of 23d February, 1893, and 23d March, 1898.) At the same time the efforts of the Jews to found and maintain their own schools are seriously obstructed by the Government and local authorities.

Public employments and all the liberal professions are closed to Jews, and they are virtually excluded from many trades. They cannot act as stock or trade brokers of any kind; they are excluded from Chambers of Commerce, and they may not be members of Artisans' Corporations. (Laws of 8th June, 1884; 24th June, 1886; 28th February, 1887; 22d June, 1893; 26th January, 1894, and 18th February, 1899.) By the Law of 15th March, 1884, they were expelled from the peddling traffic, in which 20,000 are said to have been engaged. Jewish workmen can only be admitted into factories in the proportion of one-third to two-thirds Christians (Law of 24th May, 1887), which, in view of their concentration in towns, often renders employment for large numbers of them hopeless. In 1902 an attempt was actually made to deprive them of the exercise of all handicrafts by a law (17th March) which required *inter alia* that no "foreigner" should be permitted to exercise a handicraft in Roumania unless he could show reciprocity for Roumanians in his own country. The Jews being "foreigners not under foreign protection" were unable to prove this reciprocity, and had it not been for the representations of the Powers, they would have been reduced to absolute mendicancy. The law is, however, still employed in other respects to hamper Jewish artisans in earning their daily bread.

A characteristic example of the ingenuity with which this legislation is framed in order to evade the spirit of the Treaty of Berlin, while apparently complying with its letter, is afforded by the Military Law of 21st November, 1882. By Article I of this law "all the inhabitants of the country" are liable to military service. By Article II "subjects of foreign states" are declared ineligible for the army. Hence the Jews being "inhabitants" but not "subjects of foreign states," are called upon to serve, although deprived of all civil and political rights. Promotion, however, is denied them on the ground that "service in the army is a duty, while the rank of officer is a public function reserved for Roumanian citizens." (Speech of M. Bratiano in the Roumanian Senate, 27th May, 1882.)

As alleged aliens the Jews are also liable to expulsion, not only from rural communes, but even from the country itself. This has often been resorted to in order to prevent them from agitating publicly against their disabilities. They are not permitted to ventilate their grievances in the public press. They may not hold public meetings, and they have no right of petition to Parliament or the King. They are compelled to take out certificates of residence as foreigners, and although taxed for the support of local hospitals, they have no right of entry into those institutions. Besides these legal disabilities, they suffer the harshest treatment at the hands of the local authorities, who readily take advantage of their helplessness to realize against them all the underlying anti-Semitism of the laws relating to aliens. Jews are frequently arrested and beaten without cause and with absolute impunity, and in some districts special taxes, beyond those which they pay in common with all Roumanian citizens, are levied upon them. In a word, the Roumanian Jew is a veritable outlaw from his youth upwards. (For texts of the above-mentioned laws and examples of their anti-Jewish application see Sincerus: "*Les Juifs en Roumanie*," London, 1901.)

AIMS AND CONSEQUENCES OF THE PERSECUTION.

Apart from the illegality of this régime, its barbarous purpose and the embarrassments it causes to foreign countries must render it a matter of grave concern to the Powers signatories of the Treaties of 1858 and 1878. What is its purpose? A careful examination of the laws aimed at the Jews shows that they go far beyond the alleged defensive needs of Roumanian national homogeneity, or of the social and economic interests, however extravagant, of any class of the Christian population.

The effect of these laws must be to prevent the assimilation of the Jews, to perpetuate any exclusive characteristics and tendencies they may possess, and to alienate them from the national sentiment. When it is remembered that under the pledges given to the Powers by the Roumanian Government in 1880, it is this very assimilation of the Jews which would destroy the last vestige of excuse for their non-emancipation, can we doubt that these effects have been deliberately sought by the Legislature, and that assimilation has been forcibly discouraged in order to justify the Roumanian State in resisting the Treaty of Berlin? Nothing can be more convincing on this head than the virtual exclusion of Jews from the national schools and the liberal professions. In 1879 it was complained that the Jews were "*incultes, fanatiques, ayant une autre langue, d'autres moêurs, d'autres sentiments.*" (*State Papers*, vol. lxxi, p. 1161.) In view of the illiteracy of the Roumanian people themselves—88.4 per cent (*Statesman's Year Book*, p. 984), while that of the Jews is probably less than 5 per cent—and the fanaticism of the anti-Semitic movement in the country, these are strange excuses for denying the eligibility of the Jews for the rights of Roumanian nationals. But even were they relatively well founded, how can Roumania justify her conduct in seeking to perpetuate these conditions, while pleading that they stand in the way of loyal fulfilment of her Treaty obligations and pledges? The truth is that the Jews are being systematically and intentionally barbarised and impoverished, in order to exclude them from their rights, and, if possible, to get rid of them altogether. The oppressive economic laws follow logically from the barbarising laws, for it is obviously not to the advantage of any state to retain a class of inhabitants who are alien in manners and sentiment from the bulk of the nation. Hence the efforts to make life impossible to the Jews, efforts which have already driven over 100,000 into a condition approaching vagabondage, and during the last ten years has forced over 60,000 to emigrate. The exact number of refugees for this period cannot be stated, but between 1899 and 1904 alone it was officially returned at 41,754. (*Bulletin de l'Alliance Israélite*, 1904, p. 55.)

It is chiefly through this emigration that embarrassment is caused to foreign countries. It has been felt in England, and it played no small part in the agitation which led to the enactment of the Aliens Act, 1905. It has also been felt in the United States, and it compelled the Washington Cabinet in September, 1902, to address a vigorous note to the Signatory Powers of the Treaty of Berlin, protesting against the inhuman violations of that instrument by Roumania. It is, moreover, a source of danger to the peace of the Near East, and especially to the new Constitutional régime so happily inaugurated in Turkey. The demoralizing example of Roumania is calculated to encourage and in a sense justify the reactionaries in the Ottoman Empire. It was by similar violations of the practice of Liberal states that the Softa movement against the Turkish Constitution in 1876-78 was defended. (Schulthess, *Geschichtskalender*, 1876, p. 517.) The precedent is ominous. If Europe permits a Christian state which is her own creation to exclude non-Christians from national rights, why should a Mussulman state be compelled to admit non-Mussulmans? This question was asked in 1876 with disastrous consequences, and it may quite conceivably be asked again.

The Defence of Roumania.

What is the defence of Roumania against these serious charges? It is at once simple and amazingly cynical. Roumania takes her stand on the argument that the Jews have always been aliens in the land, and that the strict letter of the Treaties of 1858 and 1878 did not alter their status. When she is reminded of the official admission to the contrary of M. Boeresco in 1879, of the formal and categorical pledges of 1880, and of the precise statement of the terms on which the three Western Powers recognised her independence, she points to the equivocal revision of Article VII of her Constitution, which was ingenuously accepted by Europe, and declares that she is bound by that alone. No attempt is made to hide the bad faith of this astonishing plea. Indeed, Roumanian writers of eminence boast of it. "*Le traité de Berlin,*" writes M. Suliotis in the *Journal du droit internationale privé* (vol. xiv, p. 563), "*a cru faire merveille en faveur des étrangers mais la Roumanie a cru habilement eluder les enconvenients qui pouvaient resulter de l'application de l'article VII dans le sens du traité de Berlin, qui n'a eu d'autres resultats que de rendre plus difficile la situation des étrangers.*" No enemy of Roumania could ask for a more damaging statement of the case against her. Nor does this stand alone. Writing in the *Romanul* of 25th December, 1881, M. Rosetti, an ex-Minister and one of the leading statesmen of the Kingdom, also boasted of the trick which had been successfully played on Europe. "We may congratulate ourselves to-day," he writes, "on having solved the Jewish question in a national sense, and that—we may now avow loudly—contrary to the manifest will of the Powers and even contrary to the spirit of the Treaty of Berlin."

Are the Jews Aliens?

Notwithstanding the confidence thus shown in the letter of the Treaties, it may well be questioned whether even in this technical respect Roumania is on safe ground. The Treaty of Berlin, it is true, does not specifically recognise the Jews as nationals, but that Treaty is governed by the Convention of Paris of 1858, and it is certain that Article XLVI of that instrument accepted all native

Christians and non-Christians alike as Moldo-Wallachs, and conferred on them equal civil rights. It is idle to pretend in reply to this that the Jews of the Principalities were at that time aliens by law. In the first place it is very doubtful whether they were, seeing that as natives they were often distinguished from foreigners in the pre-1858 legislation. But even if they were, a new era was inaugurated by the Convention of 1858, which swept away the old Organic Laws and organized the autonomy of the Principalities on an entirely new and modern basis. For it must be remembered, as Lord Clarendon pointed out in 1870, that the Convention was not a mere enumeration of incidental stipulations, but was avowedly the fundamental basis of the public law of the Principalities in their new condition. Nothing of the old régime inconsistent with its provisions could survive. If the national status of Jews can be denied to-day on the ground that it existed in the Organic Laws, many other disabilities which weighed on Christians as well, in the first half of the nineteenth century, and which gave rise to the Roumanian revolution of 1848, might be revived. The solidarity of the Jews and Christians in this respect is indeed strikingly illustrated by the fact that the revolutionary Government of Wallachia in 1848 actually proclaimed the emancipation of the Jews, whose sons and grandsons to-day are declared aliens. (*State Papers*, vol. lxxi, p. 1153.) This alone suffices to destroy the contention that all the Jews of Roumania were foreigners in the eye of the law in 1858.

Nor are the Roumanians justified in assuming that if the absence of any recognition of native Jews as Roumanian subjects in Article XLIV of the Treaty of Berlin stood alone, it would sanction the Roumanian assumption of their alien status. That this is not the case is indeed clear from the protocols of the Congress. The ideas and intention which guided the Powers were expressed with as much precision as eloquence by M. Waddington at the sitting of the Conference of 28th June, 1878. On the question that an Article exactly similar in terms to Article XLIV should be imposed on Servia, Prince Gortschakoff objected to the granting of "civil and political rights" to the Jews of both Servia and Roumania. Thereupon the French plenipotentiary said:

He considered it important to seize this solemn opportunity to procure an affirmation by the Representatives of Europe of the principles of religious liberty. His Excellency added that Servia, which demands to enter into the European family upon the same footing as the other States, should in the first place acknowledge the principles which form the basis of social organization in all the States of Europe, and accept them as a necessary condition of the favor she solicits. (*Protocols of the Berlin Congress*, C-2083, p. 120.)

It was on this principle that the Powers acted when the effects of Article XLIV were considered. Their idea was that the emancipation of native Jews in Roumania should be assimilated to the like emancipations in Western Europe. This view, indeed, was at once adopted by Servia, where Jews had previously been persecuted and oppressed in the same way and on the same grounds as in Roumania. Moreover, it must be obvious that when the Powers stipulated for religious equality " in matters relating to the enjoyment of civil and political rights," they could not have contemplated the exclusion of Jews *quâ* Jews from the fundamental right of nationality.

It should also be observed—though this is quite a minor matter —that even if the Roumanian contention is sound, the treatment of the Jews is none the less a violation of Article XLIV. The concluding *alinéa* of that Article provides for the equal treatment of all foreigners. This the Jews do not enjoy even in their alleged capacity of foreigners, for apart from the unequal incidence of the Roumanian legislation relating to aliens, the Jews are compelled to serve in the army, while other aliens are exempt, and their civil status is arbitrarily regulated by Roumanian law, while that of other foreigners is subject to the law of their respective countries.

Conclusion.

On these grounds the Jewish communities of Great Britain venture to hope that His Majesty's Government will be able to see their way to submit this grave question to the Signatory Powers of the Treaty of Berlin, and to seek with them for a solution which will put an end to a situation which is not only a source of much human suffering, but also a scandalous defiance of the will of Europe as embodied in solemn Treaties. Of all violations of the Treaty of Berlin which have taken place during the last thirty years, the worst are assuredly those which have set at nought the liberating spirit which is of the very essence of that compact. Territorial changes and changes in the political status of the various territories of South-Eastern Europe are of subsidiary consequence. The Treaty of Berlin is above all a great charter of emancipation, especially of civil and religious equality. This principle is embodied in no fewer than five of its Articles, relating to every political division of the vast region with which it deals, and in each case it is asserted as the fundamental basis of the liberties conferred on the various states. Hence to violate this principle is the gravest blow which can be struck at the Treaty, besides being a menace to the peace and social stability of the Near East, and an offence against international morality. To-day this principle has been loyally complied with by all the States of South-Eastern Europe with the single exception of Roumania. In that Kingdom, over 200,000 human beings, languishing in a bondage worse than ever oppressed the Christians of the Ottoman Empire, still invoke the liberating spirit of the Charter of 1878. The Great Powers of Europe assuredly cannot be insensible to this cry, at a moment when they are about to consider the revision of this very Charter.

INDEX.

Abell, W. Maitland, ref. to paper by, 80 (note).
"Abrogation of the Russian Treaty," 62d Congress, 2d Session, House Report No. 179, alluded to, 6 (note).
"Acte si documente relative la Istoria Renascerei Romaniei" (Sturdza), ref. to, 139.
Adams, John, 5 (note).
A. d'Avril, alluded to, 48 (note).
Adee, Alvey A., 1 (note).
Adler, Dr. Cyrus, 1 (note).
  preface by, ix-x.
  work by, alluded to, 4 (note).
  ref. to, 41, 80 (note).
  correspondence relating to the Jewish question in Roumania, 84, 86-92.
Adler, Chief Rabbi Hermann, 24.
Alexander, Prince, of Bulgaria, 79.
Alexander, Prince, of Serbia, letter of, to King Charles of Roumania, 74.
Alexander Pasha, 121.
Algeciras Conference, U. S. at, makes plea in behalf of Jews 88.
Ali Pasha, 121.
"Allgemeine Zeitung des Judentums," ref. to, 3 (note), 16 (note), 35 (note), 44 (note), 49 (note), 71.
Alliance Israélite Universelle, 2, 7, 22, 24, 29, 35, 36, 39, 44, 47, 48, 49, 50, 52, 53 (note), 65, 70, 72, 73, 74, 82 (note), 111.
  Memorial of, to the Congress of Berlin, 44, 105-107.
"American contributions toward the Removal of Jewish Disabilities in the Balkan States," by Max. J. Kohler and Simon Wolf, ix.

American contributions toward removal of Jewish disabilities in the Balkan States, ix, 1, 2, 3, 6, 7, 8, 9, 10, 11, 12, 13, 14, 16, 17, 18, 19, 20, 21, 22, 23, 24, 25, 26, 27 and (note)-28 (note), 29, 30, 31, 32, 33, 34, 36, 37, 38, 39, 41, 42, 43, 55 (note), 80-93, 108-114, 114-137.
  See also under United States.
"American Hebrew," ref. to, 44 (note), 48 (note), 82 (note).
"American in Roumania, An," ref. to, 78 (note).
American Jewish Committee, x.
  correspondence relating to the Jewish question in Roumania, 83-92.
American Jewish Historical Society, 1 (note).
American Jewish Historical Society, Publications of, ref. to, 3 (note), 4 (note), 6 (note), 21 (note), 41 (note), 80 (note), 89.
"American Jewish Year Books," ref. to, 4 (note), 6 (note), 78 (note), 80 (note), 82 (note), 83 (note), 116, 131.
"American Law Review," ref. to, 6 (note).
"American Progress in Jurisprudence" (Field), quoted, 6 (note).
American Roumanian Committee, 24.
American Roumanian Society, 11.
"American Spirit, The" (Straus), cited, 5 (note).
  ref. to, 94 (note).
Andrassy, Count Gyula, 44, 50, 51, 64, 66, 120, 121.

155

Anglo-Jewish Association, 22, 29, 34, 39, 45 and (note), 46, 93, 137.
"Annales du Sénat de la Chambre des Deputés," quoted, 54 (note).
Astruc, Chief Rabbi Elie-Aristide, 29, 30.
Argyle, Duke of, ref. to work by, 49 (note).
"Around the World with General Grant" (Young), ref. to, 49 (note).
"Aus dem Leben Königs Karls von Rumänien" (ed. S. Whitman), alluded to, 3 (note), 47 (note), 76 (note).
  quoted, 75.
  ref. to, 16 (note).
  cited, 74.
Austria-Hungary, treatment of Jews by, 4 (note).
  and the Jewish question in Roumania and the Balkan States, 19, 20, 51, 76 (note), 102, 110, 125, 126, 134, 142, 144.
  champions religious liberty at the Congress of Berlin, 44, 64.
  and the Jewish question at the Congress of Berlin, 50, 108, 115.
Austro-Prussian War of 1866, 48 (note).

Balkan States. Congress of Berlin decrees establishment of religious liberty in, ix, 95, 121, 122.
  disabilities and persecution of the Jews in, 1, 2, 85.
  Jewish question in, and the Congress of Berlin, 54 (note).
  and the Balkan Wars of 1912-1913, 83-92, 93-94.
  See also under: Bulgaria; Danubian Principalities; Greece; Montenegro; Roumania; Serbia.
"Balkans, The" (Sloane), alluded to, 80 (note).
"Balkan Wars and the Jews," ref. to, 80 (note).

Balkan Wars of 1912-1913, and the Jewish question in the Balkan States, 83-92, 93-94.
Bamberger, Leopold, 27.
Bamberger, Ludwig, 16, 56 (note).
Bancroft, George, 21.
Bayard, Thomas F., quoted, 5 (note).
"Beaconsfield" (Brandes), alluded to, 57 (note).
"Beaconsfield" (Froude), alluded to, 57 (note).
Beaconsfield, Lord (Benjamin Disraeli), 24, 41, 45 and (note), 46, 51, 53 (note), 56 (note), 57 (note), 60 (note), 66, 71 and (note), 121.
Beck, Dr. M., 82.
Belgium, and the Jewish question in the Balkan States, 102.
Benisch, Dr. A., 12 (note).
Bennet, William S., 83.
Berlin, Congress of, ix, 1, 39, 40-74, 75, 76 (note), 77, 82, 85, 95, 120, 135.
  Memorial of Alliance Israélite Universelle, to, 105-107.
Berlin, Treaty of, 24, 42, 79, 80, 81, 85, 93, 94, 108, 112, 114, 115, 128, 129, 131, 133, 134, 137, 140, 141, 142, 143, 144, 145, 146.
"Berliner Kongress, Der" (Milobar), alluded to, 48 (note).
Bessarabia, 52, 65, 66.
"Bismarck" (Hahn), ref. to, 49 (note), 54 (note), 60 (note).
Bismarck, Prince [Otto von], 35 and (note), 40, 46, 47, 50, 51 and (note), 52, 53 (note), 55 (note), 56 and (note), 59 (note), 60, 61, 63, 64, 65, 66, 67, 69, 71, 75, 76 (note), 120, 121.
Blaine, [James G.], dispatch to Charles Emory Smith, quoted, 113.
Bleichroeder, Baron Gerson von, 47 and (note), 48 (note), 50, 51, 52, 55 (note), 76 (note).
Bleichroeder, Julius, 12 (note), 25, 28 (note), 47 (note).

Blowitz, M. de, "Memoirs" of, alluded to, 49 (note).
  cited, 53 (note).
Bluntschli, [Johann Kaspar], alluded to, 48 (note), 97.
  work by, quoted, 76-77.
B'nai B'rith, Independent Order of, 9, 11, 22.
Boeresco, Roumanian Foreign Minister, 124, 126, 128, 142, 150.
Bolingbroke, Lord, quoted, 1.
Bonfils, alluded to, 97.
Board of Delegates of American Israelites, 3, 8, 11, 12 and (note), 22, 26, 28 (note), 31, 36, 37, 39, 47 (note).
  correspondence between Secretary of State Evarts and, 32-34.
Board of Delegates on Civil Rights of the Union of American Hebrew Congregations, 81.
Brandeis, Alter, 14, 15.
Brandes, Georg, work by, alluded to, 57 (note).
Bratiano, 52, 65, 73, 148.
Brunswik, B., work by, alluded to, 48 (note).
Brussels, Jewish Conference at, in behalf of Roumanian Jews, 24, 25-29, 47 (note).
Bryce, [James], work by, alluded to, 57 (note).
Bucharest, Peace Conference at, of 1913, 2, 92, 93.
Buchner, Adolph, 8, 9, 12 (note).
Buckle. *See* Monypenny and Buckle.
Bulgaria, disabilities and persecutions of the Jews in, 2, 107.
  Congress of Berlin and establishment of religious liberty in, 42, 53-55, 56, 57, 58, 59, 61, 65, 68, 69-70, 71, 92.
  status of Jews in, after the Congress of Berlin, 73, 74, 78-79, 92, 93.
  United States and religious liberty in, 91.
"Bulgaria and Her People" (Monroe), quoted, 79.
"Bulgarie, La" (Chaunier), alluded to, 79 (note).

"Bulletin de l'Alliance Israélite," ref. to, 149.
"Bulletin" of the New York Public Library, alluded to, 49 (note).
Bülow, Baron Bernhard von, 35 and (note), 44 (note), 49, 51, 65, 121.
Buzeo, Roumania, 15, 19.

Cairoli, Signor, 126, 144.
"Cambridge Essays for 1856," alluded to, 55 (note).
Caradja, John, Code of, 116.
Carathéodory Pasha, 58, 60, 61.
  work by, alluded to, 48 (note).
"Career and Correspondence of Sir William White" (Edwards), ref. to, 78 (note).
"Carte Commérciale de la Bulgarie," ref. to, 78-79.
Casserly, Senator, 11.
Castelar, Emilio, ref. to work by, 7 (note).
"Century Magazine," ref. to, 7 (note), 57 (note).
"Ces ques les Juifs Roumains doivent à la Prusse" (alluded to), 76 (note).
Chandler, Hon. Walter M., speech in the House of Representatives on "The Jews of Roumania and the Treaty of Berlin," 80 (note), 83, 114-137.
Charles, King, of Roumania, 2, 13, 14, 15, 17, 74, 75, 76 (note).
Charles, Prince, of Roumania. *See* Charles, King, of Roumania.
Chaunier, work by, alluded to, 79 (note).
"Church and State in the United States" (Schaff), alluded to, 6 (note).
"Cinquante ans d'histoire. L'Alliance Israélite Universelle, 1860-1910" (Leven), alluded to, 34.
"Civil Disabilities of the Jews" (Macaulay), alluded to, 7 (note).
Clapp, Moses E., 83.
Clarendon, Lord, 151.
Code Cahmachi, 116.

Cogalniceanu (Kogalniceano), M., 36, 38, 52, 65, 73, 101, 117.
Cole, Senator, 11.
"Congrès de Berlin, Le," ref. to, 48 (note).
"Congrès de Berlin, Le" (French Yellow Book, 1886), alluded to, 48 (note).
ref. to, 72 (note).
Congress, and the Jewish question in Roumania, 8-9, 16, 17, 83, 114-115.
"Congressional Globe," ref. to, 8 (note), 16 (note).
"Congressional Record," alluded to, 6 (note).
ref. to, 83 (note), 114 (note).
Constantinople, Conference of, 29, 30, 43, 49, 50, 118, 119, 139, 140.
appealed to on behalf of Jews, 29, 30, 34, 102-105.
"Contemporary France" (Hanotaux), ref. to, 48 (note), 54 (note).
Conybeare, F. C., ref. to work by, 78 (note).
alluded to, 83 (note).
Cortelyou, George B., 82.
Corti, Count, 121.
Costaforo, Roumanian premier, 26.
Cowen, E[lfrida], alluded to, 28 (note).
Cox, Samuel S., 16, 17.
Crémieux, Adolphe, 2, 7, 9, 12 (note), 22, 25, 26, 29, 30, 39, 44, 47, 54 (note).
Curtin, U. S. Minister at St. Petersburg, 112.

Damascus, United States protests against persecution of Jews in, 4, 5, 88, 94.
Dan II, 100.
Danubian Principalities, Jewish question in, 102, 103.
See also under Balkan States.
Davis, Israel, work by, alluded to, 78 (note).
de Bar, L., ref. to work by, 77 (note).

"Debats parlementaires," ref. to, 4 (note).
Decazes, Duke, 35.
Decebalus, 100.
"Declaration of Rights of Man and of Citizens, The" (Farrand), alluded to, 7 (note).
de Hirsch, Baron, 39.
De Mouy, Charles, ref. to work by, 48 (note).
"Denkrede über Benj. F. Peixotto" (Stern), alluded to, 9 (note), 12, 22.
ref. to, 25 (note).
Derby, Earl of (Lord Stanley), alluded to, 3 (note).
quoted, 34, 104, 112.
Derby, Lord. *See* Derby, Earl of.
Dérenbourg, Joseph, 30.
Désprez, Félix, 57, 68, 69, 121.
Deutsch, Prof. Gotthard, alluded to, 28 (note).
ref. to, 56 (note).
de Worms, Baron Henry (Lord Pirbright), 29, 30, 45 and (note), 46, 48 (note), 53 (note), 77.
ref. to work by, 59 (note).
"Dictionary of National Biography," ref. to, 45 (note).
"Digest of International Law" (Moore), ref. to, 60 (note).
Diplomatic correspondence of the United States, Jews in, 4-5, 13, 17, 18, 19, 20, 21, 30, 31, 34, 36-38, 41-42, 43, 71-72, 80, 81, 82, 84-92, 108-114, 133-134.
"Diplomatist, A; Nationalism and the War in the Near East," alluded to, 80 (note).
Disabilities, Jewish, in the Balkan States, 1, 2-3, 23, 37, 62, 63, 78, 79, 87, 95, 98, 99, 102, 103, 104, 105, 106, 108, 109, 110, 111, 112, 115, 116, 117, 119, 120, 122, 123, 124, 127, 128, 129-131, 132, 134, 135, 139, 140, 141, 145, 146, 147, 148, 149, 150, 151, 152.
See also under: Bulgaria, Greece, Montenegro, Roumania, Serbia.

Disraeli, Benjamin. *See* Beaconsfield, Lord.
"Doctrine of Intervention, The" (Hodges), cited, 94.
D'Oubril, Paul, 121.
Dufaure, M., 72.
Duggan, S. P., work by, alluded to, 49 (note).

"Eastern Question, The" (Duggan), alluded to, 49 (note).
"Eastern Question, The" (Duke of Argyle), ref. to, 49 (note).
Eastern Roumelia. *See* Roumelia, Eastern.
Edwards, work by, alluded to, 78 (note).
"Elements of International Law" (Wheaton), ref. to, 94 (note).
"Encyclopedia Britannica," ref. to, 48 (note), 56 (note).
Enfield, Lord, 139.
England and the Jewish question in Roumania and the Balkan States, 2, 19, 20, 21, 34, 43, 49, 55 (note), 74, 76 (note), 77, 79, 81, 89, 90, 91, 93, 102, 104, 110, 125, 126, 134, 142, 144.
insists on equal rights for English Jews in Switzerland, 3 (note).
and the Jewish question at the Congress of Berlin, 46, 56 (note), 57 (note), 108, 115.
champions religious liberty at the Congress of Berlin, 53 (note), 62, 66, 75.
"England's Policy in the East" (de Worms), alluded to, 45 (note).
ref. to, 59 (note).
English Jewish Year Book for 1903, alluded to, 45 (note).
"Erklärung der Menschen—und Bürgerrechte, Die" (Jellinek), alluded to, 7 (note).
"Essays in Jurisprudence and Ethics," alluded to, 7 (note).
"Essays on Some Disputed Questions in Modern International Law" (Lawrence), alluded to, 94 (note).
"Essentials of International Public Law" (Hershey), ref. to, 97 (note).
"European Concert in the Eastern Question" (Holland), alluded to, 48 (note).
Evarts, William M., correspondence relating to Jews in the Balkan States, 32-34, 36-38.

Farrand, M., work by, alluded to, 7 (note).
Fay, [Theodore], 3.
Ferrero, Prof., alluded to, 48 (note).
Field, David Dudley, work by, quoted, 6 (note).
"Final Report of Board of Delegates of American Israelites," ref. to, 25 (note).
alluded to, 39 (note).
Fish, Hamilton, diplomatic correspondence of, relating to Jews in Roumania, 16, 17, 18, 19, 20, 21, 31, 110, 112-113.
Fluegel, Rabbi Maurice, 26.
"Foreign Relations of the United States, 1867," ref. to, 3 (note).
"Foreign Relations of the United States, 1872," ref. to, 20 (note), 21 (note), 110, 113.
"Foreign Relations of the United States, 1877," ref. to, 31 (note).
"Foreign Relations [of the United States], 1878," ref. to, 41 (note), 42 (note), 43 (note), 49 (note), 57 (note), 71.
"Foreign Relations of the United States, 1880," ref. to, 75 (note), 76 (note).
"Foreign Relations of the United States, 1891," quoted, 113.
"Foreign Relations of the United States, 1902," ref. to, 80 (note).
Forsyth, John, diplomatic correspondence of, on behalf of Jews of Damascus, 4-5, 94.

France, and the Jewish question in Roumania and the Balkan States, 2, 16, 19, 21, 43, 49, 55 (note), 74, 76 (note), 81, 82 (note), 102, 110, 125, 126, 134, 142, 144.
    insists on equal treatment for French Jews in Switzerland, 3 (note), 4 (note).
    influence of United States on religious liberty in, 7 (note).
    and the emancipation of Jews in the Orient, 36.
    and the Jewish question at the Congress of Berlin, 53 and (note)-55 (note), 70-71, 108, 115.
    champions religious liberty at the Congress of Berlin, 60, 61, 63, 65, 66, 70-71, 151.
Franchi, Cardinal, Papal Secretary of State, 72.
Franco, M., on the status of the Jews of Bulgaria, 78-79.
Freeman, Edward A., alluded to, 57 (note).
Freidus, A. S., alluded to, 28 (note).
French Yellow Books, alluded to, 48 (note), 78 (note).
    ref. to, 72 (note).
Friedenberg, Albert M., ix.
    alluded to, 28 (note).
Friedenwald, Dr. Herbert, correspondence relating to Jewish question in Roumania, 84, 86-89.
Froude, [James A.], work by, alluded to, 57 (note).
"Fürst Bismarck's Verhältniss zum Glauben insbesondere zum Judenthum," alluded to, 56 (note).

Gaster, Dr. Moses, 82.
German Union of Jewish Congregations, 71.
Germany, and the Jewish question in Roumania and the Balkan States, 19, 21, 35, 43 and (note), 44, 46, 49, 51, 55 (note), 74, 76 (note), 81, 102, 110, 125, 126, 134, 142, 144.
    and the Jewish question at the Congress of Berlin, 46, 47 and (note), 51 and (note), 53 (note), 55 (note), 59 (note), 76 (note), 108, 115.
    champions religious liberty at the Congress of Berlin, 61, 64, 66, 67, 75.
"Geschichte der Serben" (Jiriček), alluded to, 80 (note).
"Geschichtskalender" ("Schulthess"), ref. to, 149.
Ghika, Gregory, 117, 118, 119, 122, 127, 139, 145.
Giurgewo, Roumania, 36, 37, 38.
Gladstone, [William E.], 56 (note), 57 (note), 71 (note).
Gloucester, Bishop of, 16.
Godefroi, Michael H., 3 (note).
Goldfogle, Henry M., 83.
Goldschlager, David, 14, 15.
Goldsmid, of Vienna, 22.
Goldsmid, Sir Francis, 2, 12 (note), 15 (note), 16, 22, 24, 25, 26, 28 (note).
Gorchakov, Prince. See Gortschakoff, Prince.
Gortschakoff (Gorchakov), Prince, 62, 63, 64, 66, 69, 82, 121, 151.
Grant, President U[lysses] S., and the Jewish question in Roumania, 8, 9, 12-13, 110, 112.
Granville, Earl of, 16, 21, 146.
Granville, Lord. See Granville, Earl of.
Green, J., English consul at Bucharest, 19.
Great Britain. See England.
"Great Britain, Foreign Office: Correspondence relating to the Congress of Berlin. . . . ." ref. to, 48 (note).
"Great Britain, Parliamentary Papers," ref. to, 78 (note).
Great Britain, State Papers, ref. to, 3 (note), 15 (note).
    alluded to, 16 (note), 20 (note).
Greece protests against persecution of Jews in Roumania, 19, 110.
    position of the Jews in, 87, 92, 93.
    United States and religious liberty in, 91.

Index. 161

Greek Catholic Church, 85, 87.
Grey, Sir Edward, and memorandum prepared by English Jews on the treaty rights of the Jews of Roumania, 89, 93, 94, 137-153.
Guedemann, Dr. Moritz, 47.
"Gunton's Magazine," ref. to, 80 (note).

"Ha-Carmel," ref. to, 28 (note).
Hahn, ref. to work by, 49 (note), 54 (note), 60 (note).
Hall, alluded to, 96, 97.
Hallgarten, Adolph, 11.
Hanotaux, ref. to work by, 48 (note), 54 (note).
Hansard's Debates, ref. to, 3 (note), 15 (note), 16 (note), 71 (note).
Harrison, President [Benjamin], and the persecution of the Jews in Russia, 85, 112, 113.
Hay, John, 111.
   Roumanian Note of, 2, 80-82, 86, 87, 94, 133-134.
Haymerle, Baron von, 121.
Hearings before the Committee on Foreign Affairs of the House of Representatives, Dec. 11, 1911, on "Termination of the Treaty of 1832 between the United States and Russia," alluded to, 6 (note).
"Hebrews in America" (Markens), alluded to, 9 (note).
Hellman, George S., ref. to, 48 (note).
Hershey, work by, ref. to, 97 (note).
"Histoire des Israélites roumains et le droit d'intervention" (Stambler), alluded to, 77 (note), 78 (note).
"History of the Alliance Israélite Universelle" (Leven), alluded to, 25 (note), 29 (note).
"History of the Jews in America" (Wiernik), ref. to, 80 (note).
Hodges, H. C., work by, cited, 94; quoted, 95 and (note), 96 and (note), 97 and (note).

Hohenlohe-Schillingsfürst, Prince, 51 and (note), 121.
   "Memoirs" of, alluded to, 47 (note).
   ref. to, 51 (note).
   quoted, 62 (note), 75 (note)-76 (note).
Holland rebukes Switzerland for anti-Jewish discriminations, 3 (note).
   and the Jewish question in Roumania and the Balkan States, 16 (note), 102.
Holland, T. E., work by, alluded to, 48 (note).
Horowitz, Leon, work by, alluded to, 28 (note).
House Executive Documents, 1872, 42d Congress, 2d Session, No. 318, ref. to, 17 (note).
House of Commons, Great Britain. See Parliament, British.
House of Representatives, Committee on Foreign Affairs of, hearings on "The Jews of Roumania," 83.
   See also Congress.
Hühner, Leon, alluded to, 28 (note).
"Humanitarian Diplomacy of the United States" (Straus), ref. to, 5 (note), 94 (note).
Hungary. See Austria-Hungary.

Illoria, Italian consul at Bucharest, 19.
Immigration of Roumanian Jews, to the United States, 25, 26, 27 and (note)-28 (note), 29, 80, 134, 149.
   to England, 149.
"International Law" (Oppenheim), quoted, 95 (note)-96 (note).
   ref. to, 97 (note).
"International Law and the Discriminations Practiced by Russia under the Treaty of 1832" (Kuhn), quoted, 4 (note).
Intervention, doctrine of, in behalf of the persecuted, 94, 95, 96 and (note), 97 (note).

12

Isaacs, Lewis M., 1 (note), 12 (note).
Isaacs, Myer S., 12 (note), 24, 27 (note), 28 (note), 31, 33, 39.
Isidor, Chief Rabbi Lazard, 29.
Ismail, Roumania, 14, 15.
"Israelitische Wochenschrift," ref. to, 44 (note), 46, 47 (note), 54 (note).
alluded to, 56 (note).
Italy, and the Jewish question in Roumania and the Balkans, 16, 19, 35, 43, 44, 49, 55 (note), 76 (note), 81, 102, 110, 125, 126, 134, 142, 144.
and the Jewish question at the Congress of Berlin, 51, 53 (note), 108, 115.
champions religious liberty at the Congress of Berlin, 64, 66.

Jacobs, Rev. Henry S., 39.
Jay, John, 20.
Jellinek, George, work by, alluded to, 7 (note).
"Jewish Chronicle" of London, quoted, 24.
ref. to, 39 (note), 44 (note), 45 (note), 47 (note), 71 (note), 74 (note), 76 (note), 77 (note), 93 (note).
"Jewish Encyclopedia," ref. to, 3 (note), 44 (note), 47 (note), 56 (note), 57 (note), 78 (note), 79 (note).
alluded to, 9 (note), 45 (note), 48 (note).
cited, 76 (note).
"Jewish Immigrants—Report of a Special Committee of the National Jewish Immigration Council...." cited, 83 (note).
"Jewish Immigration to the United States from 1881 to 1910" (Joseph), cited, 82.
"Jewish Times," ref. to, 7, 8 (note), 9 and (note), 11, 16 (note), 24 (note), 25 (note), 26 (note), 29 (note).
alluded to, 12, 39 (note).

"Jewish World," ref. to, 48 (note).
"Jews in the Diplomatic Correspondence of the United States" (Adler), alluded to, 4 (note).
ref. to, 41.
"Jews in Roumania, The" (Davis), alluded to, 78 (note).
"Jews in Roumania, The. Account of the Proceedings of the Trial of the Jews at Busen," alluded to, 15 (note).
"Jews of Roumania and the Treaty of Berlin," speech by Hon. Walter M. Chandler in the House of Representatives, 83, 114-137.
Jiriček, work by, alluded to, 80 (note).
Joseph, Samuel, work by, cited, 82.
"Journal du droit international privé," ref. to, 150.
"Journal officiel de la République Française," ref. to, 72 (note).
alluded to, 76 (note).
"Judaeans, The," alluded to, 48 (note).
"Juden in Bulgarien" (Segall), ref. to, 79 (note).
"Juden in Rumänien, Die" (Lazare), alluded to, 78 (note).
"Judenfrage in den Donaufürstenthümern, Die" (Levy), alluded to, 3 (note).
"Juifs en Roumanie" (Sincerus), alluded to, 78, 148.
ref. to, 117.

Kallimachor, Code of, 116.
Kanitz, ref. to work by, 80 (note).
Kann, M., 47, 50, 51.
Karl Anton, Prince, 74, 75.
Karolyi, Baron, 121.
Kasson, John A., diplomatic correspondence of, and the Jews of Roumania, 41, 42, 43, 71, 72, 85.
Kayserling, Dr. M[yer], ref. to, 3 (note).

Index.

"Kirchlich-religiöse Leben bei den Serben, Das" (Razhichlich), alluded to, 79 (note).

Kogalniceano, M. *See* Cogalinceanu.

Kohler, Max J., ref. to work by, 6 (note).

Kohler, Max J., and Wolf, Simon, on "American Contributions toward the Removal of Jewish Disabilities in the Balkan States, ix.

Kompert, Dr. Leopold, 25.

Königswarter, Baron Moritz von, 22, 28 (note).

Krauskopf, Rev. Dr. Joseph, alluded to, 80 (note).

Kristeller, Dr. Samuel, 29.

Kuhn, Arthur K., work by, cited, 4 (note).
alluded to, 28 (note).

Kuranda, Dr. Ignaz, 44.

Landsberg, Dr., 30.

Lasker, Eduard, 16, 43 and (note), 44 (note), 46, 56 (note).

Launay, Count de, 51, 64, 68, 69, 121.

Laurence, J. M., 29.

"Law of Nations" (Twiss), ref. to, 48 (note).

Lawrence, T. J., work by, alluded to, 94 (note).

Lazare, work by, alluded to, 78 (note).

Lazarus, Emma, ref. to work by, 57 (note).

Lazarus, Prof. Moritz, 22, 25, 28 (note).

Le Souard, G., French consul at Bucharest, 19.

Lesseps, Ferdinand de, 4 (note).

Leven, Narcisse, 12 (note), 22, 30.
work by, alluded to, 25 (note), 29 (note), 34, 48, 50, 70, 74.
ref. to, 71.
quoted, 73.

Lévy, Arthur, 29.

Levy, Bernard, work by, alluded to, 3 (note).

"Life and Letters of Bayard Taylor, ref. to, 42 (note).

Lilienthal, Dr. Max, 11.

Lippe, Dr. C., 82.

"List of Works Relating to the History and Condition of the Jews in Various Countries" (Freidus), ref. to, 28 (note).

"List of Works Relating to the Near Eastern Question and the Balkan States," alluded to, 49 (note).

Littauer, Hon. Lucius N., 81.

Loeb, Isidore, 12 (note).
work by, alluded to, 3 (note), 30.
ref. to, 16 (note), 34, 35 (note), 50, 116, 117.

Loewy, A[lbert], 22, 30.
See also Marks, D. W., and Löwy, Albert.

London, peace conference in, 84, 85, 86, 88, 90, 91.

London Board of Deputies of British Jews, 45, 46, 93, 137.

London Roumanian Committee, 24.

Ludwig, King of Hungary, 100.

Lupashku, Prefect, 37.

Luzzatti, Signor, 88.

Macaulay, [Thomas Babington], work by, alluded to, 7 (note).

Majoresco, M., 93.

Mannheimer, Prof. S., ref. to, 56 (note).

Markens, [Isaac], work by, alluded to, 9 (note).

Marks, D. W., and Löwy, Albert, work by, alluded to, 3 (note).
ref. to, 24.

Marsh, Mr., 43.

Marshall, Louis, 1 (note).
correspondence relating to the Jewish question in Roumania, 83, 84-86.

Martens, de, work by, ref. to, 49 (note).
alluded to, 97.

Marx, Prof. Alexander, ix.

Mayhew, Jonathan, alluded to, 109.

Maynard, Horace, diplomatic correspondence of, relating to the Jews in the Balkan States, 30, 31, 33-34.

Melegari, Minister of Foreign Affairs of Italy, 35.
"Memoir of Sir Francis Henry Goldsmid" (Marks and Löwy), alluded to, 3 (note).
ref. to, 24.
"Memoirs of David Blaustein," ref. to, 78 (note).
"Memoirs of M. de Blowitz," alluded to, 49 (note).
Memorial of Alliance Israélite Universelle to the Congress of Berlin, 44, 105-107.
Memorial on behalf of Jews presented to the Constantinople Conference of 1877, 30, 31, 34, 35, 102-105.
"Menorah, The," ref. to, 9 (note), 15 (note).
cited, 12.
"Messages and Papers of the Presidents" (Richardson), ref. to, 9 (note), 17 (note).
Metternich, Prince, 4 (note).
Milan, Prince, 67.
Milobar, work by, alluded to, 48 (note).
Moldavia, the Jewish question in, 2, 20, 37, 102, 103, 104, 112, 117-118, 138, 139.
Monize, Alexander, 116.
Monroe, W. S., work by, quoted, 79.
Montefiore, J. M., 45.
Montefiore, Sir Moses, 2, 12 (note), 22, 48 (note).
Montenegro, Congress of Berlin decrees establishment of religious liberty in, 68, 70, 71, 92, 122, 135.
status of Jews in, after the Treaty of Berlin, 79, 93.
United States and religious liberty in, 91.
Moore, J. Hampton, 83.
Moore, J[ohn] B[assett], ref. to work by, 60 (note).
correspondence relating to the Jewish question in Roumania, 84, 89-92, 94.
Morocco, United States helps Jews in, 88.

Morris, Mr., U. S. Minister at Constantinople, 3.
Münster, Count, 121.
"My First Years as a Frenchwoman" (Waddington), ref. to, 49 (note), 53 (note).
"My Recollections" (Princess Radziwill), quoted, 75 (note).

Napoleon III, protests against persecution of Jews in Roumania, 2-3.
"National Review," ref. to, 78 (note).
alluded to, 83 (note).
Neanes, Greek consul at Bucharest, 19.
Netter, Charles, 12 (note), 30, 35, 36, 47, 48 (note), 50, 65, 72, 73.
"Neueste Geschichte des jüdischen Volkes" (Philippson), ref. to, 79 (note).
"Nouveau Recueil Général" (Martens), ref. to, 49 (note).

"Observations concernant la preuve de la nationalité et l'expulsion par le gouvernement roumains d'Israélites nés et domiciliés en Roumanie" (de Bar), ref. to, 77 (note).
"Official Documents extracted from the Diplomatic Correspondence of 2/14 September, 1878, 17/29 July, 1880," ref. to, 142.
Oppenheim, work by, cited, 95 and (note), 96 (note), 97 (note).
Order Zion, Roumanian society, 22, 23.
Orloff, Prince, 35.
Otis, James, alluded to, 109.
Owens, O. L., work by, alluded to, 60 (note).

Paris, Convention of, 98, 102, 103, 105, 118, 119, 122, 127, 137, 138-140, 141, 150.
Paris, International Jewish conference at, in 1876, 29-36, 43, 45 (note).

memorializes Constantinople Conference on behalf of Jews of Eastern Europe, 30, 31, 34, 35, 102-105.
Paris, International Jewish Conference at, in 1878, 39.
Paris, Treaty of, 102.
Parliament, British, and the Jewish question in Roumania, 15 (note), 16, 139.
"Passport Question, The," ref. to, 6 (note).
Peixotto, Benjamin F., 1, 2, 7 (note), 9-15, 17-24, 25, 26, 27, 39.
"Persecutions of the Jews in Roumania, The" (Schloss), alluded to, 78 (note).
Petition of Roumanian Jews to Chamber of Deputies, 98-101.
"Phases in the History of Religious Liberty in America with Special Reference to the Jews" (Kohler), ref. to, 6 (note).
Philippson, M., ref. to work by, 79 (note).
Phillimore, work by, cited, 96 (note).
Pirbright, Lord. See de Worms, Baron Henry.
Plotke, work by, alluded to, 78 (note).
Poindexter, Miles, 83.
Pollock, Sir Frederick, work by, alluded to, 7 (note).
Powderly, T. V., Commissioner General of Immigration, 109.
"Primacy of the Great Powers, The" (Lawrence), alluded to, 94 (note).
"Protection of American Foreign Missionaries by the United States" (Owens), alluded to, 60 (note).
"Protestant Church and Religious Liberty in France" (Waddington), alluded to, 55 (note).
"Protocols of the Berlin Congress," ref. to, 152.
"Question Israélite en Roumanie, La" (Rey), alluded to, 78 (note).

Rachic, work by, alluded to, 79 (note).
Radziwill, Princess, work by, quoted, 75 (note).
Razhichlich, work by, alluded to, 79 (note).
Reichstag, German, and the Jewish question in Roumania, 16, 43, 44.
"Religious Liberty" (Ruffini), alluded to, 7 (note).
"Religious Liberty in the United States" (Straus), quoted, 5 (note).
Rémusat, M. de, 21, 30.
"Réunion au Faveur des Israélites de l'Orient," ref. to, 29 (note).
"Revue des Deux Mondes," ref. to, 48 (note).
"Revue du droit international," ref. to, 77 (note).
"Revue du droit international public," alluded to, 48 (note).
Rey, work by, alluded to, 78.
Richardson, ref. to work by, 9 (note), 17 (note).
Ristitch, 52, 67, 72.
Roggenbach, alluded to, 51 (note).
Roosevelt, President Theodore, and the Jewish question in Roumania, 81, 82, 111-114.
Root, Elihu, alluded to, 80 (note).
Rosenbach, Dr. A. S. W., ix.
Rosenfeld, Lazarus, 11.
Rosetti, M., quoted, 128-129, 150.
Rothschild, Baron, 28 (note).
Rothschild, Lionel de, 45.
Roumania, the United States and the Jewish question in, ix, 1, 2, 3, 6-24, 25, 26, 27, 28, 30-34, 36-38, 39, 41-42, 43, 80, 81, 82-93, 108-114, 114-115, 133-134, 136, 149.
disabilities and persecutions suffered by Jews in, 2-3, 6, 8, 14-16, 29, 32, 36, 37, 78, 81, 87, 88, 95, 99-101, 102, 103, 104, 105, 106, 107, 108, 109, 110, 111, 112-113, 115, 116-120, 122, 123, 127, 128, 129-131, 132, 133, 134, 135, 138,

139-140, 141, 145, 146-148, 149.
European Powers and the Jewish question in, 15-21, 24, 32, 34, 35, 43, 44, 45, 73, 74, 75, 82 (note), 104, 110.
Jews of, petition for civil and political rights, 25, 28, 98-101.
three international Jewish conferences in behalf of Jews in, 25-39.
the Jewish question in, and the Congress of Berlin, 41, 42, 43, 49, 50, 52, 66, 68, 69, 76 (note), 95, 108, 114, 151-152.
Jews render patriotic services in, 47 (note), 99, 107.
Congress of Berlin decrees establishment of religious liberty in, 65-67, 70, 71, 85, 92, 114, 122-124, 140-141.
the Jewish question in, after the Congress of Berlin, 73, 74, 75, 76 and (note), 77, 93-94, 95, 108-114, 124-126, 127, 128, 129, 135, 136, 137, 142-146, 148-153.
speech of Hon. Walter M. Chandler on the Jews of, and the Treaty of Berlin, 83, 114-137.
memorandum presented by English Jews to Sir Edward Grey on the Treaty rights of the Jews of, 89, 93, 137-153.
promises full rights to Bulgarian Jews transferred to her, 92, 93.
and the right of intervention in behalf of persecuted Jews, 95, 96.
"Roumania and America" (Horowitz), alluded to, 28 (note).
"Roumania and the Legal Status of the Jews in Roumania" (Bluntschli), quoted, 76-77.
"Roumania as a Persecuting Power" (Conybeare), ref. to, 78 (note).
Roumanian Emigration Society, 26.
Roumanian Note of John Hay, 2, 80-82, 86, 87, 133-134, 149.

"Romanul," ref. to, 128, 150.
Roumelia, Eastern, religious liberty in, and the Congress of Berlin, 42, 55, 56, 58, 59 and (note), 60, 61.
status of Jews in, after the Congress of Berlin, 73, 79.
Jews persecuted in, 107.
"Royaume de Serbie, Le" (Rachle), alluded to, 79 (note)-80 (note).
Ruffini, Francesco, work by, alluded to, 7 (note).
"Rumänische Post," alluded to, 12 (note), 22.
"Rumänischen Juden unter dem Fürsten und König Karl, Die" (Plotke), alluded to, 78 (note).
Russell, Lord, 51, 121.
Russell, Lord John, 51.
Russia, United States abrogates treaty with, 6 (note).
and the Jewish question in Roumania and the Balkan States, 15 (note), 16, 21, 35, 76 (note), 81, 115, 134, 146.
position of the Jews in, 47 (note), 63, 64, 96, 113.
and the Jewish question at the Congress of Berlin, 49, 50, 61, 63, 108.
attitude toward religious liberty at the Congress of Berlin, 58, 61, 64, 66-67.
Russo-Turkish War, 36, 39, 40, 120.

Sadullah Bey, 121.
St. Vallier, de, 50, 70, 121.
Salisbury, Lord. See Salisbury, Marquess of.
Salisbury, Marquess of, 30, 46, 49, 56 (note), 58, 59, 60, 61, 62, 67, 68, 71 and (note), 77, 121.
Salonika, 87.
Salomon, Barnett L., 11.
San Stefano, Treaty of, 40, 41, 46, 52, 54 (note), 56 (note), 59 (note), 61, 120.
Schaff, Rev. Dr. Philip, work by, alluded to, 6 (note).
Schenck, Robert C., 21.
Schechter, Solomon, 82.

Schiff, Jacob H., 1 (note), 39, 81, 111.
   letter from Oscar S. Straus to, on the Jewish question in Roumania, 108-111.
Schlechta, Austro-Hungarian consul at Bucharest, 19.
Schloss, D. F., work by, alluded to, 78 (note).
Schouvaloff (Shuvalov), Count, 47 (note), 56, 58, 61, 64, 121.
   work by, alluded to, 48 (note).
Schulthess, ref. to work by, 149.
Schurz, Carl, 11.
Schwarzfeld, Elie, 82.
   ref. to work by, 78 (note).
Segall, ref. to work by, 79 (note).
Seligman, Isaac, 12 (note), 25, 26.
Seligman, Jesse, 11.
Seligman, Joseph, 11, 12 (note).
Seligman, William, 29, 30.
Senate, United States. *See* Congress.
Serbia, disabilities and persecutions suffered by Jews in, 2, 3, 29, 31, 34, 63, 102, 103, 105, 106, 107.
   the Jewish question in, and the Congress of Berlin, 49, 50, 52, 63, 67, 151-152.
   Congress of Berlin decrees establishment of religious liberty in, 61, 62, 63, 64, 65, 68, 70, 71, 92, 122.
   status of Jews in, after the Congress of Berlin, 72-73, 74, 79, 92, 93, 135.
   United States and religious liberty in, 91.
"Serbien und das Serbenvolk" (Kanitz), ref. to, 80 (note).
"Servia and the Servians" (Stead), ref. to, 80 (note).
Seward, William H., 3.
Shaftesbury, Earl of, 16.
   quoted, 112.
Shaftesbury, Lord. *See* Shaftesbury, Earl of.
Shuvalov, Count. *See* Schouvaloff, Count.
Silberman, Jacob, 14, 15.
Simon, Sir John, 15 (note).

Sincerus, work by, ref. to, 117, 121, 129, 130, 131.
   alluded to, 78 (note), 148.
Singer, B., 30.
"Situation, La des Israélites en Turquie, en Serbie et en Roumaine" (Loeb), alluded to, 3 (note), 30.
   ref. to, 116.
"Situation of the Jews in Roumania since the Treaty of Berlin," ref. to, 78 (note).
Sloane, work by, alluded to, 80 (note).
Smith, Charles Emory, U. S. Minister to Russia, 113.
Solomons, Adolphus S., 12 (note).
"Souvenirs inédits du Congrès de Berlin" (Carathéodory Pasha), alluded to, 48 (note).
"Souvenirs inédits du Congrès de Berlin" (Schouvaloff), alluded to, 48 (note).
Spear, Rev. Dr. Samuel T., quoted, 5 (note).
Stambler, work by, alluded to, 77 (note), 78 (note), 94 (note); ref. to, 97 (note).
Stanley, Lord. *See* Derby, Earl of.
"Stateman's Year Book," ref. to, 149.
Stead, ref. to work by, 80 (note).
Stefan III, 100.
Stern, Dr. Adolf, 27, 82.
   work by, alluded to, 9 (note), 12, 22.
   ref. to, 25 (note), 26 (note).
   correspondence regarding persecution of Jews in Roumania, 36-38.
Stern, Myer, 39.
Stöcker, 75 (note), 76 (note).
"Story of the Roumanian Mission" (Peixotto), cited, 12.
Straus, Oscar S., 1 (note).
   work by, cited, 5 (note).
   ref. to, 48 (note), 94 (note).
   alluded to, 80 (note).
   and the Jewish question in Roumania, 81, 82, 108-114.
Stroock, S. M., ref. to work by, 3 (note).

"Studies in Contemporary Biography" (Bryce), alluded to, 57 (note).
"Studies in International Law" (Holland), alluded to, 49 (note).
Sturdza, ref. to work by, 139.
Sullotis, M., quoted, 128, 150.
Sumner, Charles, 8, 11, 94.
Switzerland, foreign governments insist on equality for their Jewish subjects in, 3 and (note), 4 (note).
and the Jewish question in the Balkan States, 102.
"Switzerland and American Jews" (Stroock), ref. to, 3 (note).

Taft, President William H., and the Jewish question in Roumania, 84.
"Tagebuchblätter" (Busch), alluded to, 47 (note), 56 (note).
Taylor, Bayard, 42.
"Termination of the Treaty between the United States and Russia," alluded to, 6 (note).
"Theory of Persecution" (Pollock), alluded to, 7 (note).
Thidan, German consul at Bucharest, 19.
"Times, The," of London, ref. to, 60 (note).
Toizé, M., 51.
"Traité de Berlin annoté et commenté" (Brunswik), alluded to, 48 (note).
"Treaty of 1832 with Russia," alluded to, 6 (note).
Tripoli, 5 (note).
Turkey, demands equality of treatment for Ottoman Jews from Austria, 4 (note).
and the Jewish question in Roumania and the Balkan States, 21, 31, 81, 115, 134.
position of non-Musselman subjects in, 31, 34, 35, 39, 53 (note)-54 (note), 55 (note), 57 (note), 58, 59 and (note), 60 (note), 61, 66, 67-68, 84, 85, 87, 102, 103, 105, 106, 149, 150.

religious liberty in, and the Congress of Berlin, 53 (note)-54 (note), 55 (note), 57 (note), 58, 59 and (note), 60, 61, 74.
acquiesces in independence of Serbia, 61-62.
champions religious liberty at the Congress of Berlin, 64, 67, 108.
Twiss, ref. to work by, 48 (note).

United States, the protagonist of religious liberty, ix, 1, 3, 4-5 and (note), 6 and (note), 7 (note), 8, 13, 18, 20, 30, 42, 80, 86, 88, 89, 94, 102, 112-113, 132.
and the Jewish question in Roumania and the Balkan States, 1, 2, 3, 6, 7-14, 15-21, 32-34, 41, 42, 55 (note), 75, 79, 80-93, 110, 111-114, 133-134, 135, 136, 149.
secures equality of rights for Jews in Switzerland, 3.
aids persecuted Jews of Damascus, 4, 88.
insisting on equal treatment of all citizens abroad, abrogates treaty with Russia, 6 (note).
diplomatic correspondence of, relating to Jews in the Balkan States, 13, 18, 19-20, 21, 30, 31, 32-34, 36-38, 41, 42, 71-72, 80, 112-113, 133-134, 149.
aids persecuted Jews of Morocco, 88.
pleads for persecuted Jews at the Algeciras Conference, 88, 89.
urges establishment of religious liberty in the Balkan States at the Conference of Bucharest, 92-93.
United States House of Representatives. See Congress.
United States Senate. See Congress.
U. S. Senate Document, 1872, 42d Congress, 2d Session, No. 75, ref. to, 17 (note).
"U. S. Senate Document No. 611, 63d Congress, 2d Session," cited, 83 (note).

U. S. Senate Hearings before Committee on Foreign Relations on "Treaty of 1832," alluded to, 6 (note).

"Unveiling and Consecration of the John Hay Memorial Window at the Temple of the Reform Congregation Keneseth Israel, Philadelphia," 80 (note).

Van Buren, Martin, 4.
Veneziani, F., 30, 39, 47, 50.
Vilcova, Roumania, 19.
von Beust, Count, 45 (note).

Waddington, Mary King, ref. to work by, 49 (note), 53 (note).
Waddington, William Henry, 53 and (note), 54 (note), 55 (note), 56, 57, 58, 59, 60, 62, 63, 64, 65, 66, 70, 72, 76 (note), 121, 151.
Wahrmann, Moritz, 44.
Wallachia, the Jewish question in, 20, 102-103, 104, 112, 117-118, 138, 139, 151.
"Was the Earl of Beaconsfield a Representative Jew?" (Lazarus), ref. to, 57 (note).
Washburne, Elihu B., 20, 21, 30.
Washington, [George], 5 (note).
Watchorn, Robert, report of, on immigration of Roumanian Jews to the United States, 109, 111.

Wertheimer, Ritter Josef von, 12 (note), 22.
"What Shall We Do with Our Immigrants?" (Peixotto), quoted, 13-14.
Wheaton, ref. to work by, 94 (note).
White, Andrew D., quoted, 43 (note)-44 (note).
White, Sir William, 124, 142.
Whitman, S., work by, alluded to, 3 (note).
Wiernik, [Peter], ref. to work by, 80 (note).
William I, Emperor of Germany, 56 (note), 75 and (note), 76 (note).
Wilson, President Woodrow, and the Jewish question in Roumania, 84.
Winchester, Mr., 8.
Wolf, Lucien, ref. to, 47 (note), 56 (note).
alluded to, 57 (note).
Wolf, Simon, 7, 8, 9, 11, 12 and (note), 13, 21, 24, 33, 81.
See also Kohler, Max J., and Wolf, Simon.

Young, J. R., ref. to work by, 49 (note).

"Zeitschrift für Demographie und Statistik der Juden," ref. to, 79 (note).

The Bloch Publishing Company, 40 E. 14th Street, New York City, is selling agent for the Society.

Publication No. 1, 1893 (143 pp.), containing the following papers:

Address of the President. *Hon. Oscar S. Straus.*
The Settlement of the Jews in Georgia. *Chas. C. Jones, Jr., LL. D.*
Mickvé Israel Congregation of Philadelphia. *Rev. Sabato Morais, LL. D.*
Some Unpublished Material relating to Dr. Jacob Lumbrozo, of Maryland. *Dr. J. H. Hollander.*
Beginnings of New York Jewish History. *Max J. Kohler, M. A.*
Notes on the Jews of Philadelphia, from Published Annals. *Prof. Morris Jastrow, Jr.*
The First Publication of a Jewish character printed in Philadelphia. *Prof. Morris Jastrow, Jr.*
Jews Mentioned in the Journal of the Continental Congress. *Dr. Herbert Friedenwald.*
A Landmark. *N. Taylor Phillips, LL. B.*
An Act allowing Naturalization of Jews in the Colonies. *Hon. Simon W. Rosendale.*
Jewish Beginnings in Kentucky. *Lewis N. Dembitz.*
A Document Concerning the Franks Family. *Hon. Simon W. Rosendale.*
Jews in the American Plantations between 1600 and 1700. *Dr. Cyrus Adler.*
Americana at the Anglo-Jewish Exhibition. *Dr. Cyrus Adler.*
A Political Document of the Year 1800. *Dr. Cyrus Adler.*
The Settlement of Jews in Canada. *Andrew C. Joseph.*
Notes and Index.

2d edition, postpaid, $1.50.

No. 2, 1894 (207 pp.), containing the following papers:

Address of the President. *Hon. Oscar S. Straus.*
A Sketch of Haym Salomon. *Prof. Herbert B. Adams, Ph. D.*
On the History of the Jews of Chicago. *Dr. B. Felsenthal.*
The Jewish Congregation in Surinam. *Dr. B. Felsenthal.*
A Sermon by Moses Mendelssohn, printed in Philadelphia 130 years ago. *Dr. B. Felsenthal.*
The Civil Status of the Jews in Maryland, 1634-1776. *J. H. Hollander, Ph. D.*
Family History of the Reverend David Mendez Machado. *N. Taylor Phillips, LL. B.*
Note concerning David Hays and Esther Etting his Wife, and Michael Hays and Reuben Etting, their Brothers, Patriots of the Revolution. *Solomon Solis-Cohen.*
The Colonization of America by the Jews. *Dr. M. Kayserling.*
Phases of Jewish Life in New York before 1800. *Max J. Kohler.*
The Lopez and Rivera Families of Newport. *Max J. Kohler.*
A Letter of Jonas Phillips to the Federal Convention. *Herbert Friedenwald, Ph. D.*
Jacob Isaacs and his Method of Converting Salt Water into Fresh Water. *Herbert Friedenwald, Ph. D.*
Memorial presented to the Continental Congress. *Herbert Friedenwald, Ph. D.*
Columbus in Jewish Literature. *Prof. R. J. H. Gottheil.*
Settlement of the Jews in Texas. *Rev. Henry Cohen.*
Aaron Levy. *Mrs. Isabella H. Rosenbach and Abraham S. Wolf Rosenbach.*
Documents from the Public Record Office (London). *Dr. Charles Gross.*
Memoir of John Moss. *Lucien Moss.*

Postpaid, $2.00.

No. 3, 1895 (176 pp.), containing the following papers:

Address of the President. *Hon. Oscar S. Straus.*
Some further References relating to Haym Salomon. *Dr. J. H. Hollander.*
The Earliest Rabbis and Jewish Writers of America. *Dr. M. Kayserling.*
The American Jew as Soldier and Patriot. *Hon. Simon Wolf.*
Points in the First Chapter of New York Jewish History. *Albion Morris Dyer.*
An Early Ownership of Real Estate in Albany, New York, by a Jewish Trader. *Hon. Simon W. Rosendale.*
Phases of Jewish Life in New York before 1800. II. *Max J. Kohler.*
Correspondence between Washington and Jewish Citizens. *Lewis Abraham.*
The Relation of Jews to our National Monuments. *Lewis Abraham.*
Early Jewish Literature in America. *George Alexander Kohut.*
Notes. *Morris Jastrow, Jr., Herbert Friedenwald, Cyrus Adler.*

Postpaid, $1.50.

No. 4, 1896 (243 pp.), containing the following papers:

Chronological Sketch of the History of the Jews in Surinam. *Dr. B. Felsenthal and Prof. Richard Gottheil.*
The Jews in Texas. *Rev. Henry Cohen.*
The Jews of Richmond. *Jacob Ezekiel.*
Trial of Jorge de Almeida by the Inquisition in Mexico (with a fac-simile illustration). *Dr. Cyrus Adler.*
Incidents Illustrative of American Jewish Patriotism. *Max J. Kohler.*
Jewish Martyrs of the Inquisition in South America. *George Alexander Kohut.*
The Levy and Seixas Families of Newport and New York. *N. Taylor Phillips.*
A Biographical Account of Ephraim Hart and his son Dr. Joel Hart, of New York. *Gustavus N. Hart.*

Postpaid, $2.00.

No. 5, 1897 (234 pp.), containing the following papers:

Frontispiece: *Portrait of Isaac Franks.*
Address of the President. *Hon. Oscar S. Straus.*
Documents relating to the Career of Colonel Isaac Franks. *Professor Morris Jastrow, Jr.*
Some Cases in Pennsylvania wherein Rights claimed by Jews are affected. *John Samuel.*
Henry Castro, Pioneer and Colonist. *Rev. Henry Cohen.*
Material for the History of the Jews in the British West Indies. *Dr. Herbert Friedenwald.*
Naturalization of Jews in the American Colonies under the Act of 1740. *Dr. J. H. Hollander.*
Who was the First Rabbi of Surinam? *George A. Kohut.*
Isaac Aboab, the First Jewish Author in America. *Dr. M. Kayserling.*
The Jews and the American Anti-Slavery Movement. *Max J. Kohler.*
Documents relative to Major David S. Franks, while Aid-de-camp to General Arnold. *Abraham S. Wolf Rosenbach.*
Notes on the First Settlement of Jews in Pennsylvania, 1655-1703. *Abraham S. Wolf Rosenbach.*
Notes. *Herbert Friedenwald, J. H. Hollander, A. S. Wolf Rosenbach.*

Postpaid, $2.00.

No. 6, 1897 (180 pp.), *containing the following papers:*

Address of the Corresponding Secretary. *Dr. Cyrus Adler.*
A Memorial sent by German Jews to the President of the Continental Congress. *Dr. M. Kayserling.*
Documents relating to the Attempted Departure of the Jews from Surinam in 1675. *Dr. J. H. Hollander.*
A Modern Maccabean. *Rev. Henry Cohen.*
Notice of Jacob Mordecai, Founder and Proprietor from 1809 to 1815 of the Warrenton (N. C.) Female Seminary. *Gratz Mordecai.*
Some Newspaper Advertisements of the Eighteenth Century. *Dr. Herbert Friedenwald.*
The Jews in Newport. *Max J. Kohler.*
Civil Status of the Jews in Colonial New York. *Max J. Kohler.*
The Oldest Tombstone Inscriptions of Philadelphia and Richmond. *George A. Kohut.*
A Literary Autobiography of Mordecai Manuel Noah. *George A. Kohut.*
The Congregation Shearith Israel. An Historical Review. *N. Taylor Phillips.*
Growth of Jewish Population in the United States. *David Sulzberger.*
Notes.

Postpaid, $1.50.

No. 7, 1899 (134 pp.), *containing the following:*

Trial of Gabriel de Granada by the Inquisition in Mexico, 1642-1645. Translated from the original by *David Fergusson*, of Seattle, Washington. Edited with notes by *Cyrus Adler.*

Postpaid, $1.50.

No. 8, 1900 (168 pp.), *containing the following papers:*

Address of the President. *Hon. Oscar S. Straus, LL. D.*
Asser Levy, A Noted Jewish Burgher of New Amsterdam. *Leon Hühner, A. M., LL. B.*
Site of the First Synagogue of the Congregation Shearith Israel of New York. *Albion Morris Dyer.*
The Jewish Pioneers of the Ohio Valley. *David Philipson, D. D.*
A Brave Frontiersman. *Rev. Henry Cohen.*
Some Early American Zionist Projects. *Max J. Kohler, A. M., LL. B.*
Ezra Stiles and the Jews. *Rev. W. Willner.*
Notes on Myer Hart and Other Jews of Easton, Pennsylvania. *Gustavus N. Hart.*
Some References to Early Jewish Cemeteries in New York City. *Elvira N. Solis.*
Persecution of the Jews in 1840. *Jacob Ezekiel.*
Notes. *Herbert Friedenwald.*

Postpaid, $1.50.

No. 9, 1901 (190 pp.), containing the following papers:

Address of the President. *Dr. Cyrus Adler.*
A Plea for an American Jewish Historical Exhibition. *Joseph Jacobs, B. A.*
Fray Joseph Diaz Pimienta, alias Abraham Diaz Pimienta, and the Auto-de-Fé held at Seville, July 25, 1720. *Prof. Richard Gottheil.*
The Early Jewish Settlement at Lancaster, Pennsylvania. *Henry Necarsulmer, A. M., LL. B.*
Jews and the American Anti-Slavery Movement. II. *Max J. Kohler, A. M., LL. B.*
Isaac Levy's Claim to Property in Georgia. *Herbert Friedenwald, Ph. D.*
The History of the First Russian-American Jewish Congregation. *J. D. Eisenstein.*
Whence came the First Jewish Settlers of New York? *Leon Hühner, A.M., LL. B.*
The German-Jewish Migration to America. *Max J. Kohler, A. M., LL. B.*
Francis Salvador, a Prominent Patriot of the Revolutionary War. *Leon Hühner, A. M., LL. B.*
Notes on the History of the Earliest German-Jewish Congregation in America. *Rev. Dr. Henry Berkowitz.*
Contributions to the History of the Jews in Surinam. (Illustrated.) *Prof. Richard Gottheil.*
Notes. *Prof. Richard Gottheil, Rev. H. P. Mendes, Miss Elvira N. Solis, Rev. G. A. Kohut, Max J. Kohler, Herbert Friedenwald, H. C. Ezekiel.*

Postpaid, $1.50.

No. 10, 1902 (202 pp.), containing the following papers:

Address of the President. *Dr. Cyrus Adler.*
References to Jews in the Diary of Ezra Stiles. *Prof. Morris Jastrow, Jr.*
A Method of Determining the Jewish Population of Large Cities in the United States. *George E. Barnett, Ph. D.*
Jewish Activity in American Colonial Commerce. *Max J. Kohler, A. M.*
The Jews of Georgia in Colonial Times. *Leon Hühner, A. M., LL. B.*
The Cincinnati Community in 1825. *David Philipson, D. D.*
New Light on the Career of Colonel David S. Franks. *Oscar S. Straus, LL.D.*
Sampson Simson. *Myer S. Isaacs.*
The Damascus Affair of 1840 and the Jews of America. *Joseph Jacobs, B. A.*
Solomon Heydenfeldt: A Jewish Jurist of Alabama and California. *Albert M. Friedenberg, B. S.*
The Jews in Curacao. *G. Herbert Cone.*
Notes. *Max J. Kohler, Herbert Friedenwald, Leon Hühner.*

Postpaid, $2.00.

No. 11, 1903 (238 pp.), containing the following papers:

Address of the President. *Dr. Cyrus Adler.*
Switzerland and American Jews. *Sol. M. Stroock, A. M.*
Phases in the History of Religious Liberty in America with Special Reference to the Jews. *Max J. Kohler, A. M., LL. B.*
The Jews of New England (other than Rhode Island) prior to 1800. *Leon Hühner, A. M., LL. B.*
The Jews and the American Sunday Laws. *Albert M. Friedenberg, B. S., LL. B.*
The Jews of Chicago. *H. Eliassof.*
New Matter relating to Mordecai M. Noah. *G. Herbert Cone.*
Note on Isaac Gomez and Lewis Moses Gomez, from an Old Family Record. *Miss Elvira N. Solis.*
Report of the Committee on Collections of the American Jewish Historical Society. *Joseph Jacobs.*
Items relating to the History of the Jews of New York. *N. Taylor Phillips, LL. B.*
The Trial of Francisco Maldonado de Silva. *George A. Kohut.*
Notes.

Postpaid, $2.00.

No. 12, 1904 (205 pp.), containing the following papers:

Address of the President. *Dr. Cyrus Adler.*
The Inquisition in Peru. *Elkan Nathan Adler.*
The Jews of South Carolina from the Earliest Settlement to the End of the American Revolution. *Leon Hühner, A. M., LL. B.*
Judah P. Benjamin: Statesman and Jurist. *Max J. Kohler, A. M., LL. B.*
Calendar of American Jewish Cases. *Albert M. Friedenberg, B. S., LL. B.*
The Jews in Boston till 1875. *Joseph Lebowich.*
A History of the Jews of Mobile. *Rev. Alfred G. Moses.*
A Jewish Army Chaplain. *Myer S. Isaacs.*
The Development of Jewish Casuistic Literature in America. *J. D. Eisenstein.*
Jewish Heretics in the Philippines in the Sixteenth and Seventeenth Century. *George Alexander Kohut.*
Outline of a Plan to Gather Statistics Concerning the Jews of the United States. *Wm. B. Hackenburg.*
Notes and Necrology. *Leon Hühner, Louis Grossman, Joseph Lebowich, Helen Wise Molony, A. M. Friedenberg, and I. S. Isaacs.*

Postpaid, $2.00.

No. 13, 1905 (107 pp.), containing the following papers:

Naturalization of Jews in New York under the Act of 1740. *Leon Hühner, A. M., LL. B.*
Phases of Religious Liberty in America with Particular Reference to the Jews. II. *Max J. Kohler, A. M., LL. B.*
Are There Traces of the Ten Lost Tribes in Ohio? *David Philipson.*
Jewish Beginnings in Michigan Before 1850. *Hon. David E. Heineman.*
"Old Mordecai"—The Founder of the City of Montgomery. *Rabbi A. J. Messing, Jr.*
The History of the Jews of Montgomery. *Rabbi Alfred G. Moses.*
A German Jewish Poet on America. *Albert M. Friedenberg, B. S., LL. B.*
Judah Touro, Merchant and Philanthropist. *Max J. Kohler, A. M., LL. B.*
Isaac De Pinto. *Leon Hühner, A. M., LL. B.*
Additional Notes on the History of the Jews of Surinam. *J. S. Roos, Rabbi of Dutch Congregation, Paramaribo.*
Notes.

Postpaid, $1.50.

No. 14, 1906 (262 pp.), containing the following:

The Two Hundred and Fiftieth Anniversary of the Settlement of the Jews in the United States. Addresses delivered at Carnegie Hall, New York, on Thanksgiving Day, MCMV, together with other Selected Addresses and Proceedings.

Postpaid, $1.50.

(5)

No. 15, 1906 (122 pp.), *containing the following:*

Jews in the Diplomatic Correspondence of the United States. Being the Address Delivered by *Cyrus Adler, Ph. D.,* President of the American Jewish Historical Society, at the Thirteenth Annual Meeting held in Cincinnati, Ohio, February 27, 1905.

Postpaid, $1.00.

No. 16, 1907 (230 pp.), *containing the following papers:*

Address of the President. *Dr. Cyrus Adler.*
Some Further Notes on the History of the Jews in Surinam. *Rev. P. A. Hilfman.*
Some Jewish Factors in the Settlement of the West. *Max J. Kohler, A. M., LL. B.*
The Struggle for Religious Liberty in North Carolina, with Special Reference to the Jews. *Leon Hühner, A. M., LL. B.*
Jacob Philadelphia, Mystic and Physicist. *Julius F. Sachse.*
Jacob Philadelphia and Frederick the Great. *Prof. Dr. Ludwig Geiger.*
An Early Jewish colony in Western Guiana, 1658-1666; And its Relation to the Jews in Surinam, Cayenne and Tobago. *Samuel Oppenheim.*
Notes.

Postpaid, $2.00.

No. 17, 1909 (300 pp.), *containing the following papers:*

Address of the President. *Dr. Cyrus Adler.*
Dr. Rodrigo Lopez, Queen Elizabeth's Jewish Physician, and his Relations to America. *Max J. Kohler, A. M., LL. B.*
Original Unpublished Documents Relating to Thomas Tremino de Sobremonte (1638). *Dr. Cyrus Adler.*
The Jews of New Jersey from the Earliest Times to 1850. *Albert M. Friedenberg, B. S., LL. B.*
A Contemporary Memorial Relating to Damages to Spanish Interests in America Done by Jews of Holland (1634). *Dr. Cyrus Adler.*
An Early Jewish Colony in Western Guiana: Supplemental Data. *Samuel Oppenheim.*
General Ulysses S. Grant and the Jews. *Joseph Lebowich.*
The Correspondence Between Solomon Etting and Henry Clay. *Walter H. Liebmann.*
The Jews of Georgia from the Outbreak of the American Revolution to the Close of the 18th Century. *Leon Hühner, A. M., LL. B.*
Lincoln and the Jews. *Isaac Markens.*
Some Notes on the Early History of the Sheftalls of Georgia. *Edmund H. Abrahams.*
The First Jew to Hold the Office of Governor of One of the United States. *Leon Hühner, A. M., LL. B.*
Notes.

Postpaid, $2.00.

No. 18, 1909 (276 *pp.*), *containing the following papers:*

The Early History of the Jews in New York, 1654-1664, Some New Matter on the Subject. *Samuel Oppenheim.*
"A Burial Place for the Jewish Nation Forever" *Rosalie S. Phillips.*
A Memorial of Jews to Parliament Concerning Jewish Participation in Colonial Trade, 1696. *Max J. Kohler, A. M., LL. B.*
Notes on the History of the Jews in Barbados. *N. Darnell Davis, C. M. G.*
The Jews' Tribute in Jamaica. Extracted from the Journals of the House of Assembly of Jamaica. *George Fortunatus Judah.*
Notes on the History of the Jews in Surinam. *Rev. P. A. Hilfman.*
Notes.

Postpaid, $2.00.

No. 19, 1910 (285 *pp.*), *containing the following papers:*

The Jews and Masonry in the United States before 1810. *Samuel Oppenheim.*
A List of Jews Who were Grand Masters of Masons in Various States of this Country. *Albert M. Friedenberg, B. S., LL. B.*
Jews in Connection with the Colleges of the Thirteen Original States prior to 1800. *Leon Hühner, A. M., LL. B.*
The Beginnings of Russo-Jewish Immigration to Philadelphia. *David Sulzberger.*
Some Additional Notes on the History of the Jews of South Carolina. Contributed by *Leon Hühner.*
Notes.

Postpaid, $2.00.

No. 20, 1911 (209 *pp.*), *containing the following papers:*

Societies for the Promotion of the Study of Jewish History. *Alexander Marx, Ph. D.*
Unpublished Correspondence between Thomas Jefferson and Some American Jews. Contributed by *Max J. Kohler.*
Hebrew Learning among the Puritans of New England prior to 1700. *Rev. D. de Sola Pool, Ph. D.*
The Jews of Virginia from the Earliest Times to the Close of the Eighteenth Century. *Leon Hühner, A. M., LL. B.*
Joseph Simon Cohen. *Charles J. Cohen.*
A List of Jews Made Denizens in the Reigns of Charles II and James II, 1661-1687. Contributed by *Samuel Oppenheim.*
Francisco de Faria, an American Jew, and the Popish Plot. *Lee M. Friedman, A. B., LL. B.*
Documents Regarding the Thanksgiving Proclamation of Governor Hoyt, of Pennsylvania (1880). Contributed by *William B. Hackenburg.*
Rhode Island and Consanguineous Jewish Marriages. *Benjamin H. Hartogensis, A. B.*
Notes.

Postpaid, $2.00.

No. 21, 1913 (336 pp.), containing the following:

Preface and Introduction.
Biographical Sketch of Rev. Jacques Judah Lyons.
The Earliest Extant Minute Book of the Spanish and Portuguese Congregation Shearith Israel in New York, 1728-1760.
Minute Book of the Spanish and Portuguese Congregation Shearith Israel in New York, 1760-1786.
Biographical Sketch of Naphtali Phillips.
Sketch of the Spanish and Portuguese Congregation Shearith Israel, written about 1855. *Naphtali Phillips.*
Biographical Sketch of Mordecai Manuel Noah.
Address of Mordecai Manuel Noah, delivered in 1825.
Glossary and Index.
  This volume has twelve (12) illustrations, consisting of portraits, views and facsimiles.

Postpaid, $3.00.

Index, 1914 (600 pp.), containing the following:

Preface.
Index to Publications Numbers 1 to 20.
An Index to the Jewish Encyclopedia, Containing References to Articles That Deal With the History of the Jews in the United States. *Samuel P. Abelow, M. A.*
Advertisement.

Postpaid, $3.50.

No. 22, 1914 (325 pp.), containing the following papers:

Preface and Reports.
Judah Monis, First Instructor in Hebrew at Harvard University. (Illustrated by facsimile of advertisement of Monis' Grammar.) *Lee M. Friedman, A. B., LL. B.*
David Nassy of Surinam and his "Lettre Politico-Theologico-Morale sur les Juifs." *Sigmund Seeligmann.*
The Chapters of Isaac the Scribe: A Bibliographical Rarity, New York, 1772. *Samuel Oppenheim.*
The Original of Scott's Rebecca. *Joseph Jacobs, Litt. D.*
Some Phases of the Condition of the Jews in Spain in the Thirteenth and Fourteenth Centuries. *Rabbi Abraham A. Neuman, A. M., D. H. L.*
The Correspondence of Jews with President Martin Van Buren. Contributed by *Albert M. Friedenberg.*
America in Hebrew Literature. *Rev. Dr. Mendel Silber.*
Life of Hon. Henry M. Phillips. *J. Bunford Samuel.*
Jews in the Legal and Medical Professions in America prior to 1800. *Leon Hühner, A. M., LL. B.*
Notes on American Jewish History. *Rev. D. de Sola Pool, Ph. D.*
Notes. *I. Abrahams, N. Darnell Davis, Samuel Oppenheim, Albert M. Friedenberg, Leon Hühner, Max J. Kohler, David Philipson, and B. H. Hartogensis.*
Necrology.

Postpaid, $2.50.

No. 23, 1915 (257 pp.), *containing the following papers:*

Preface and Reports.

The Gratz Papers. *William Vincent Byars.*

Documents Relating to the History of the Jews in Jamaica and Barbados in the Time of William III. Contributed by *Frank Cundall, N. Darnell Davis, and Albert M. Friedenberg.*

The Startling Experience of a Jewish Trader during Pontiac's Siege of Detroit in 1763. *Hon. David E. Heineman.*

A Sketch of the Life of David Lindo. *Alicia Lindo.*

Proceedings Relating to the Expulsion of Ezekiel Hart from the House of Assembly of Lower Canada. Contributed by *Rabbi Julius J. Price.*

Some Jewish Associates of John Brown. *Leon Hühner, A. M., LL. B.*

Early Jewish Residents in Massachusetts. *Lee M. Friedman, A. B., LL. B.*

Report of the Foreign Archives Committee. *Albert M. Friedenberg, Chairman.*

Dr. Abraham Bettmann, a Pioneer Physician of Cincinnati. *Gotthard Deutsch, Ph. D.*

References to Jews in the Correspondence of John J. Crittenden. Contributed by *Cyrus Adler and Albert M. Friedenberg.*

A Spanish-American Jewish Periodical. *Rabbi Martin Zielonka.*

Unpublished Canadian State Papers Relating to Benjamin Hart. Contributed by *Rabbi Julius J. Price.*

The Sephardic Congregation of Baltimore. *Benjamin H. Hartogensis, A. B.*

Wills of Early Jewish Settlers in New York. Contributed by *Lee M. Friedman.*

Jews Interested in Privateering in America during the Eighteenth Century. *Leon Hühner, A. M., LL. B.*

Notes. *Samuel Oppenheim, D. de Sola Pool, Frank Cundall, David Philipson, J. Cassuto, Albert M. Friedenberg, Isaac E. Marcuson, and I. Abrahams.*

Necrology.

Postpaid, $2.00.

No. 24, 1916 (180 pp.), *containing the following:*

Jewish Disabilities in the Balkan States, American Contributions toward Their Removal, with Particular Reference to the Congress of Berlin. *Max J. Kohler and Simon Wolf.*

Postpaid, $1.50.

www.ingramcontent.com/pod-product-compliance
Lightning Source LLC
Chambersburg PA
CBHW020847160426
43192CB00007B/813